EssexWorks.
For a better quality of life

Please return this book on or before the date shown above. To renew go to www.essex.gov.uk/libraries, ring 0845 603 7628 or go to any Essex library.

Essex County Council

DRAW & PAINT
FANTASY ART

Vampires

Scott Purdy

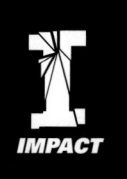
IMPACT

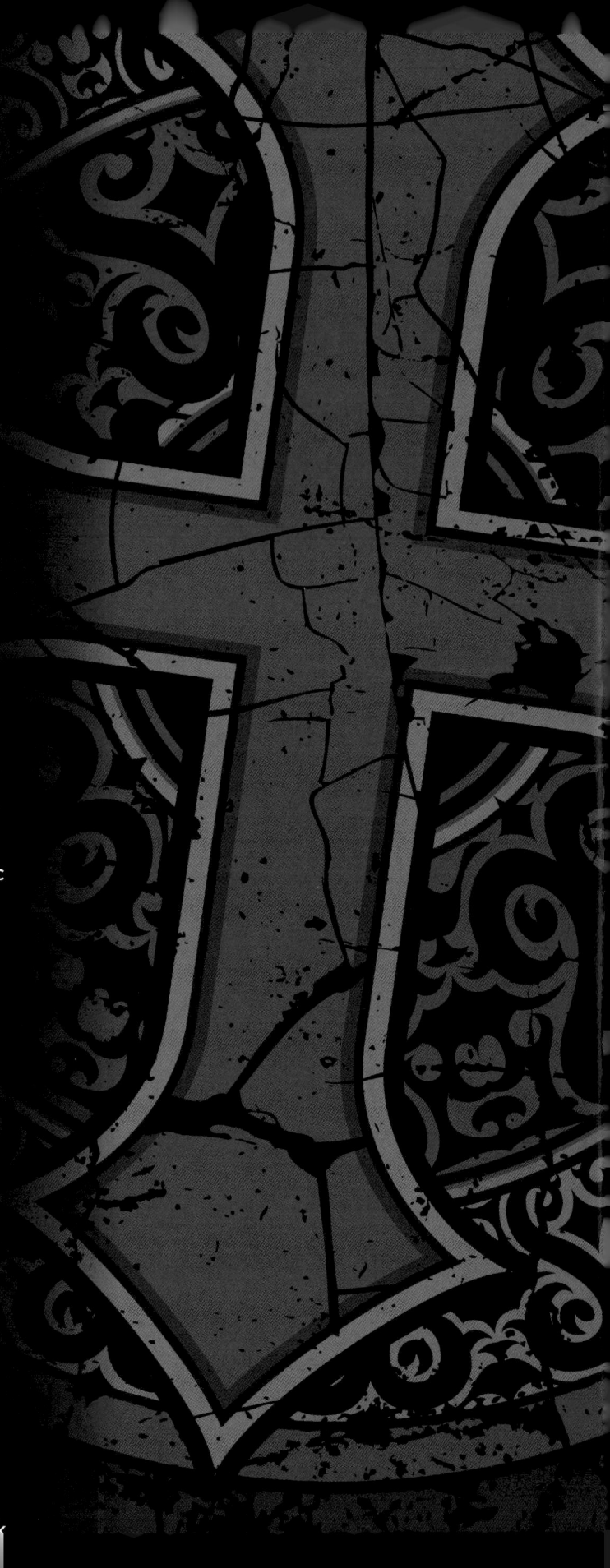

This book is dedicated to Emma, Sam and Diz!
My huge thanks to 'Monster Island' and especially
to Jon Hodgson for the extra support!
Many thanks to Elandria for the superb modelling
and photographs, and finally the D&C team for
putting up with me for one more time!

Printed in China by RR Donnelley
for David & Charles
Brunel House, Newton Abbot, Devon

Publisher: Stephen Bateman
Senior Commissioning Editor: Freya Dangerfield
Assistant Editor: James Brooks
Project Editor: Emily Pitcher
Designer: Marieclare Mayne
Production Controller: Ali Smith

David & Charles publish high quality books on a
wide range of subjects.
For more great book ideas visit: www.rubooks.co.uk

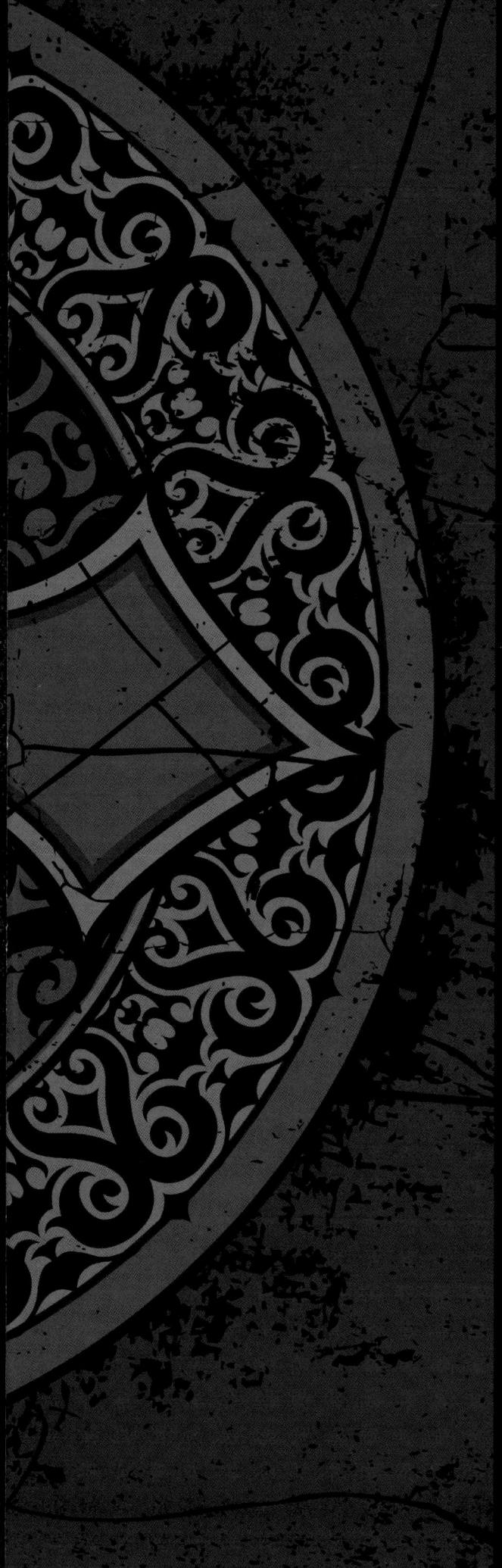

Contents

In this book we will take a fantastic ride into the world of creating your own vampire characters. We'll explore anatomy, colour, lighting and a whole host of other interesting tidbits, before showing you how to create your very own vampires with my easy to follow projects. I wish we had more room to expand on what is contained within this book, but there are only so many trees in the world that can sacrifice themselves to the will of vampire art.

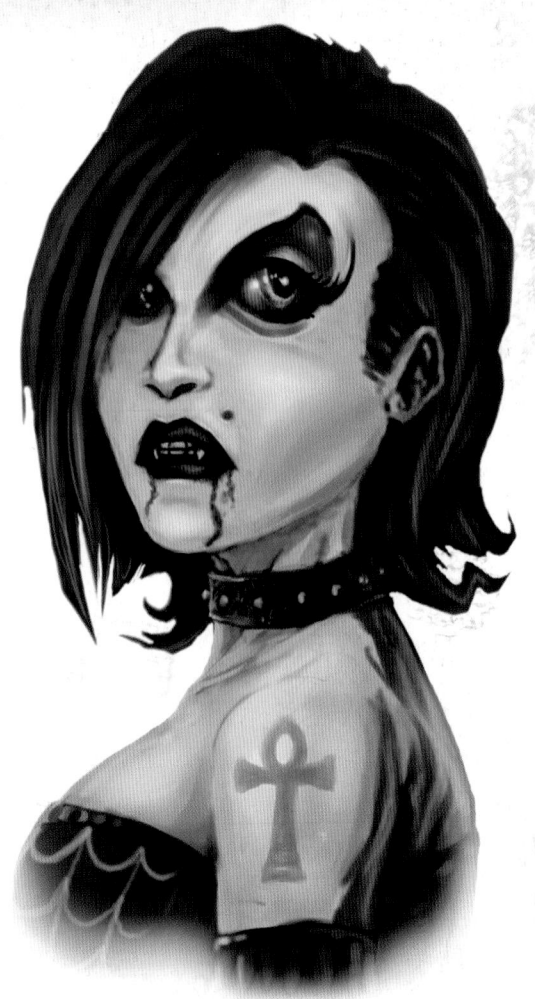

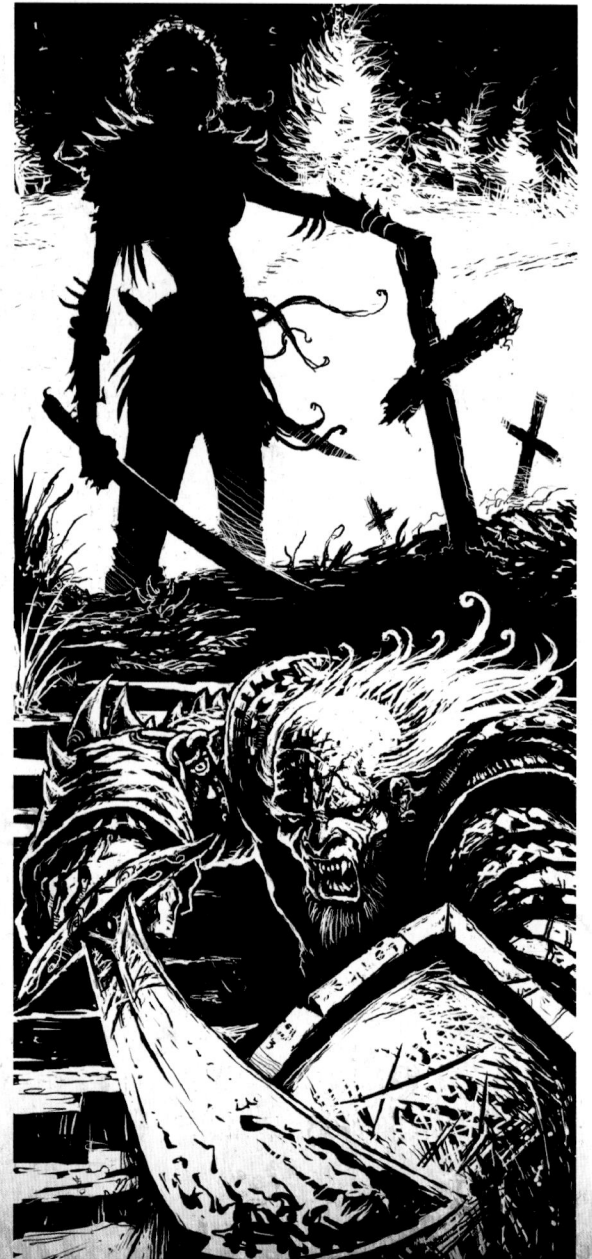

I hope you enjoy the book — my main aim when writing it was for you to have fun and learn something along the way...if I've done that for just a handful of you, then my job is complete.

Check out all of my artwork at www.scottpurdy.net

Enjoy!

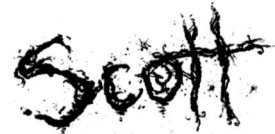

USEFUL LINKS

Artists

www.jonhodgson.com
www.andrewhepworth.co.uk
www.wrightsonart.com
www.ninjamountain.net

I'd also like to give Elandria a huge thanks for her wonderful modelling!
www.elandria.deviantart.com
www.transcendent-visions.uki.net/index.htm

Resources

Jon Schindehette, Senior Art Editor for *Wizards of the Coast*'s art blog. Includes fantasy art competitions and challenges for professionals and amateurs alike.
www.artorder.blogspot.com

Ninja Mountain Scrolls podcast: listen and learn about fantasy illustration.
www.ninjamountain.blogspot.com

Deviant Art, a huge gallery of sci-fi, horror and fantasy art. It's free to join, so what are you waiting for? Go show the world your work!
www.deviantart.com

Tools and materials

TRADITIONAL STUFF

There is a bewildering amount of equipment and media out there, and it can be confusing working out what you need to buy. If you're not sure what equipment you need it is always a good idea to ask at your local art store. Don't buy the top of the range kit until you're confident that it's what you want and you will use it often enough — until then, experiment with the cheaper materials and have fun playing with them all until you find your own style!

PENCILS

Everyone knows how to use them and they can be essential for scribbling down ideas, sketching out and planning compositions, or for producing beautiful final studies. You can choose from mechanical pencils with the loose leads, or traditional pencils in a range of weights, from the hard graphite HB, to the really soft and dark 5B.

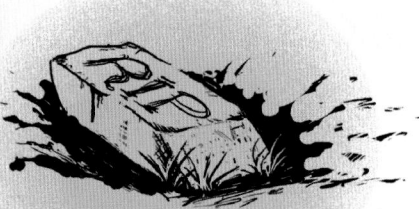

ERASER

Because we all make mistakes, right?

PEN AND INK

This medium is one of my favourites. You can buy a wide range of dip pens, biros and markers; some of my favourite pens are dip pens that I've had for around 10 years, but they do need looking after. I recommend Micron pens for producing fine details, but make sure that you buy a good quality Indian ink – other varieties can be a bit wishy washy.

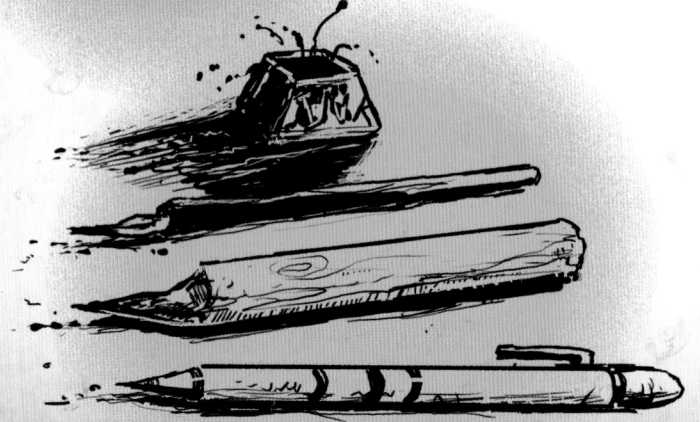

SKETCH BOOK

Where are you going to be if you have nowhere to record your ideas? Scrap paper is also great but can be easily lost (if you're as messy as me), so having your own sketch book is essential. It is also worth buying some nice quality watercolour paper or board for painting with acrylic or oils. Be prepared to make a mess!

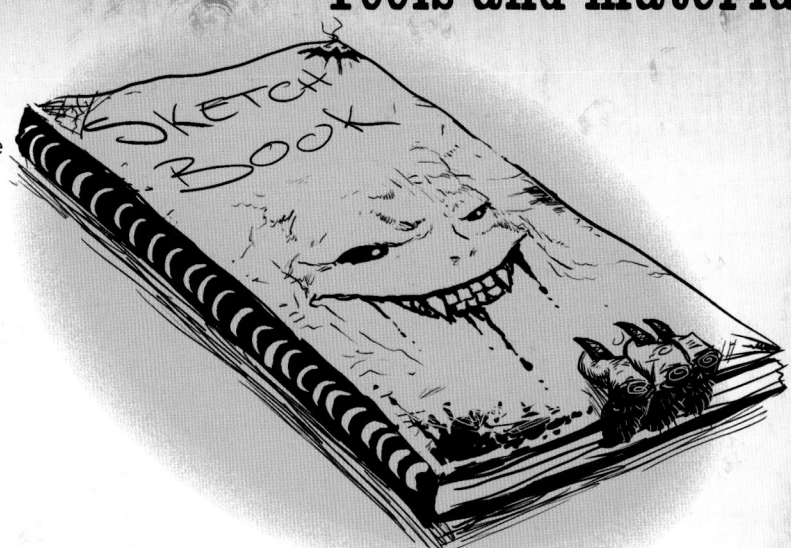

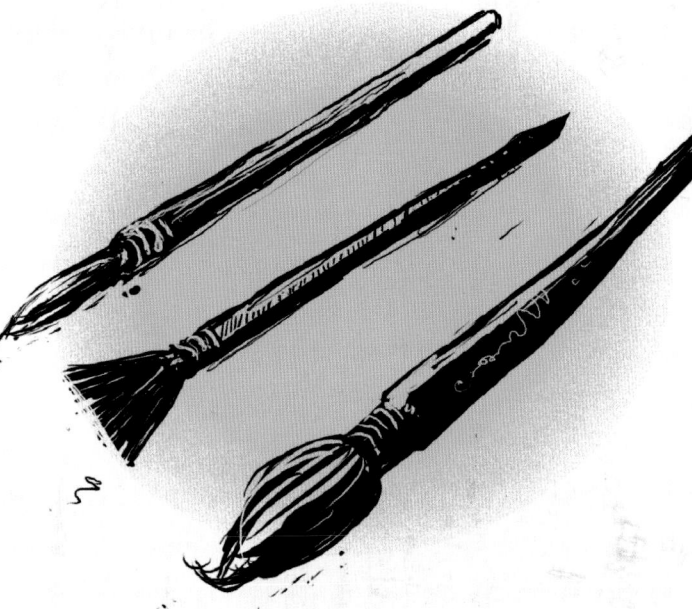

BRUSHES

There are loads of different and interesting brushes out there. Decide what kind of painting you would like to try and buy a cheap and simple paint brush pack for your chosen paint (oil, acrylic or watercolour). Don't spend lots of money on expensive brushes until you are sure which kind of painting you prefer, because each one calls for slightly different tools.

PAINTS

Let's see, oils, water soluble oils, acrylics, gouache, water colours…take your pick and see what rocks your boat. Don't be afraid to experiment until you find which ones suit you best, and that you enjoy working in. Bear in mind that you'll need a lot of old rags to keep your brushes clean, as well as thinners if you're using oils.

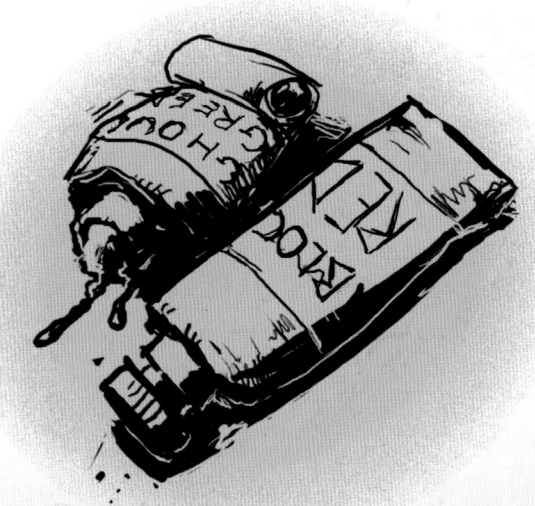

DIGITAL STUFF

You can spend all of the money in the world setting yourself up for digital painting, buying expensive computers, software and other kit. My advice is to work out what your style is, and what you enjoy creating and working with before you invest huge sums of money on gear that you're never going to use. Find your own niche style and then accessorize it selectively.

WHICH COMPUTER?

Firstly you're going to need a computer of some description, and you need to decide whether you're going to use a PC or an Apple Mac. You can buy a relatively inexpensive PC straight off the shelf, which is fine for you to start up. Make sure it has plenty of RAM (over 2 gigabytes at least) as the painting programs use a lot of memory. With a PC you also get a mouse, keyboard and generally a standard flat screen monitor that will do the job until you're a pro. Macs are more expensive but are also better than PCs in terms of graphic displays, usability and virus protection, so it's up to you to decide how much you want to spend – I use a 24' IMac and find that it's perfect for what I need.

SCANNER

You may find that you want to scan some original artwork, or begin a piece traditionally and then take it onto the computer, which means that you're going to need a decent scanner. Most scanners are A4- (US Letter-) sized, and there is a huge selection to choose from. Have a look at some online forums or ask at your computer store to find out which make and model will be the best for your needs.

The scanner I use is a CanoScan LiDE 90; it works brilliantly for me but it is quite pricey, so starting out with a cheaper one is a wise idea.

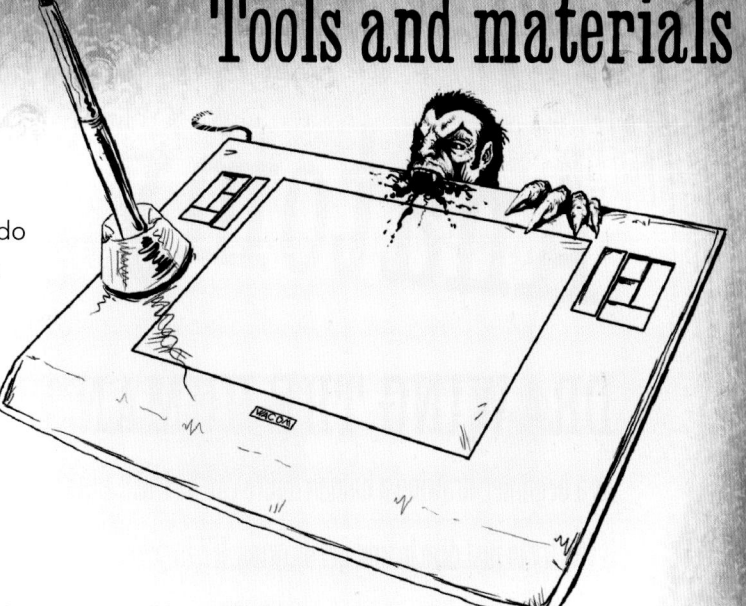

TABLET

There are loads of painting and drawing tablets on the market and the prices vary a fair bit. I use a Wacom Intuos III which is perfect for me, but again do your research on the internet before deciding which one to buy, and don't be afraid to go for a cheaper model at the outset.

SOFTWARE

There are three main pieces of software that the digital artist will find useful. They all have different strengths, weaknesses and price tags, so it is worth experimenting with them before you decide which one to get. All of the programmes listed below have either basic versions for free, or a full trial that you can download and use for a limited period.

ADOBE PHOTOSHOP

Photoshop is the big gun in the playground. It has loads of options and brushes and editing tools that makes it pretty much essential for professional designers and digital artists. The drawback is that it is hugely expensive and quite scary to use when you are first introduced to it. Luckily, Adobe make a cheaper version called Adobe Photoshop Elements, which is a stripped down version of the full programme and is a lot cheaper. Sometimes this comes bundled with tablets – have a good look online for deals!
www.adobe.com

COREL PAINTER

Unlike Photoshop, Painter is aimed directly at artists and painters. It has a lot of ready-made brushes that are perfect for painters – once you find the set that work for you you're away! There are also options included for tweaking the appearance of your brushes, so you can get them looking just right. The downside is that Corel has less editing options than Photoshop, and some people find it a little clunky to use. However, Corel is my program of choice – I flit between Painter IX and X, both of which are relatively cheap.
www.corel.com

AMBIENT DESIGN ARTRAGE

This cheap and tiny program has a wonderfully small choice of brushes. The oil brushes are quite spectacular and I don't think I've seen another program that emulates oils as realistically as this one, but it can sometimes be difficult to control them.
www.artrage.com

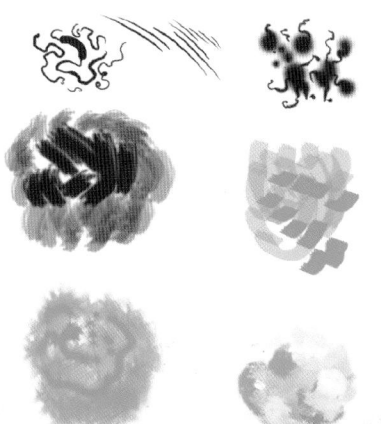

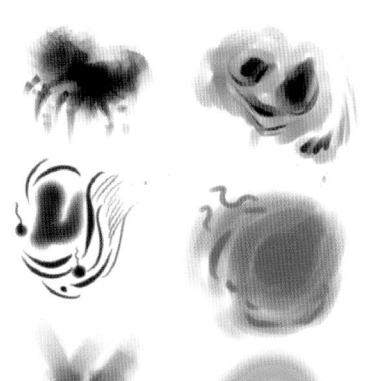

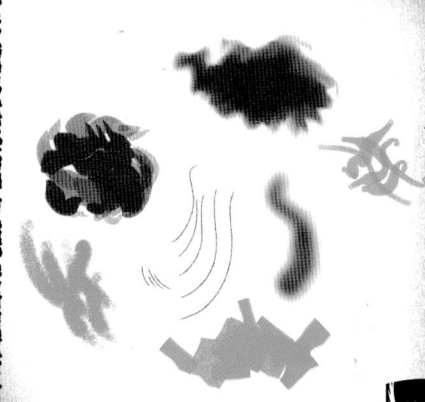

PROPORTION AND SCALE

Learning how to draw the human body with everything in proportion is essential, otherwise you're not going to be able to make your characters really believable. Even if you choose to distort your character to create more impact, it is vital that you do the distortion once you have created the character correctly in proportion. Creating a character at the outset that is out of proportion will not succeed as well as consciously increasing the size of certain aspects of the body for dramatic effect.

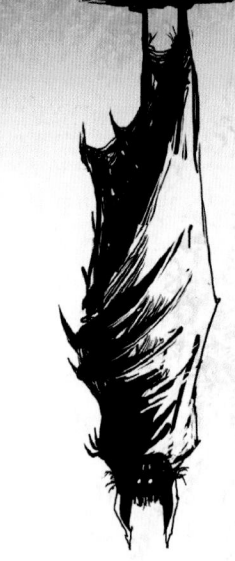

BODY SIZES

A figure can usually be broken down into head height, and stands anywhere between six and eight heads high. Alternatively, if you want your vampires to have 'heroic proportions' give them smaller heads, broader shoulders and larger bodies.

Scan in or photocopy the male and female drawings below and try it out for yourself. Notice that the woman's hips are wider, waist is smaller and shoulders are narrower than the male's.

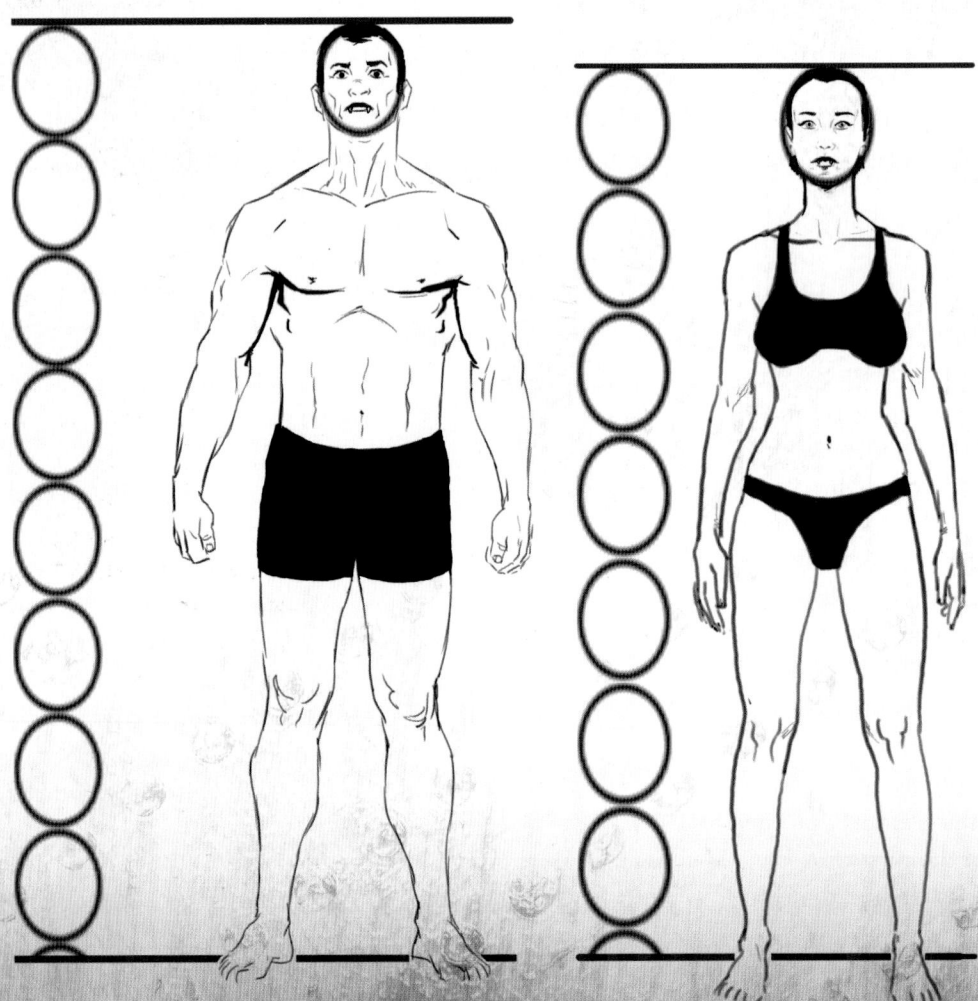

HANDS AND FEET

These can be tricky customers to draw, and some artists (myself included at times) will try to hide hands or feet within an image because it can be so difficult to get them right. It is essential, however hard they are, that you do learn how to drawn them; hands are especially important, otherwise it means you can't ever have a character holding something, and that could limit the story. Imagine how much less effective the lupine (see page 94) would be if you couldn't see it's hands.

Below are a few examples of what your character's hands could be doing, again using simple shapes to break down the form. Note the length of the fingers, where the thumb is placed in relation to them, and where the wrist connects.

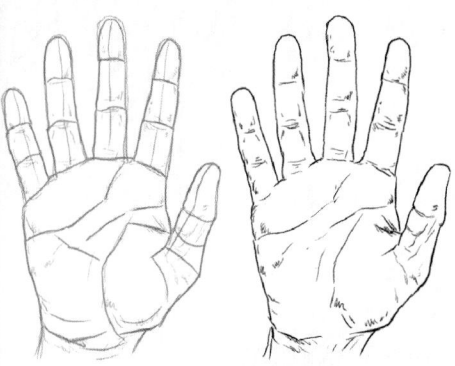

The nails could be chewed, broken or claw-like.

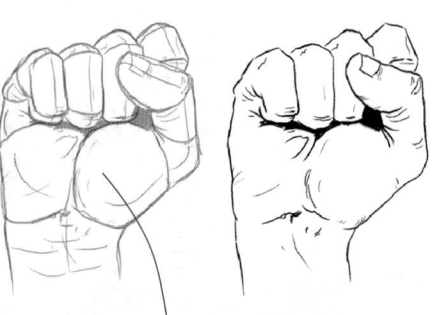

Make a fist and observe where the thumb sits over the fingers, and how the muscles of your hand bunch up.

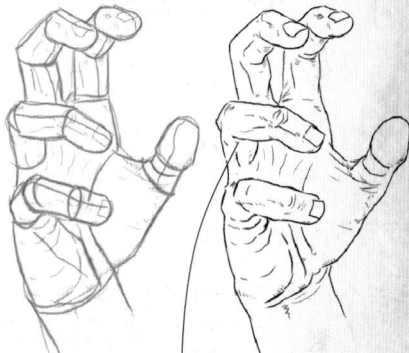

The natural bend of the fingertips has them pointing slightly inwards and down, and note how the flesh folds react.

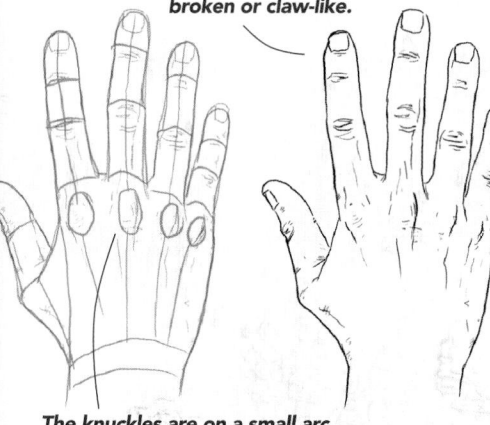

The knuckles are on a small arc, not a dead straight horizontal line.

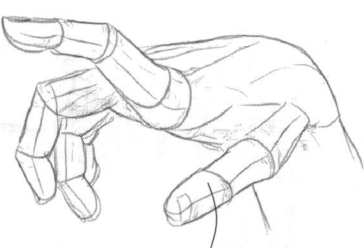

Notice how the thumb appears to be almost resting on its side.

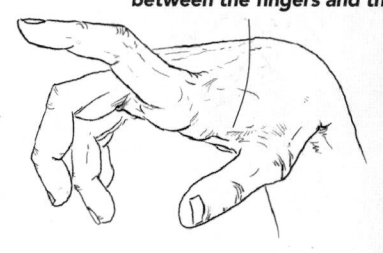

Observe how the skin flows between the fingers and thumb.

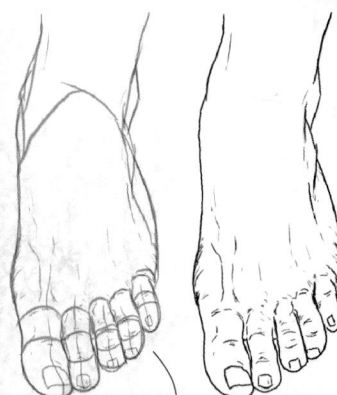

The toes are supporting and balancing the whole body and are therefore turned in together, rather than being straight or flat.

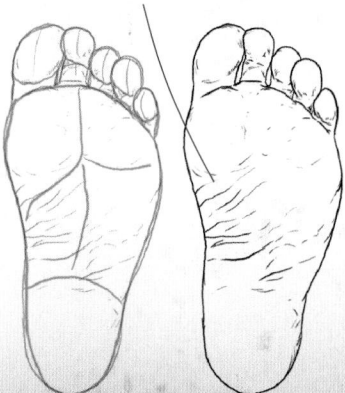

Note the folds of skin on the heel, and the arch at the base of the foot.

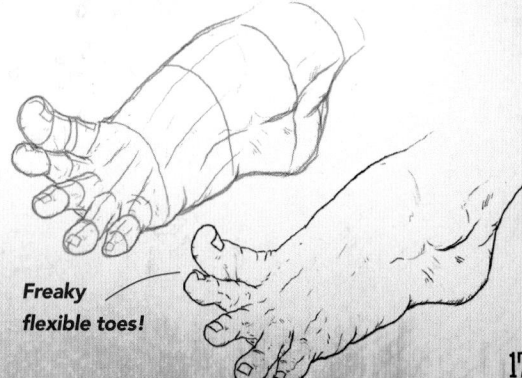

The base of your foot is as creased as your hands, with padding on the ball, heel and toes.

Freaky flexible toes!

HEADS AND FACES

The face and head can be the most interesting parts of the body to draw., and can tell so much of your story. The possibilities for facial expressions are endless and great fun to play with — try them out in the mirror and observe how the skin wrinkles and crinkles, the eyes change shape and the mouth alters in appearance as you make the most of your facial muscles.

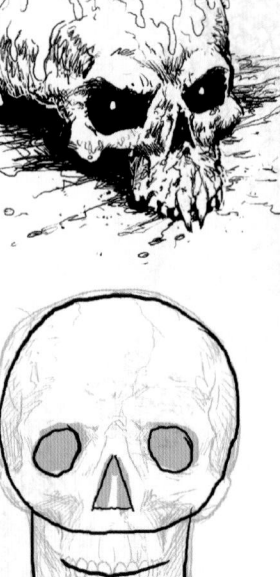

THE HUMAN SKULL

The basis of drawing good heads and faces is to learn how to draw the basic outline of the skull, and build from there. Using a simple sphere for the skull, circles for eyes, triangle for nose cavity and rough jaw shape, we have our building blocks in place.

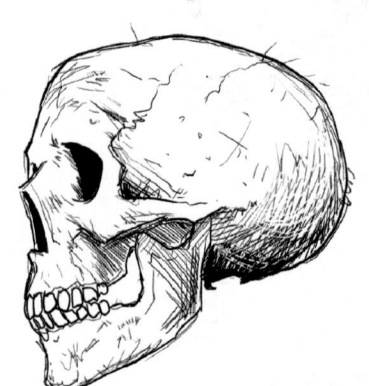

We can then draw out the head and face, placing the eyes, nose and mouth.

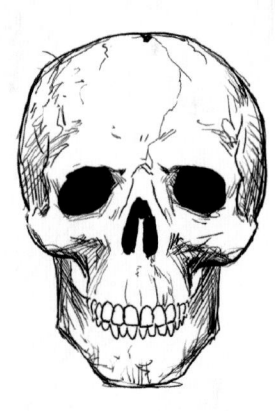

It's easy to move all of the facial elements around slightly, play with their sizes, or even leave a few out to give our vampires a tale to tell. Notice that the ears are in line with the eyes.

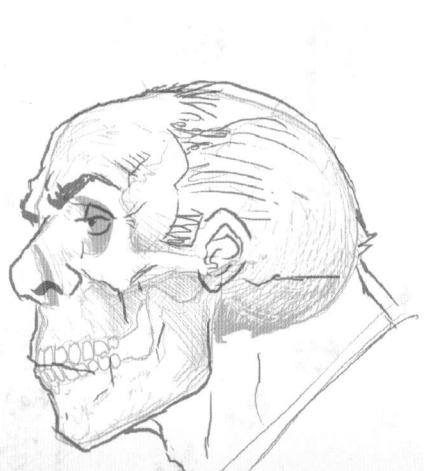

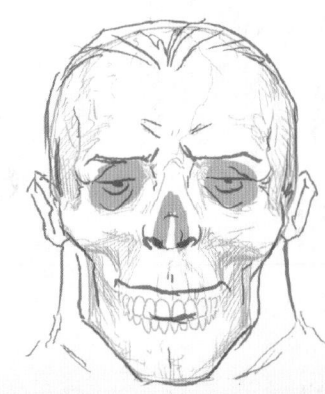

EXPRESSIONS

Happy, sad, angry, crying, surprised or confused, here are a few very simple examples using the simplest of shapes. Practise drawing these ovals and adding in the eyes, eyebrows nose and mouth to work out the expression you want to convey.

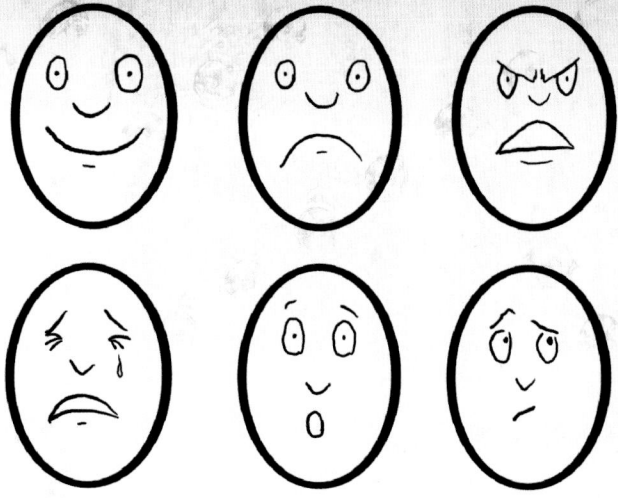

Using your basic oval expressions as the building blocks, you can soon develop them into these more detailed drawings.

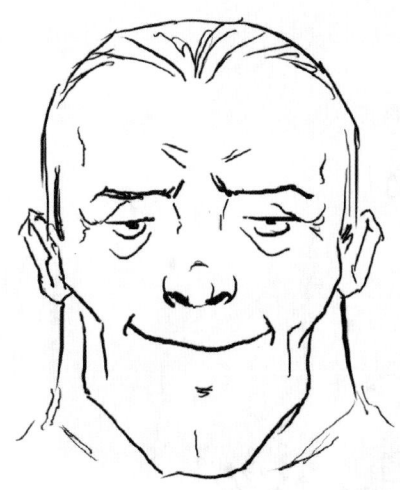
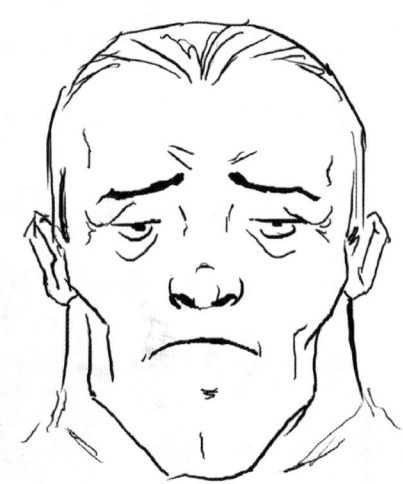
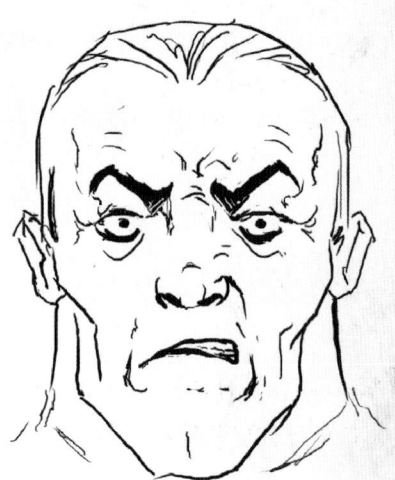

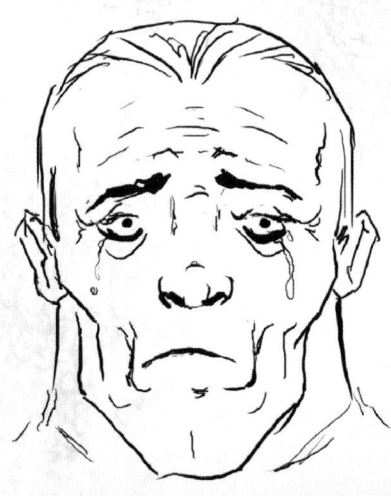
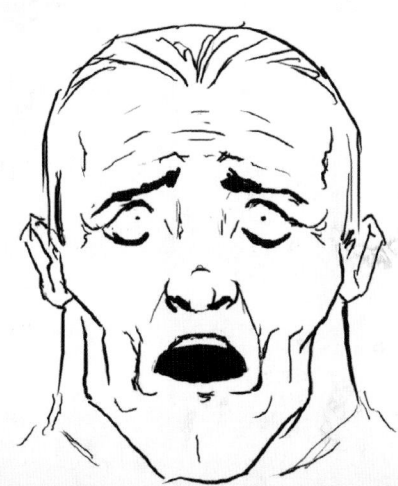
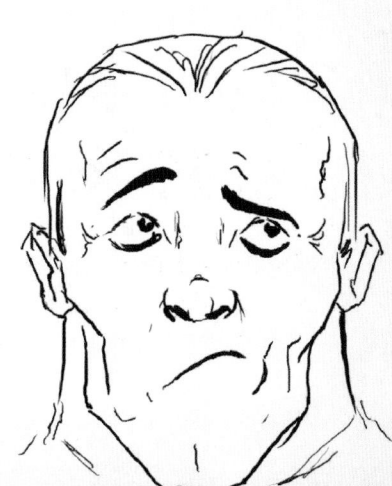

Planning

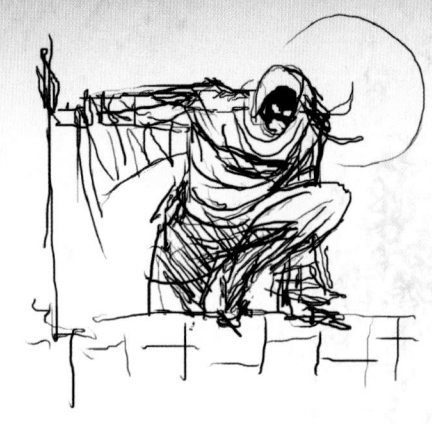

You've got all of your kit, decided on the media you want to use and you're mastering the basic techniques or rendering a figure. So what next?

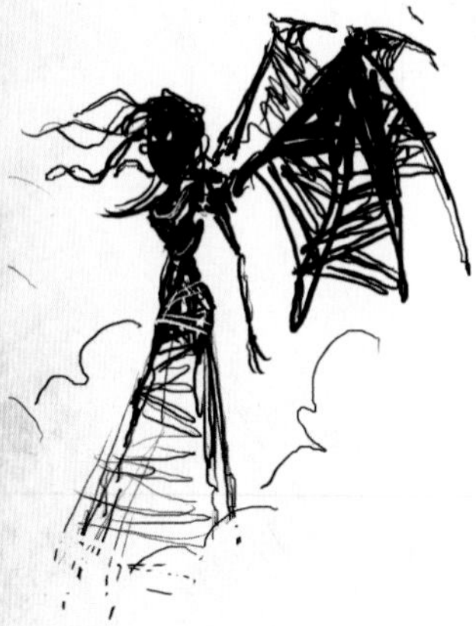

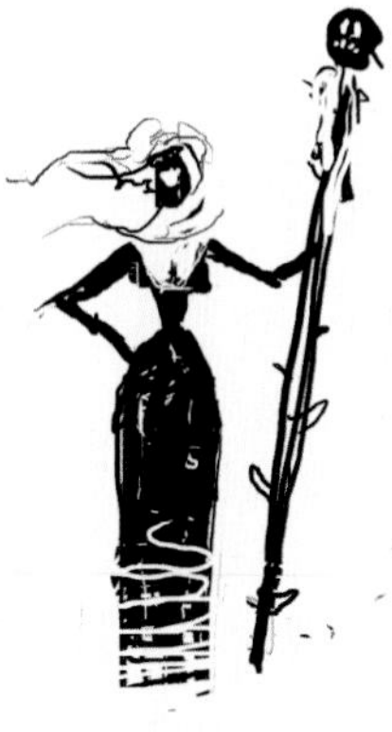

THUMBNAILS

A thumbnail sketch is a quick drawing that helps you to work out the shape, proportions and dynamism of your characters. Grab your sketchbook and start sketching simple stick men and shapes to work out what your character's pose is. Are they hunched over? Do they have massively broad shoulders? Are they wearing armour or tattered rags? Male or female? Sensual or horrific?

These are some of the things that you can work out brilliantly at this stage.

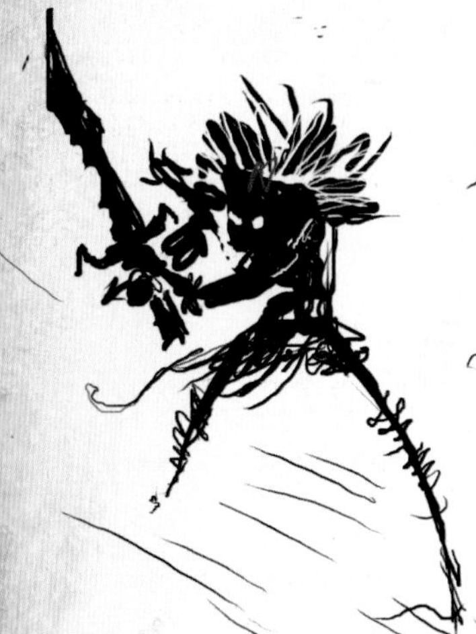

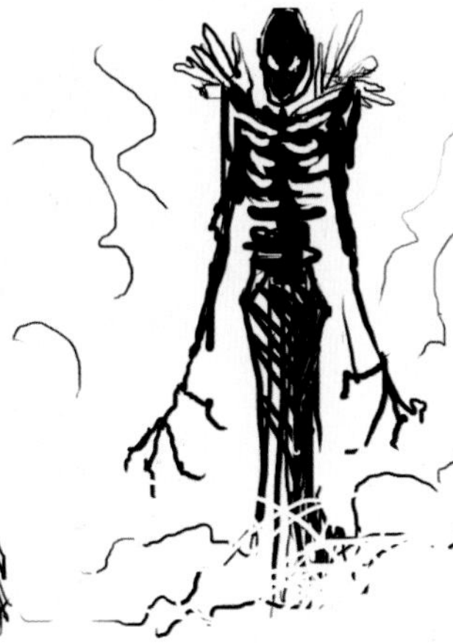

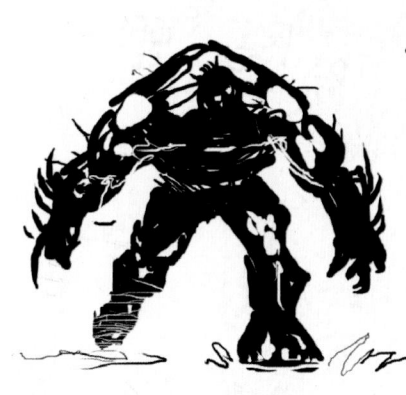

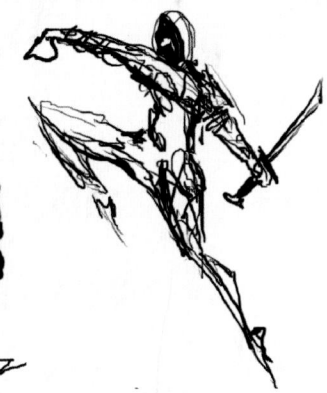

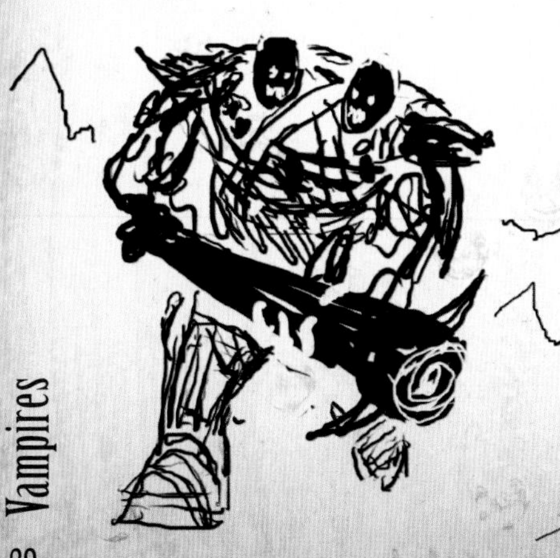

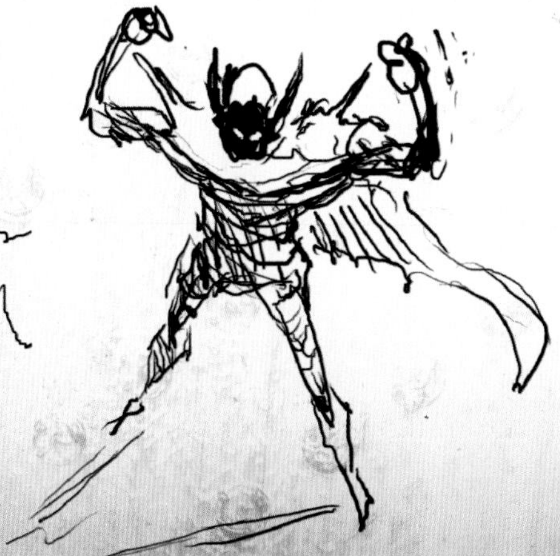

SKETCHING

This is something that you must try to do as much of as you can. Never leave the house without your sketchbook and, if something grabs your interest or you suddenly have an idea, sketch it down, make notes and then use and refine them once you're back in your studio space. Use quick lines and shapes as the foundation for your figure so that you can quickly plan out your composition and check it works before spending loads of time adding in the detail or even thinking about painting.

COMPOSITION

At the heart of any good piece of artwork is a good composition; weak composition will make your character and work less appealing to look at. Your character's pose and portrayal of the surrounding environment can help the eye rove around the painting, as can props or tools that they hold.

Try not to always put things in the middle of the page as it will tend to make your piece look static and less interesting. It is also important that the viewer's attention is kept on the character; having details at the corner of the page will distract the eye.

REFERENCE

Grab your camera and use yourself and willing friends and family as models. Use your imagination when it comes to props – broom handles or sticks can make excellent swords, while old sheets are excellent as robes or drapery.

The internet is great for artists – you can research costumes, weapons and armour, for example, or find out the history and context of any historical figures (such as Dracula) that will help you to enhance your work. Films and books are also a useful way of inspiring your story. Part of the fun is creating something yourself and really using your own imagination to tell the story.

Planning

You can see a strong dynamic triangular composition in this character, helping to move the eye round and keep you interested. There are lots more points of interest; see if you can spot them and apply similar points to your characters

Traditional painting

BASIC TECHNIQUES

Traditional painting is a difficult skill to learn, but with determination, blood, sweat and a bit of luck you can create some fantastic pieces of artwork. There will always be times within each painting where you'll be cursing the brushes, the canvas, paint and possibly your family, but never give up — take a deep breath and come back to it later. Here are some basic techniques that you need to get to grips with, but it's up to you to make a masterpiece.

STARTING

You'll need a fairly large workspace that's comfortable for you to work around. Make sure you have all of your equipment laid out in an order that is easy for you to reach – you don't want to knock your water or brush pot over as you reach for your rag. It's important to have good quality tools as well; you don't need to go out and buy the most expensive set of brushes, canvas and paints but make sure that they're all clean and undamaged and up to the job.

BRUSHES

There is a huge range of brushes out there and it can be quite confusing working out which ones to buy. Experiment with different ones until you find a set that really works for you and the way that you want to paint. There are some standard brushes, however, that are really useful for any artist's tool box. Hoghair brushes are pretty stiff, making them excellent for scrubbing the paint into the canvas, and also for painting in large texture with thick paint. Fan brushes are very good for blending your paint. As a general rule, have three flat brushes from medium to small in size for various levels of detail, and one large round brush for washing and laying in large areas of thick paint.

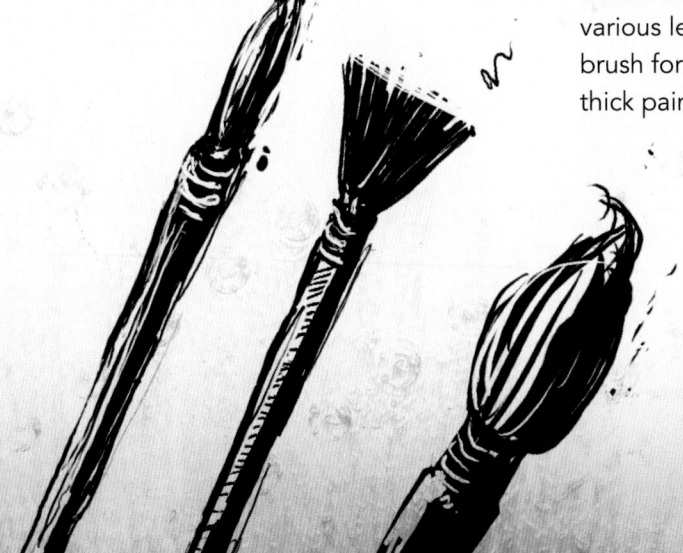

COLOUR MIXING

Mixing colours can be difficult, and it's all too easy to end up with a muddy brown colour. Use a large palette space and just one assigned brush for mixing, reserving various other brushes for picking up the paint.

You might find that paint washes can sometimes get too watered down and are difficult to control, so be careful how much water or thinner you use. Practise as much as you can, and always test the brush on a piece of scrap paper or a discreet corner before adding it to the centre of your prized artwork. If you're using the paint and finding that it's too thick, just add a little of the thinner, or water mixed in well will also help the paint flow better and not clog up the brush hairs so much.

TRADITIONAL TOOLS

The medium that you're using will dictate whether to use thinner or water. Watercolours, acrylic and gouache use water as their thinner, and oils use a thinner which can be purchased from an art store. There are also some oil paints available now that are water-soluble.

You can buy canvas quite cheaply these days, and it is best to buy it mounted on board. It is a good idea to only buy it at A4 (US Letter) and smaller, so that it can easily fit on your scanner. There is also a variety of different papers available, so why not ask at your local art store which one would be best for the medium that you're using? Again, don't buy particularly large sizes unless you specifically need to.

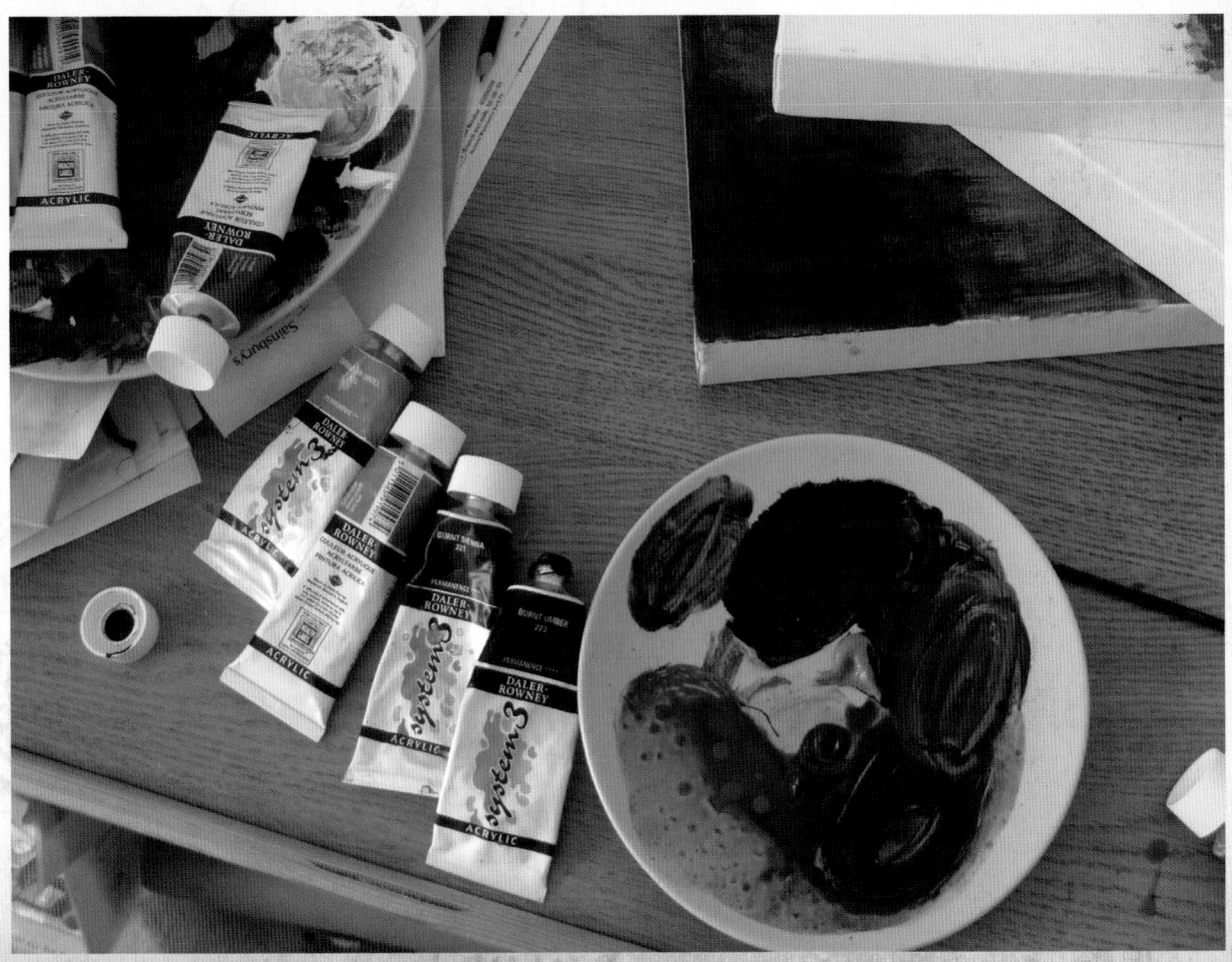

MARK MAKING

Your sketch is already planned and laid out, but you don't want to destroy that fine drawing with thick paint. In which case, go and grab your large brush, water down or thin your paint and lay down large areas of wash without ruining your pencil or ink work. If you find that your pencil lines run then you can purchase a special sealant to keep them tight.

Hold the brush near the far end for more naturally flowing brush marks, and work from your elbow and shoulder, rather than your wrist or hand. It might seem difficult at first, especially if you're used to working on a tight drawing in great detail. For this stage it's much better to relax your mark making. Make time to practise on a canvas to see what different kind of marks you can make.

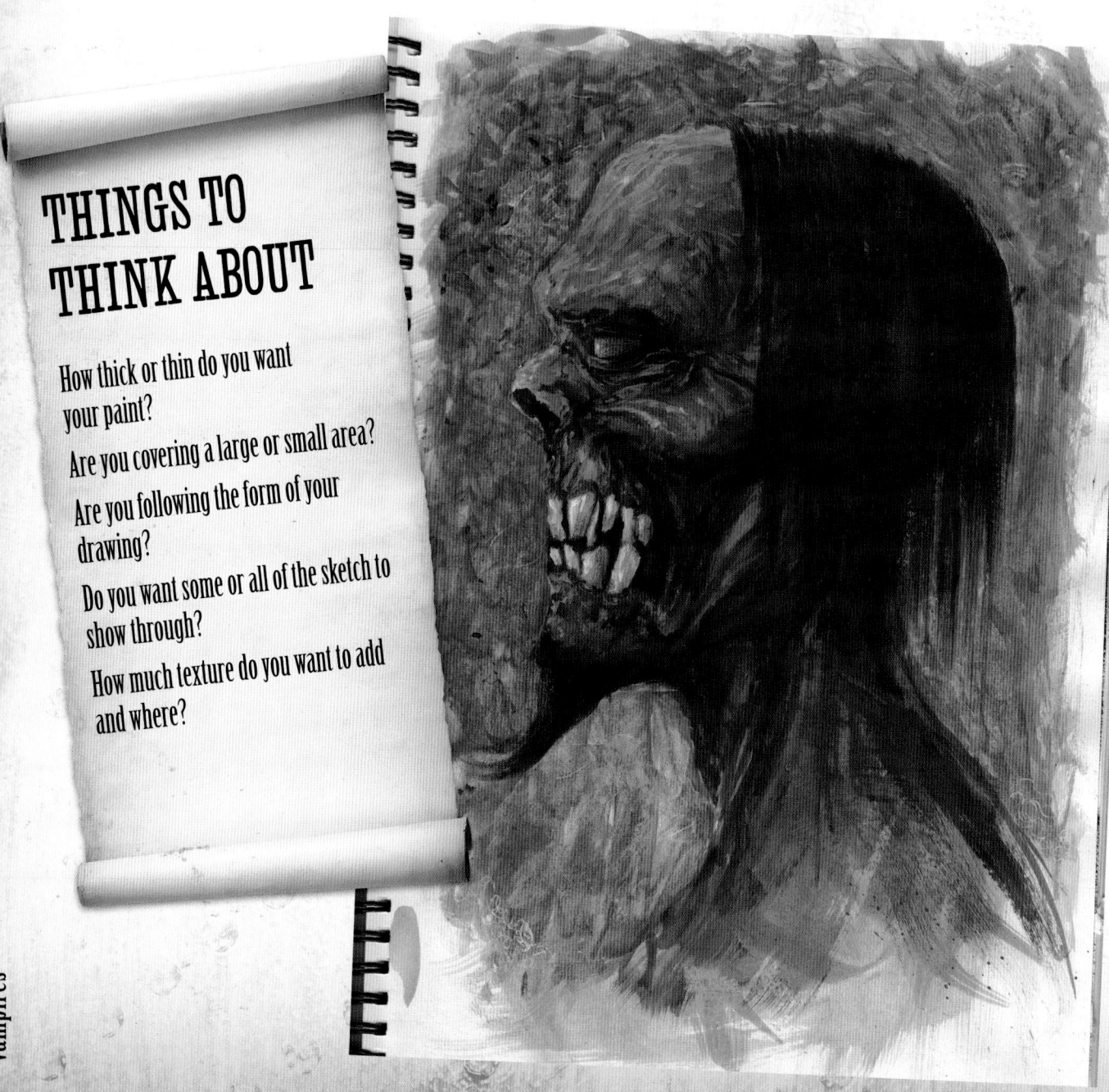

THINGS TO THINK ABOUT

How thick or thin do you want your paint?

Are you covering a large or small area?

Are you following the form of your drawing?

Do you want some or all of the sketch to show through?

How much texture do you want to add and where?

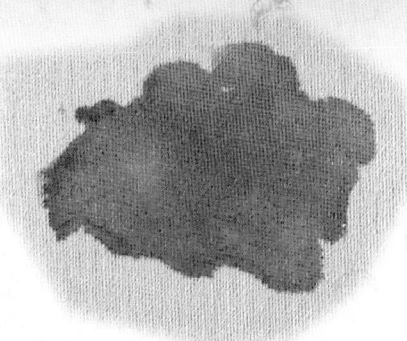

1. WASH

Two colours washed next to each other that bleed into one another. You can clearly see the canvas underneath.

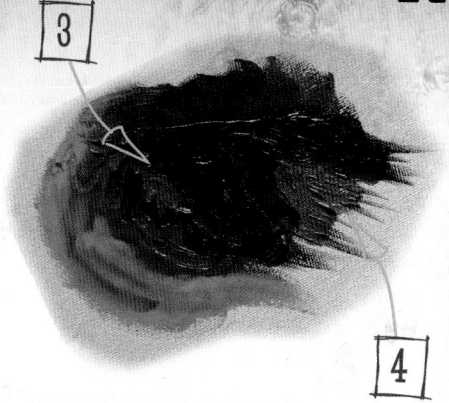

3. WASH AND OPAQUE

Using oils or acrylics, this is a little thicker and with only one colour. You can see how the white canvas shows through and is semi-transparent next to the lumpy opaque paint.

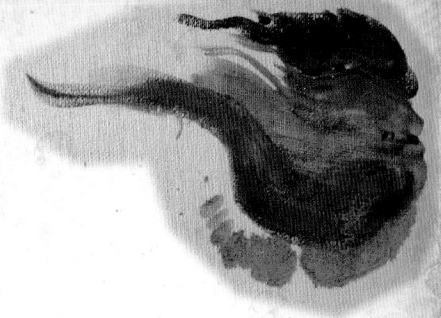

6. WAVY WET

Blending wet paints together and dragging the brush to the left until it's dry.

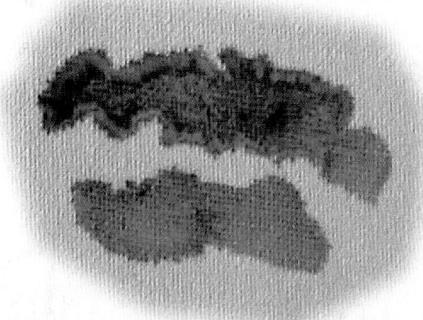

2. WASH AND OPAQUE PAINT

Two colours, one of which was thinned down and it has feathered out into the canvas, while the opaque blue bleeds slowly into the wet wash.

4. THICK, SCRATCHED AND FLICKED

The paint is laid down straight out of the tube and blended with various colours. The sharp end of the brush has been scratched into the thick paint to give the wavy line effect. The flicks on the top right were done using a dry brush loaded with paint, and flicking the thick paint up.

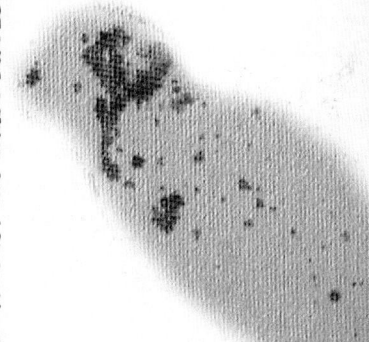

7. SPLAT

Paint that is very thin and loaded quite heavily onto the brush. Hold the brush above the surface of the canvas and flick it without touching the brush to canvas.

5. DRY AND WET BLEND

A small amount of opaque paint is brushed onto the canvas and then washed over with very thin paint to blend with the paint underneath.

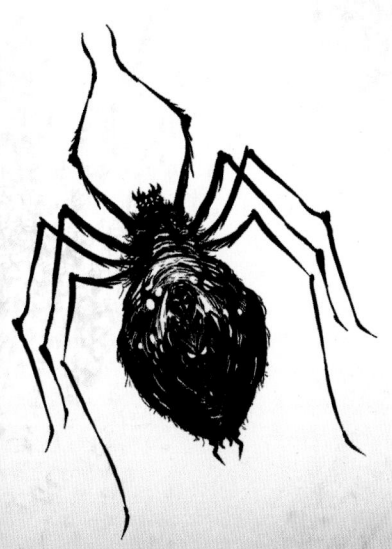

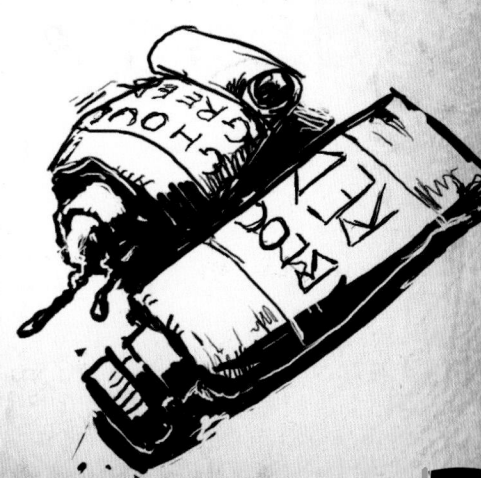

Digital painting

MASTERING THE SOFTWARE

Painter and Photoshop are the most well known programmes available to a digital artist, and the ones that I use regularly during my working day. Both have certain areas that they excel in and both work well in tandem with each other, but there are some basics that you have to master to really get the most out of any digital software.

BRUSHES

Both of the programmes have a scary number of brushes, but don't be put off by them! Take the time to really try out *every* brush, playing, experimenting and generally making a huge digital mess. From this you should be able to work out a small selection of brushes that suit the way in which you want to work. I only have seven brushes that I use in Painter, and just two round basic brushes in Photoshop.

PAINTER BRUSHES

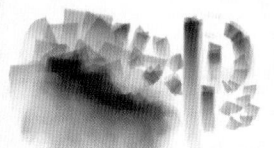

1. TAPERED OIL BRUSH

For building up sharp edges and blending.

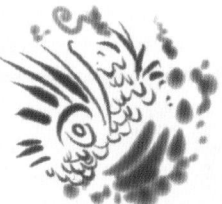

3. COVER PENCIL

Used to cover areas in flat colour or fine details.

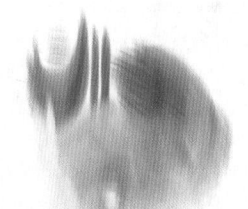

5. REAL FAN SOFT BRUSH

For blending and soft detail.

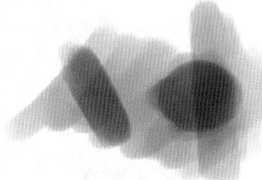

7. OIL PASTEL ON MULTIPLY LAYERS

Used for glazing or watercolour effects.

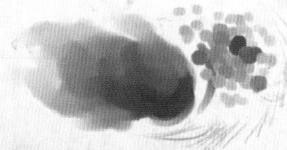

2. OIL PASTEL

For building up and soft blending.

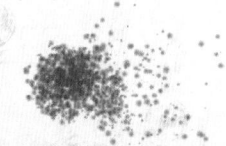

4. VARIABLE SPLATTER AIRBRUSH

For texture.

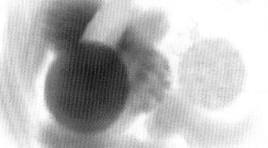

6. ROUND BLENDER BRUSH

For blending.

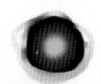

8. GLOW

For detail.

PHOTOSHOP BRUSHES

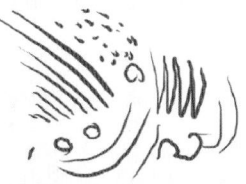

1. FINE ROUND BRUSH

Used for pencils and inking fine details.

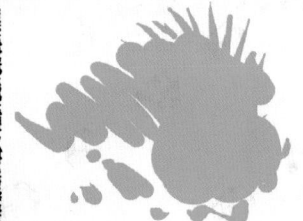

3. LARGE ROUND BRUSH

Used for inking and blocking in.

5. SOFT ROUND BRUSH

Used for foliage and blocking.

7. CUSTOM BRUSH

For large textural areas.

2. MID OPACITY ROUND BRUSH,

For washes.

4. ROUND BRUSH WITH LOW FLOW

For light texture.

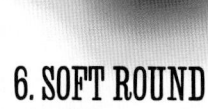

6. SOFT ROUND BRUSH

Low opacity, used for airbrushing.

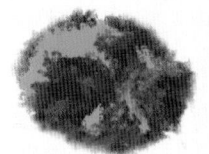

8. CUSTOM BRUSH

Painting with twocolours for large textural areas.

OPACITY

Digital brushes have a setting so that you can change the solidity of your brush marks. With a little luck, practise and skill you can get a range of beautiful marks and colour blends. High opacity marks completely cover the canvas underneath your paint, while low opacity brushes are semi transparent so you can achieve washes and layers of colour.

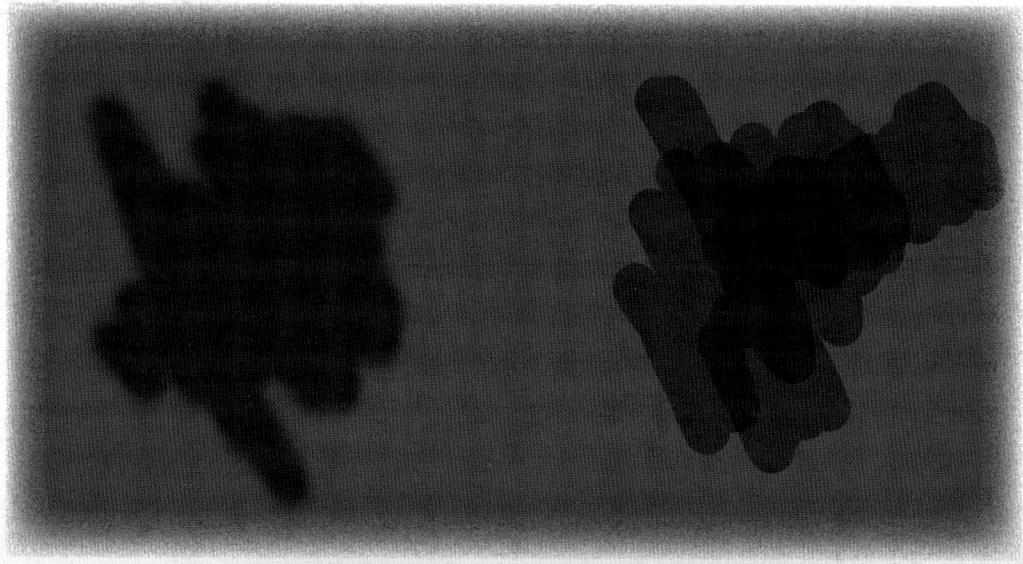

BLENDING

Digital tools are ideal for blending, as they don't make a mess and you can change your mind if you don't like it! The oil pastel brush in Painter is marvellous for painting skin and blending it on the fly. Just lay your colours down next to each other, colour pick the lightest and run gently over the colours to blend.

In Photoshop, use a very low opacity soft brush to effectively paint over, which gives the effect of blending. You'll have to think a little more if you want to blend the paint on something textured like a tree or rusty armour – practise makes perfect!

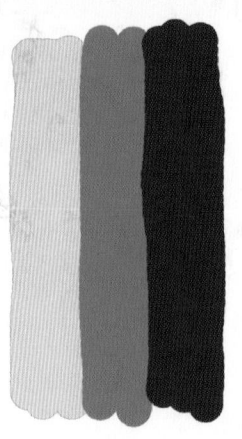 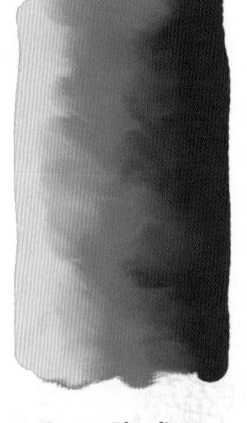 

Unblended   *Coarse Blending*   *Smooth Blending*

LAYERS

Layers are like clear sheets of plastic or glass that cover your painting. If you paint on a separate layer and then make a mistake you can easily delete your error, or even delete the entire layer, leaving your bottom, original layer of work unaffected. If you use layers effectively, you need never lose the hard work that you put in!

There are lots of different layer types that can effect the paint in different ways. The most common ones are 'normal' (or default) and 'multiply' layers. Normal layers are akin to putting a sheet of paper over the top of your canvas, but it's transparent. You can paint, blend and draw on this layer as if it's the canvas.

Working on multiply layers makes your brush marks transparent. They are ideal for washing and glazing your canvas, but be careful as they darken with each multiply layer added, and eventually your marks will turn black and run the risk of deadening the impact of your painting.

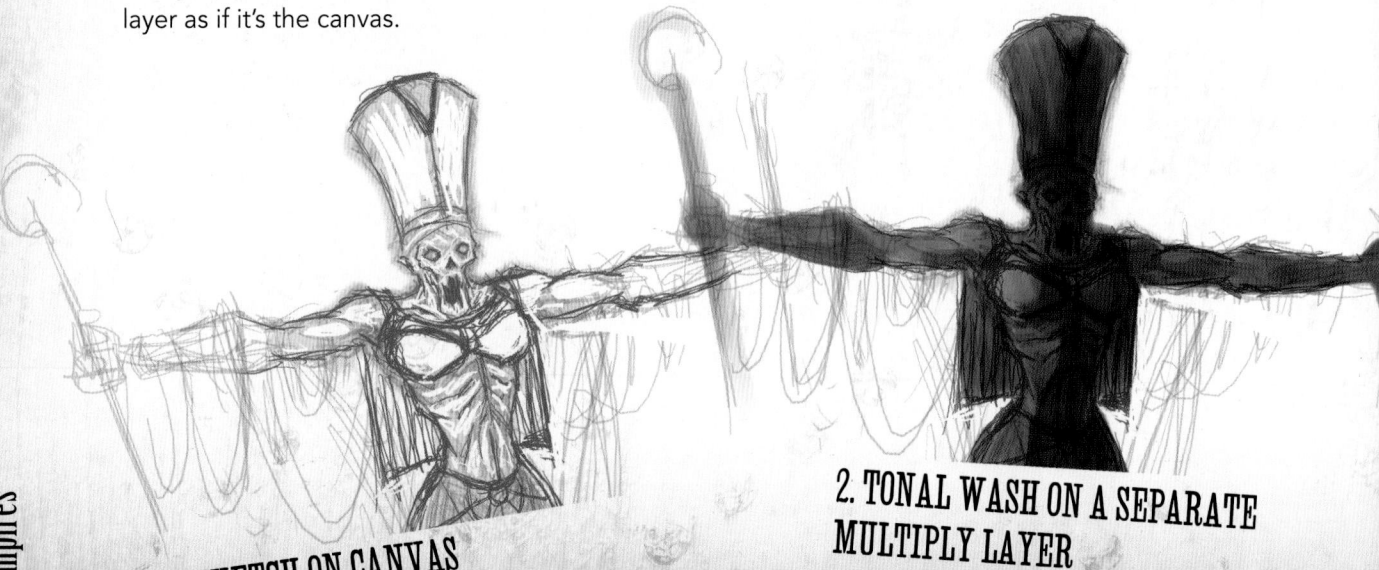

2. TONAL WASH ON A SEPARATE MULTIPLY LAYER

1. SKETCH ON CANVAS

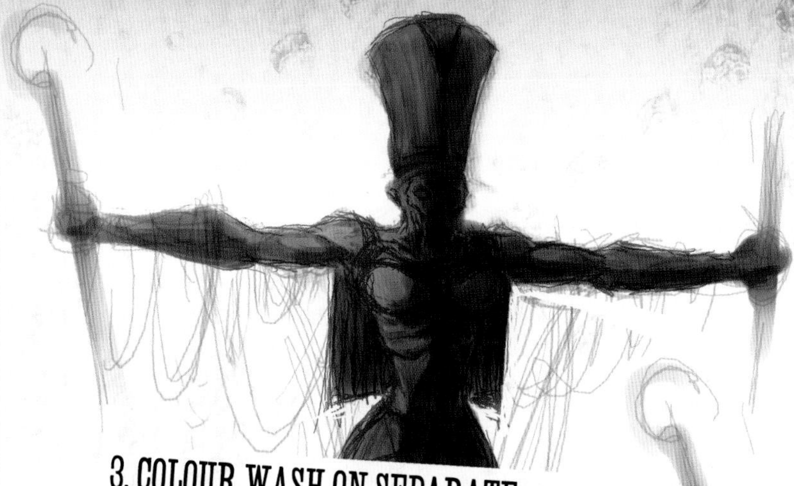

Digital painting

3. COLOUR WASH ON SEPARATE MULTIPLY LAYER

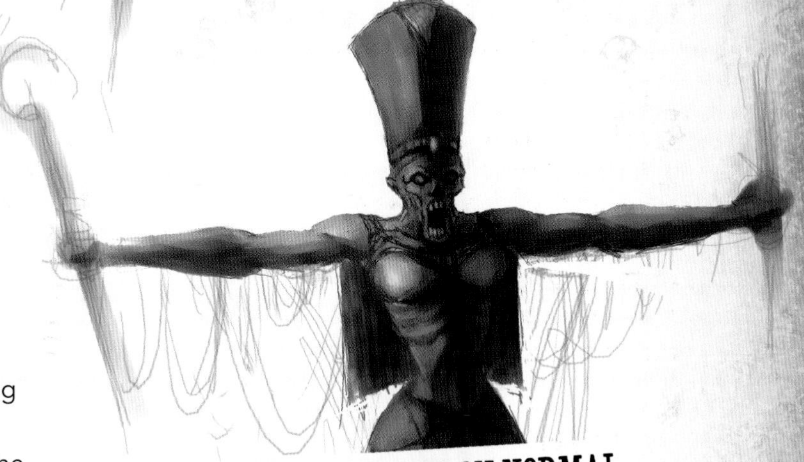

Having lots of layers is a huge memory hog on your computer. It is best to get into the habit of only using two layers at a time and flatten them to the canvas when you're happy with the results of the paint on the new layers. Huge files will slow your machine and brush marks down considerably, and this might make your programme prone to shutting down unexpectedly and your work go unsaved.

4. OPAQUE COLOURS ON NORMAL (OR DEFAULT) LAYER

DIGITAL RESOLUTION

Digital resolution is set by the number of dpi (dots per inch) or ppi (points per inch). It is most common to work at 300dpi in colour, and 600dpi with black and white line work. This will make your work of print quality, but if you don't ever want to print your work out then you can easily change the dpi of your canvas to something more suitable. Images that need to go online, either for gaming or gallery, are generally 72dpi, otherwise they are just too big to load. The most important thing is to ensure that your finished art's physical canvas size (in inches) is the size that you want to see.

The actual canvas height on these images is 15cm (6in)

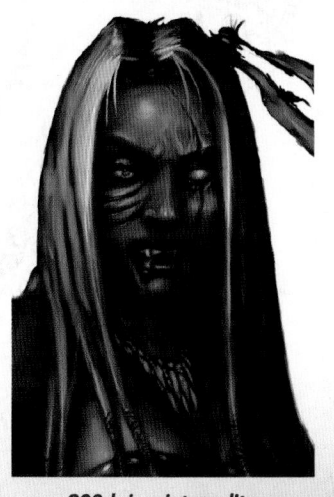

300dpi, print quality

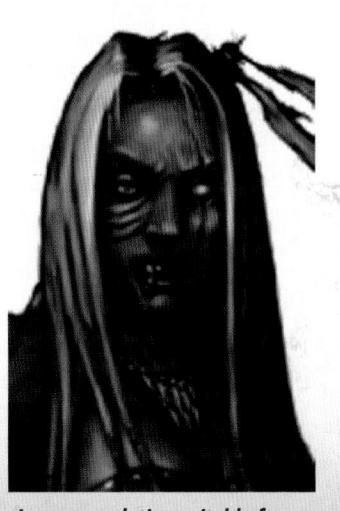

Lower resolution suitable for on screen viewing

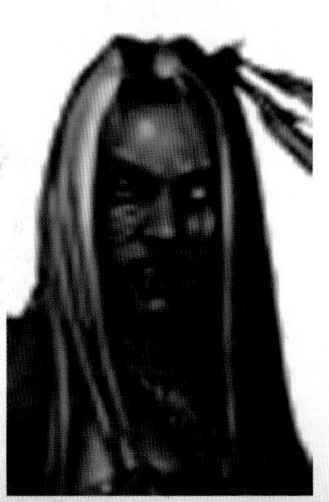

Very low resolution, suited to a thumbnail-sized image on a website

MARK MAKING

Two of the most useful marks in pencil work are cross hatching and hatching. They are very versatile and have a variety of applications, and will probably be some of the most used pencil techniques that you learn. Try to take your time with the sketching process, as rushing can limit your creativity and the natural flow of your marks.

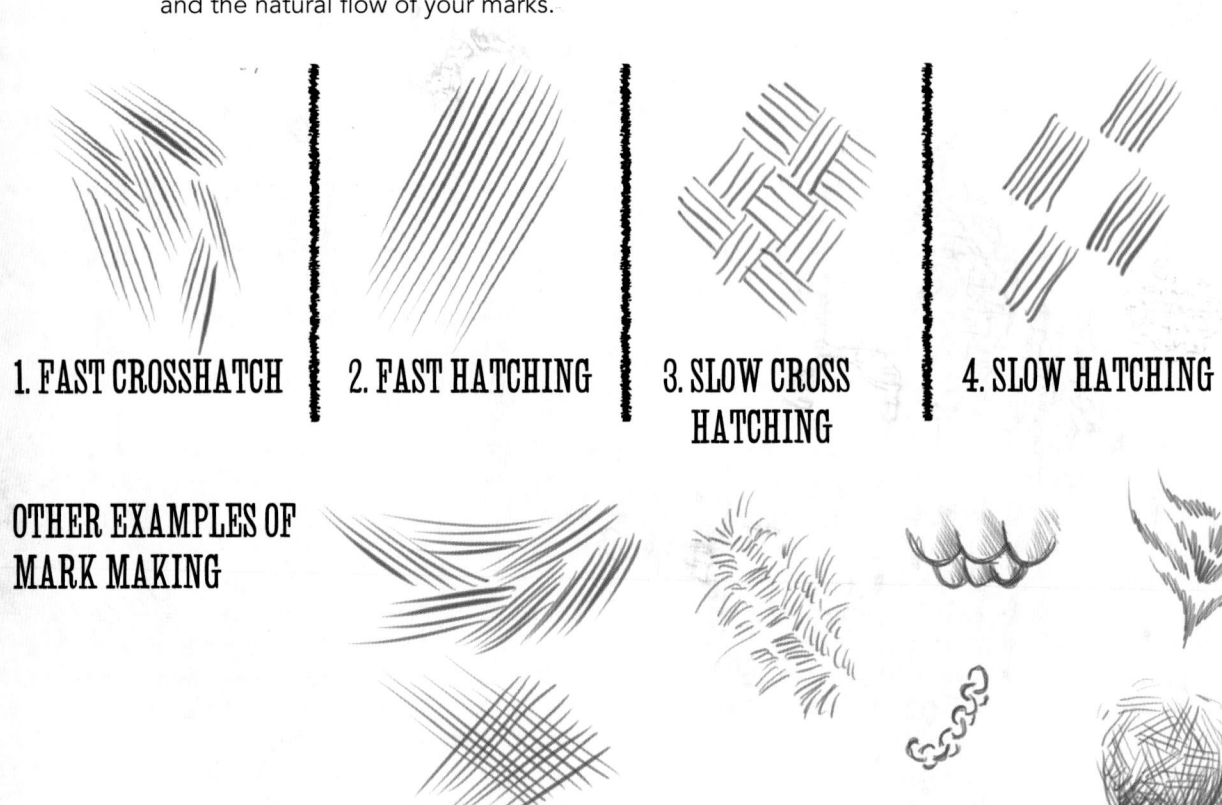

1. FAST CROSSHATCH

2. FAST HATCHING

3. SLOW CROSS HATCHING

4. SLOW HATCHING

OTHER EXAMPLES OF MARK MAKING

SHADING/TONE

A soft pencil (5B, or higher if you prefer) gently rubbed into the paper is a very effective shading technique. Try also using the side of the lead to create a deep, soft tone. Experiment with all of the different shades that can be achieved by varying the weight you apply to the pencil, using the edge of the lead, or even just having the pencil at varying sharpness – it will definitely be time well spent.

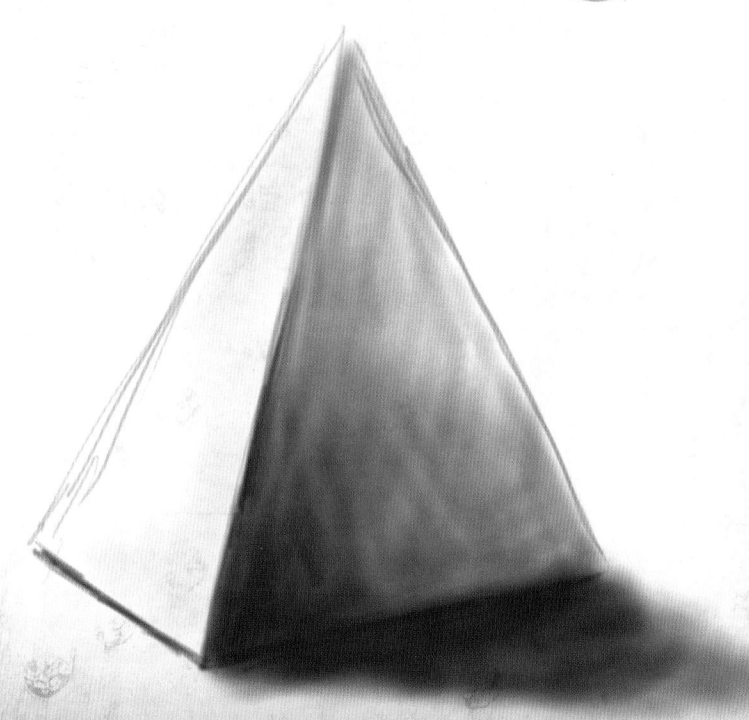

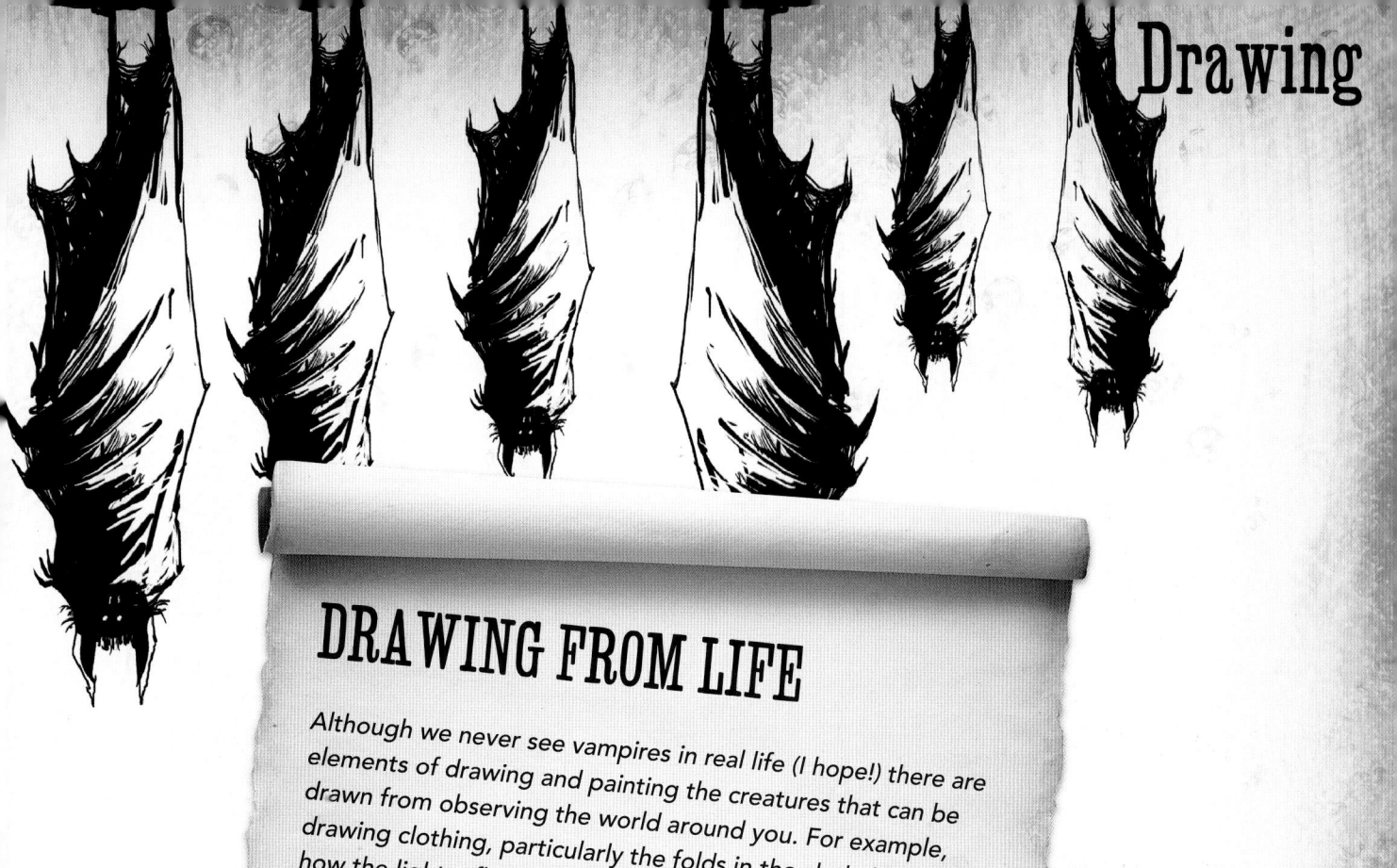

DRAWING FROM LIFE

Although we never see vampires in real life (I hope!) there are elements of drawing and painting the creatures that can be drawn from observing the world around you. For example, drawing clothing, particularly the folds in the cloth, how it hangs, how the light reflects from its surface and so on will provide excellent reference and practise. Draw as many people as you can, and study their facial expressions, body language, posture, hair, eyes, hands and feet.

Drawing from nature, observing the trees, animals, insects and so on will provide you with a catalogue of reference points for your background environments, as will drawing any interesting architecture that you come across. Always take your sketchbook out with you wherever you go, because you never know when you're going to find something useful.

It is also a good idea to take yourself out on a dedicated sketching session – go to a busy place, such as a coffee shop, and draw the sights around you. Once you're comfortable drawing in public (it can take a bit of getting used to!) take yourself off to record some interesting features of nature, or a building or graveyard, perhaps, that has grabbed your interest.

Don't forget that using photo reference for people is always very useful, but if you're going to draw an exact copy with only slight changes (fangs), then make sure that you get the photograph owner's permission beforehand!

Colour

PAINTING

So you've finished all your planning, sketched up and refined your vampire, and are now ready to paint. This can sometimes be a very scary process, especially if you're painting traditionally and you're just starting out. Here you will learn some basic principles on colour to help you on your way.

THE COLOUR WHEEL

With the entire spectrum of the rainbow, the colour wheel is an excellent aid to which colours work well together and how they relate to each other. It is a good idea to always have the wheel to hand when you are doing any colour work.

WARM/COOL

The colour wheel can be sliced into two halves, one side representing cool colour, the other side warm. Warm colours can be energetic, full of heat and passion, while cool colours are calming and soothing.

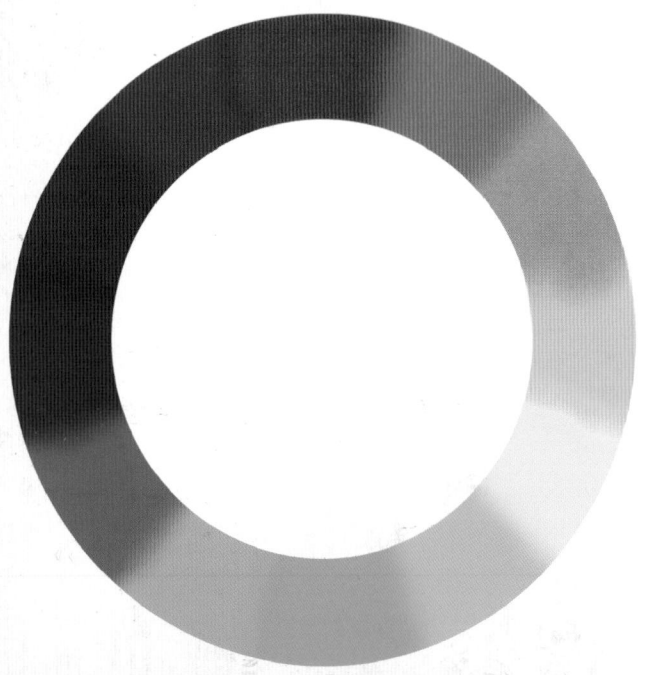

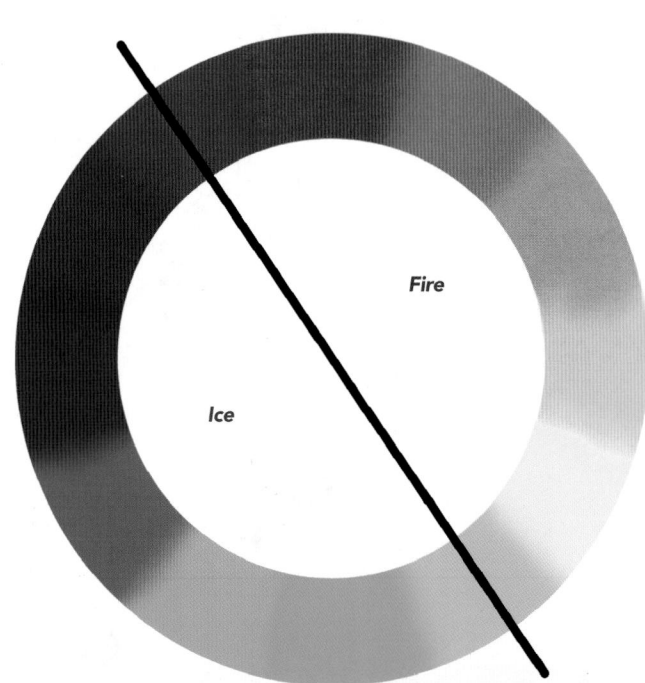

Fire

Ice

COMPLEMENTARY COLOURS

The colours that are opposite each other on the colour wheel are known as complementary. These colours contrast well with each other and have an intensifying effect. Don't be surprised if you find yourself particularly drawn to certain colours in your work – reds and greens are prevalent in my work, and I feel drawn towards them when I see them.

ANALOGOUS COLOURS

Analogous colour schemes are next to each other on the colour wheel. These colours work well together using one as your base colour, one as your highlights and the last as your darker areas. Make sure you have enough contrast if you use this technique.

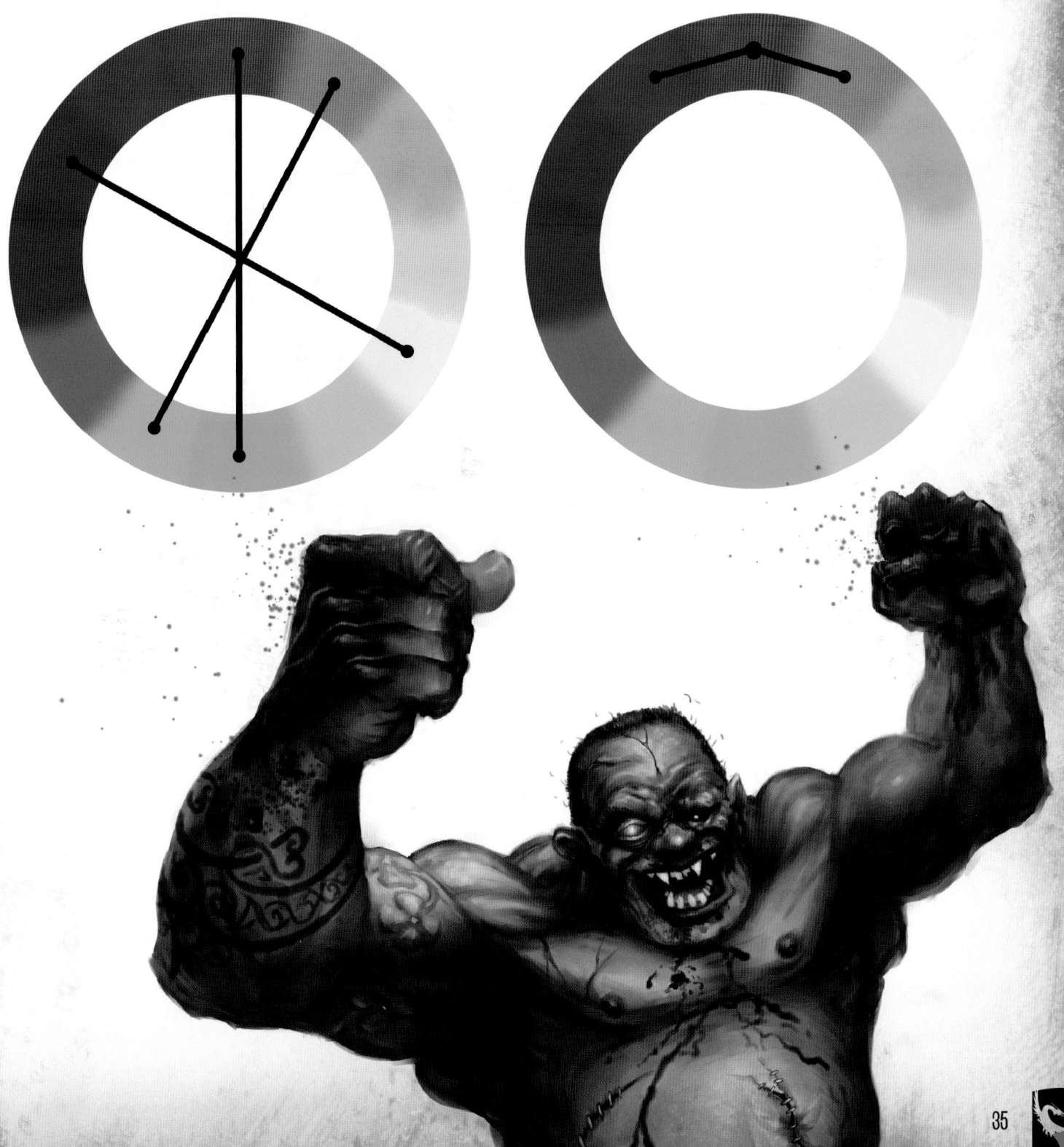

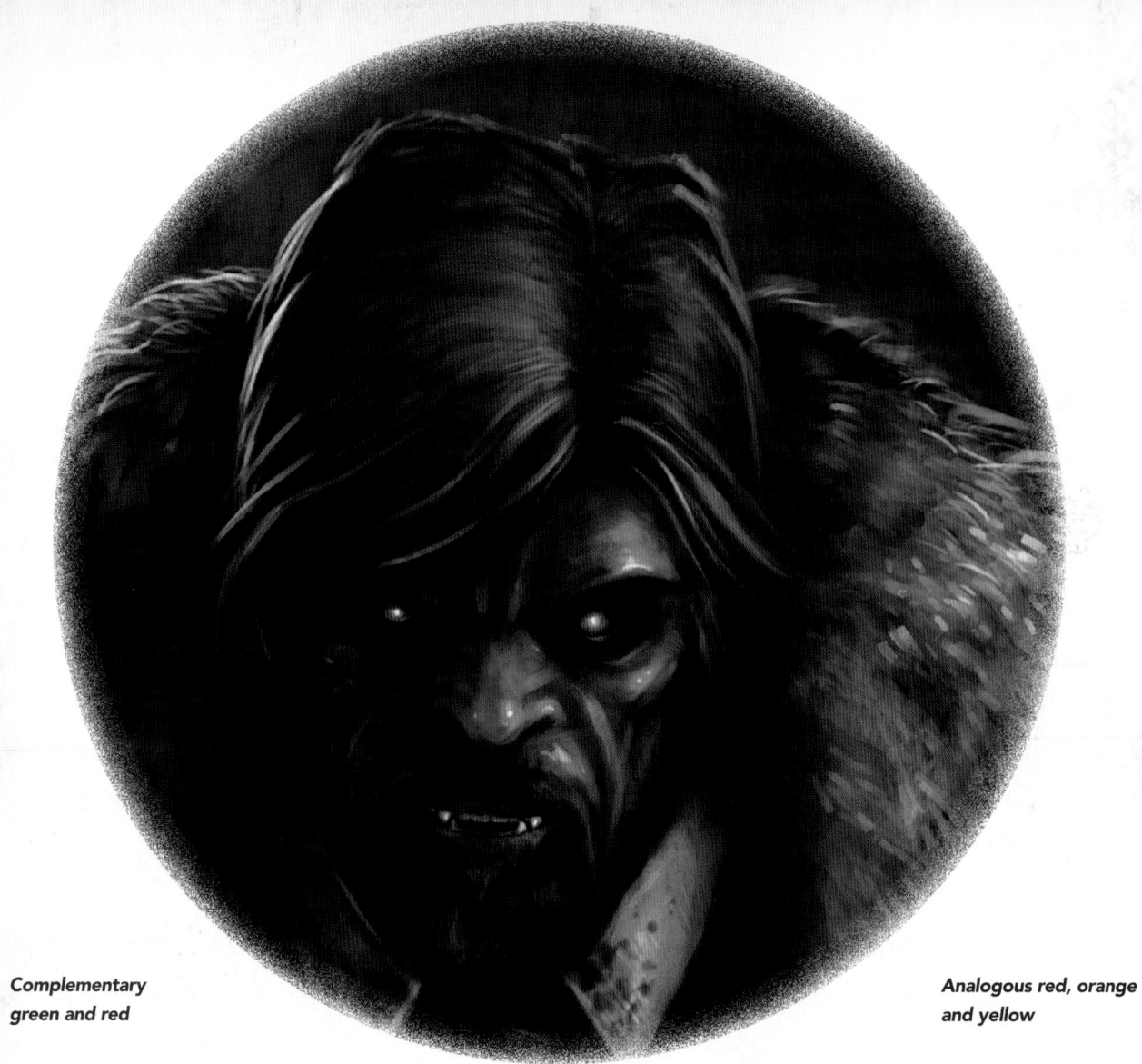

*Complementary
green and red*

*Analogous red, orange
and yellow*

COLOUR CHOICE

Keeping your palette tight and limiting the amount of colours is a
good practice, otherwise you can get yourself in a complete mess
with lots of different colours flying up all over the canvas. This can be
difficult to control, but is even more difficult to rectify and make look
good. Analogous and complementary colours are tried and tested,
so this is an excellent starting point for the amateur artist. You could
even use the analogous colours with a complementary colour for
lighting to help your image to 'pop'.

RELATIVITY

Colours can appear differently when they're placed next to or in another colour. In the image below you can see that the colour within the squares looks very different, but the smaller square is exactly the same colour in both images.

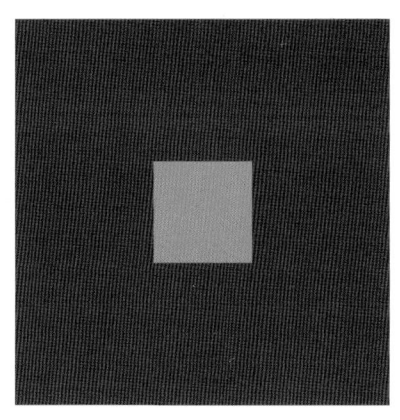

THREE IMPORTANT POINTS OF COLOUR

It is vital for any artist to understand the different aspects of colour. Here are three points that are worth remembering.

HUE

Used for all of the colours, red, green, blue etc.

VALUE

Describes the lightness or darkness of the colour. The darker a value of colour you use the lower value it will be. The lighter the colour you use, the higher the value it has.

SATURATION

The strength of the colour in use. A low saturated colour is greyish in colour, a high saturation colour is bright and strong, like the colours around the colour wheel.

THE VA

MPIRES

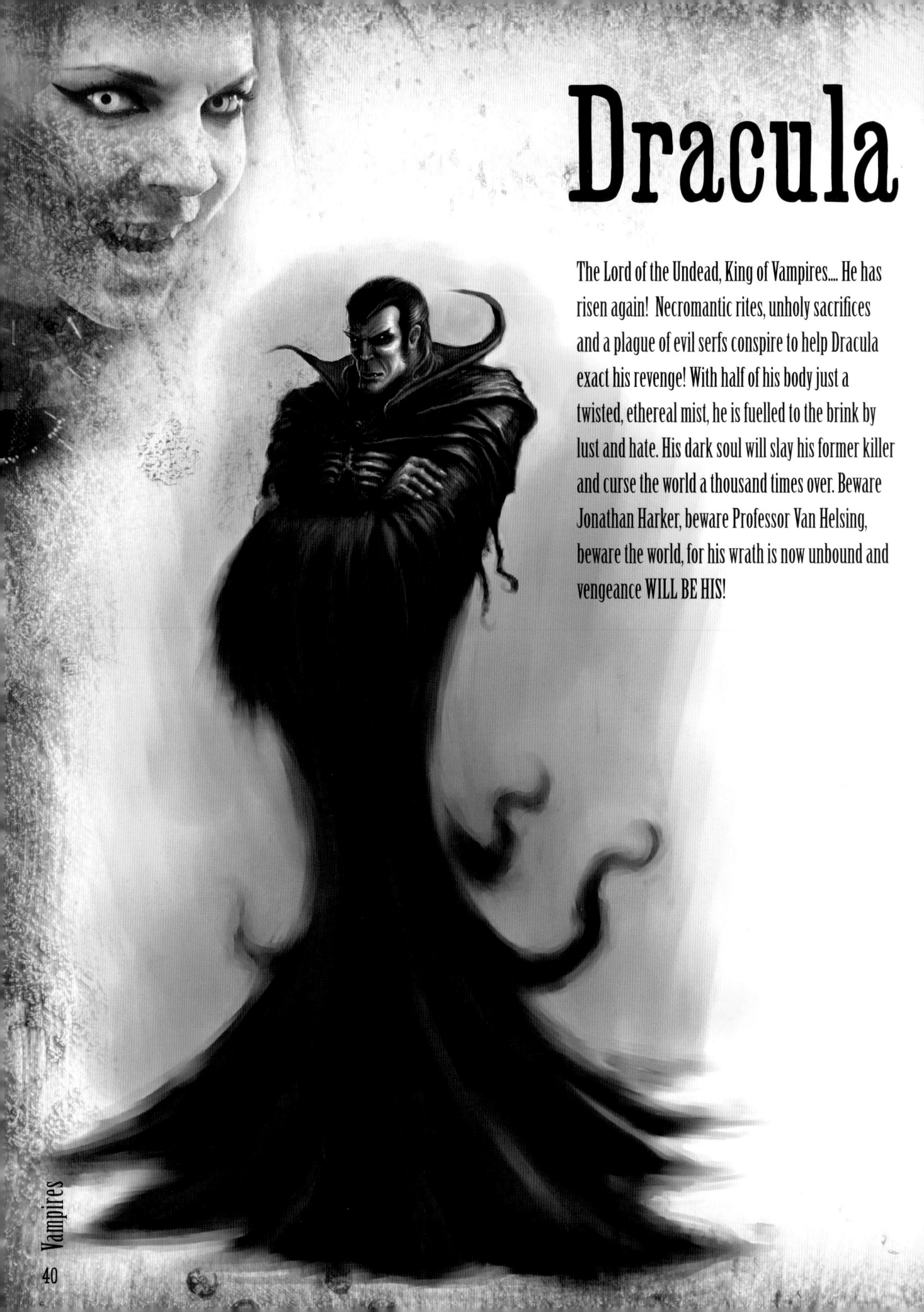

Dracula

The Lord of the Undead, King of Vampires.... He has risen again! Necromantic rites, unholy sacrifices and a plague of evil serfs conspire to help Dracula exact his revenge! With half of his body just a twisted, ethereal mist, he is fuelled to the brink by lust and hate. His dark soul will slay his former killer and curse the world a thousand times over. Beware Jonathan Harker, beware Professor Van Helsing, beware the world, for his wrath is now unbound and vengeance WILL BE HIS!

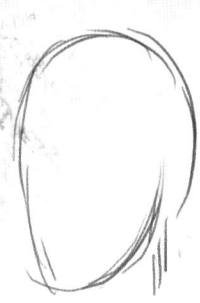

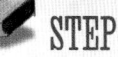

STEP 1

Draw a simple oval shape to begin the head. Give some shape to his jaw, and add a vertical line to show where his neck follows down from the base of the skull.

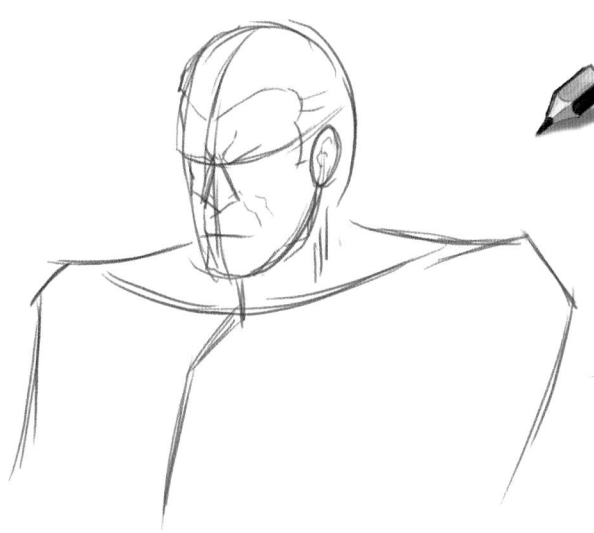

STEP 2

Use some simple curved lines, following the shape of his head, to help you place his facial features. His nose is on the vertical line, while the horizontal line shows you where the eyes will be in relation to the nose. From this you can judge exactly where to put the mouth, ears and eyes, and at what size. Now draw in a rough outline of his shoulders and the form of his chest.

STEP 3

Build up the form of his torso, especially his shoulders and arms, using simple shapes and lines. His arms are folded over his chest, so outline roughly where his fingers will be. Remember to keep your drawing really simple at this stage – this is your chance to rough out where everything is going to fall, and we will add in the detail later.

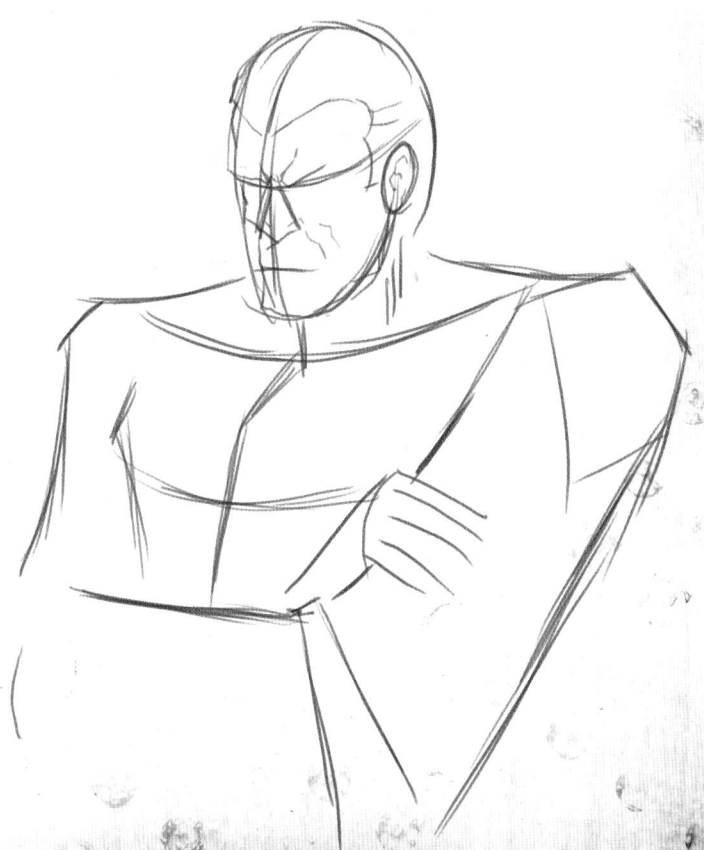

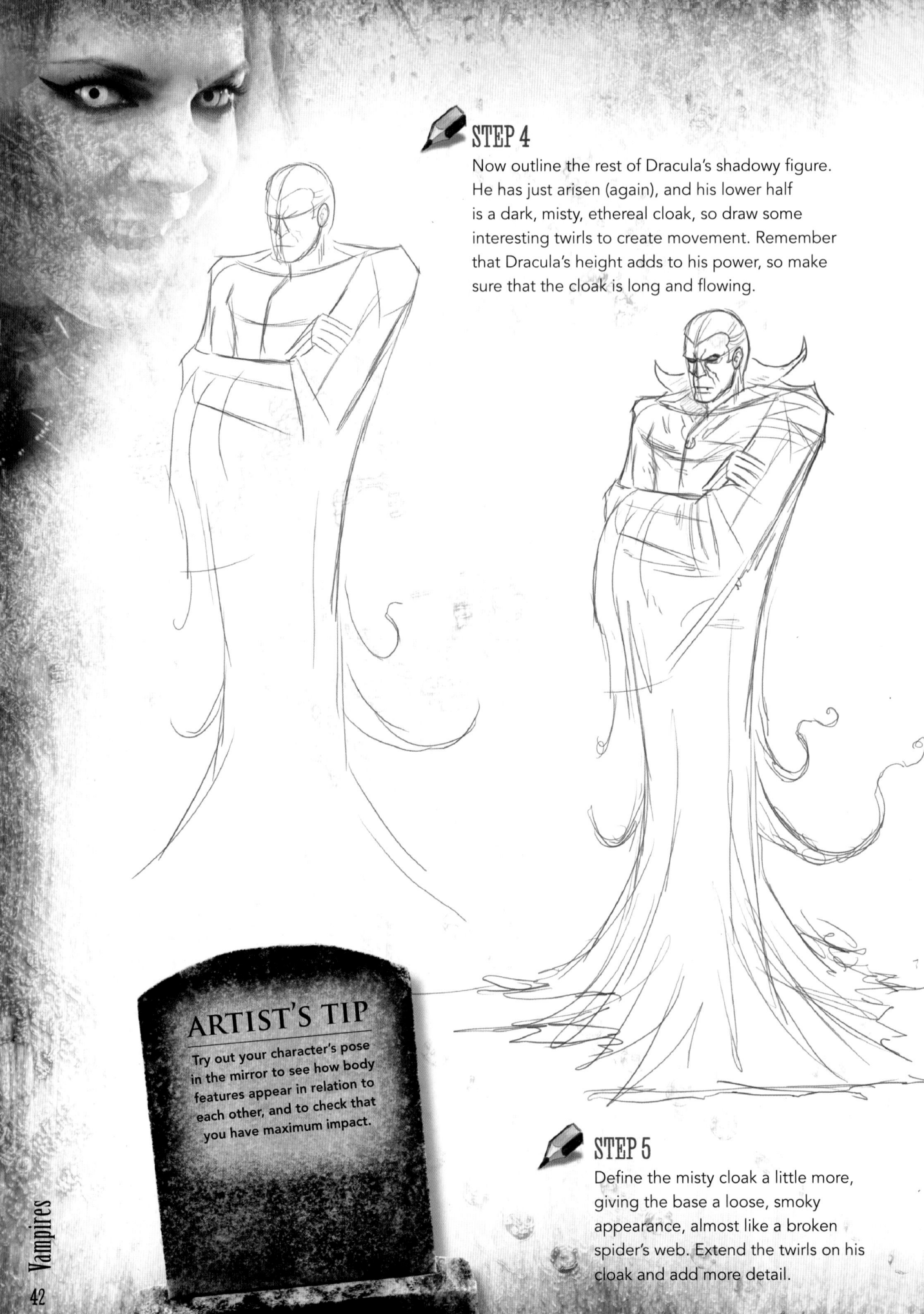

STEP 4

Now outline the rest of Dracula's shadowy figure. He has just arisen (again), and his lower half is a dark, misty, ethereal cloak, so draw some interesting twirls to create movement. Remember that Dracula's height adds to his power, so make sure that the cloak is long and flowing.

ARTIST'S TIP

Try out your character's pose in the mirror to see how body features appear in relation to each other, and to check that you have maximum impact.

STEP 5

Define the misty cloak a little more, giving the base a loose, smoky appearance, almost like a broken spider's web. Extend the twirls on his cloak and add more detail.

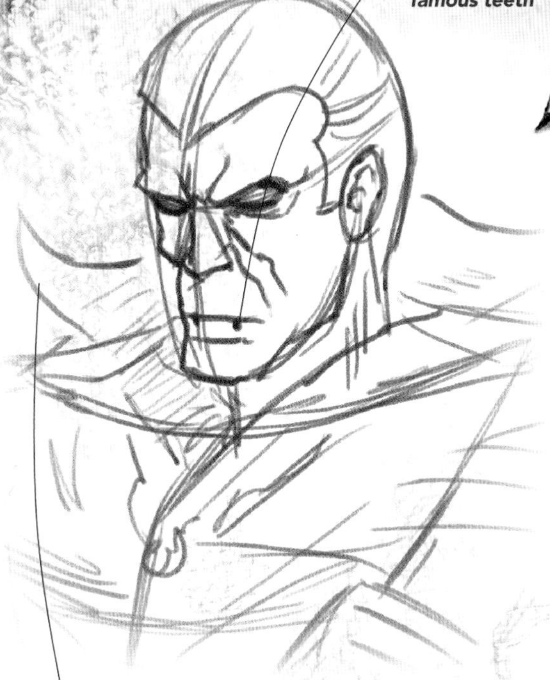

Outline his hairline more and start to work in those famous teeth

STEP 6

Dracula's not going to have a happy face, so start adding some hard facial lines to show his expression. Using an eraser, begin to remove any rough pencil lines that you're not going to use, so that the final outline is clear. If you are working traditionally transfer the final lines of the image onto your final paper with the aid of a lightbox; if you are working digitally create a new layer for the colour work to preserve your pencil sketch in case you need to revert to it at any stage.

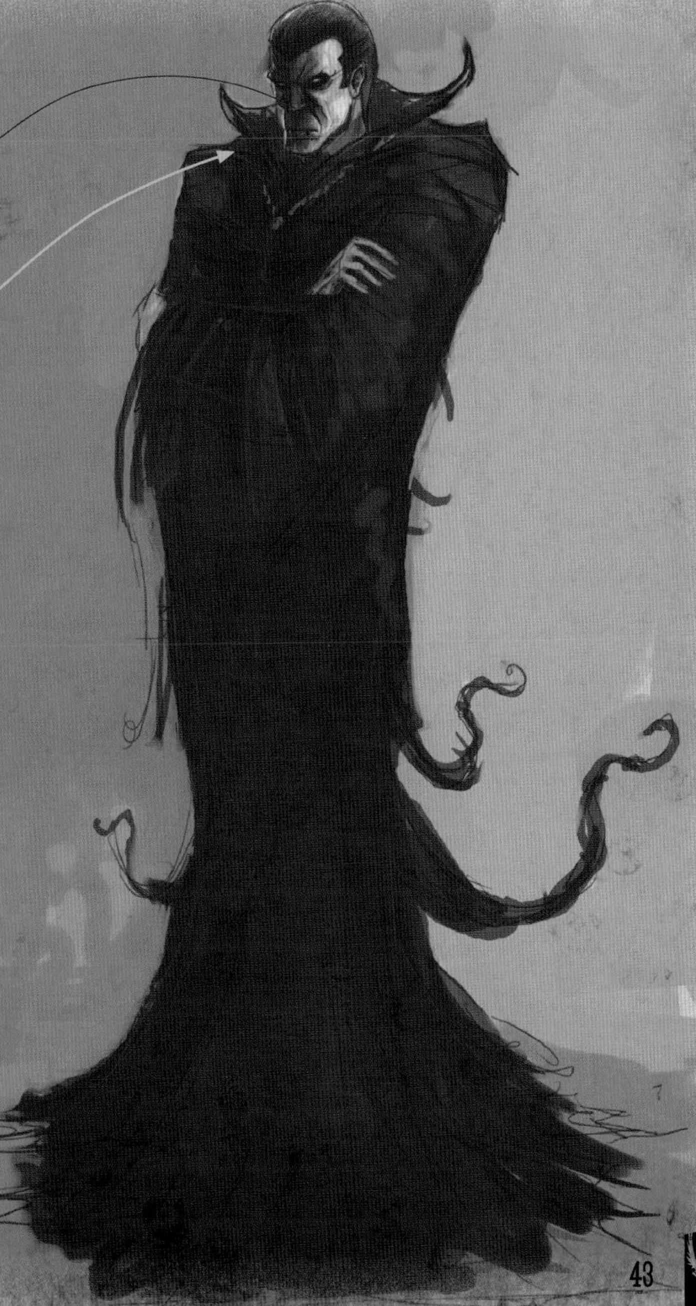

Adding a massive collar completes the look

Having the light coming in from the right lights up half of his face. Putting the other half in shadow adds to the overall evilness, but will also really accentuate his eyes

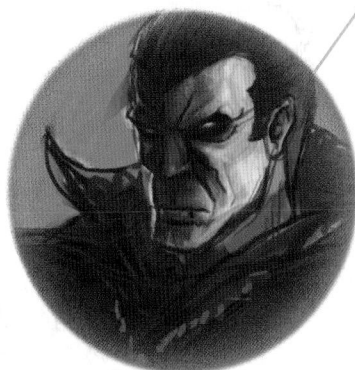

STEP 7

Now the fun part! Grab a collection of brushes and start laying down some tones! Don't worry too much about being neat and precise – you can paint over any problems that might arise. Decide where your light source is coming from and use a dark colour wash to outline the tones and areas of shadow, then go back and work in some highlights.

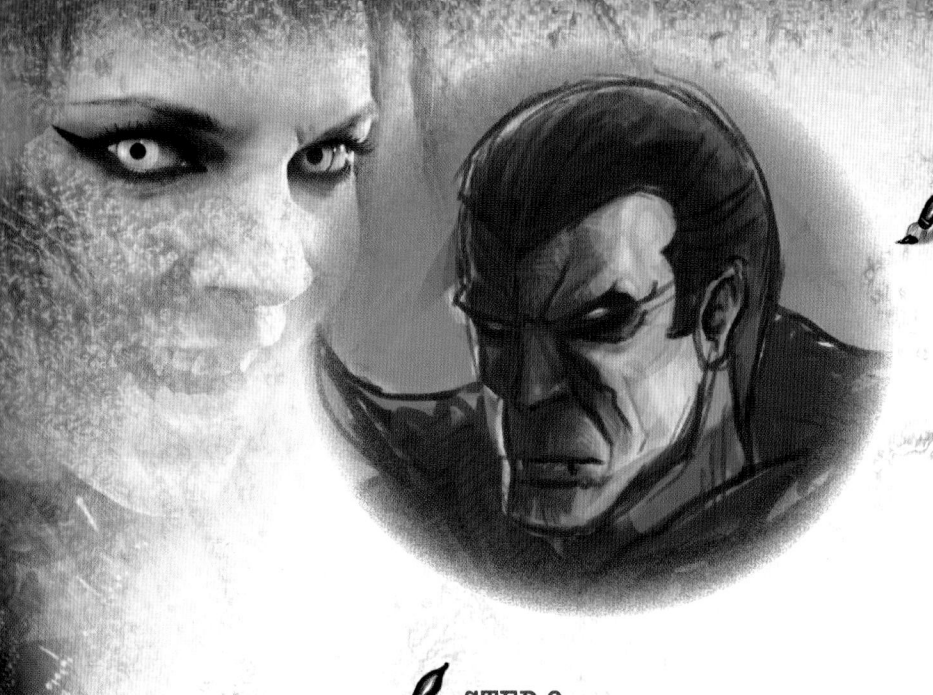

STEP 8

Use a small brush loaded with whites and greys (or 50% opaque in Photoshop) to follow the form of his features.

STEP 9

Use simple highlight lines to indicate the fingers and hand a bit more clearly – we will come back to these later to tidy them up and finish off.

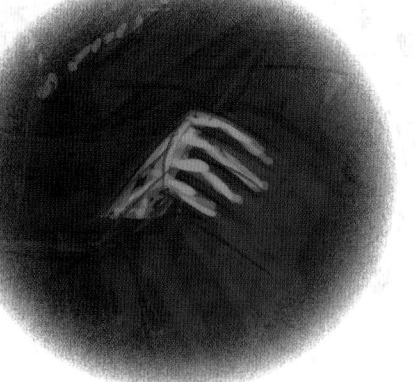

Don't worry if you go over his body a little as you can correct that later, but avoid going near the detail of his face and shoulders

STEP 10

Using a large, soft brush, paint over the background with white.

Vampires

44

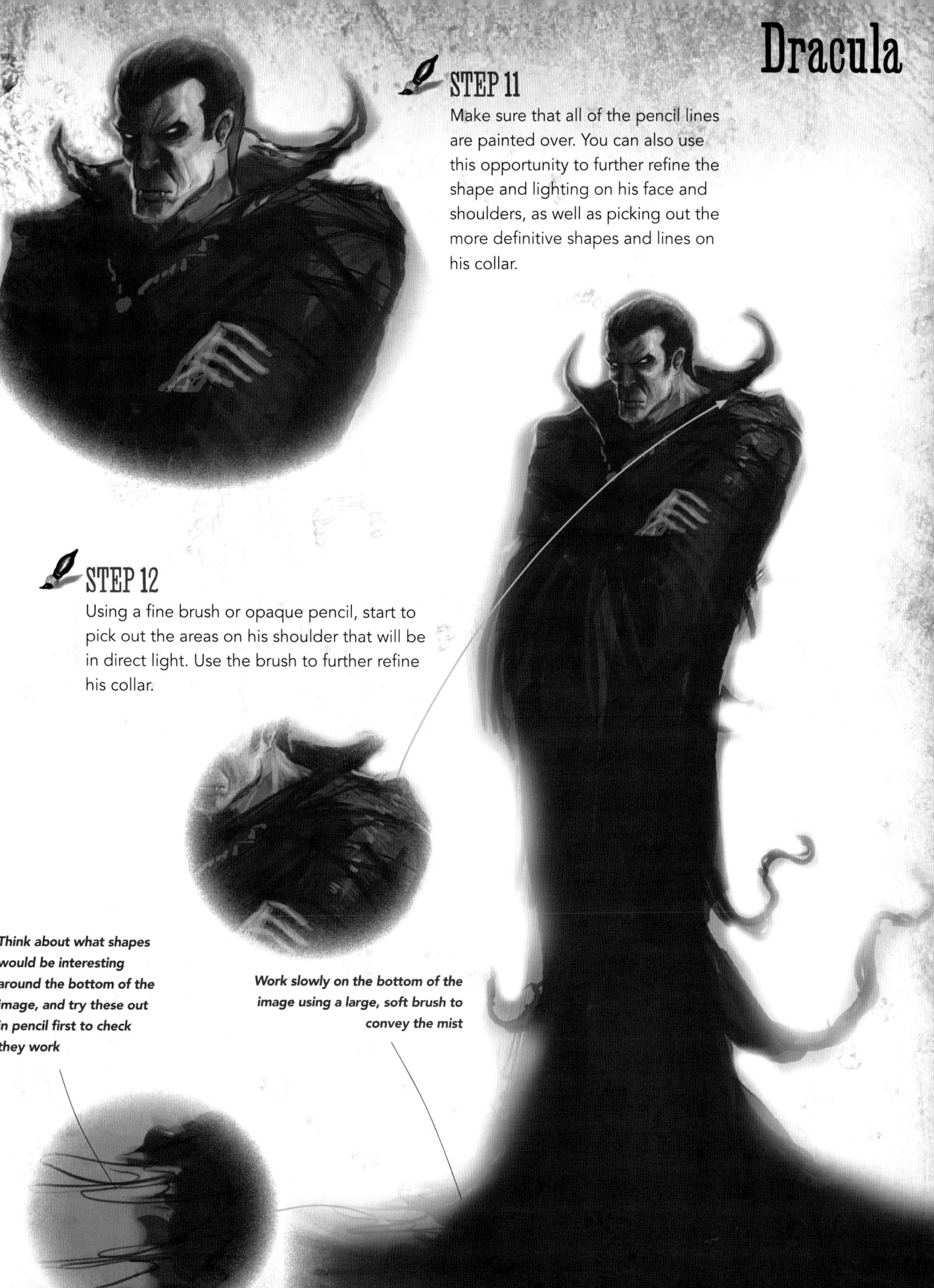

STEP 11

Make sure that all of the pencil lines are painted over. You can also use this opportunity to further refine the shape and lighting on his face and shoulders, as well as picking out the more definitive shapes and lines on his collar.

STEP 12

Using a fine brush or opaque pencil, start to pick out the areas on his shoulder that will be in direct light. Use the brush to further refine his collar.

Think about what shapes would be interesting around the bottom of the image, and try these out in pencil first to check they work

Work slowly on the bottom of the image using a large, soft brush to convey the mist

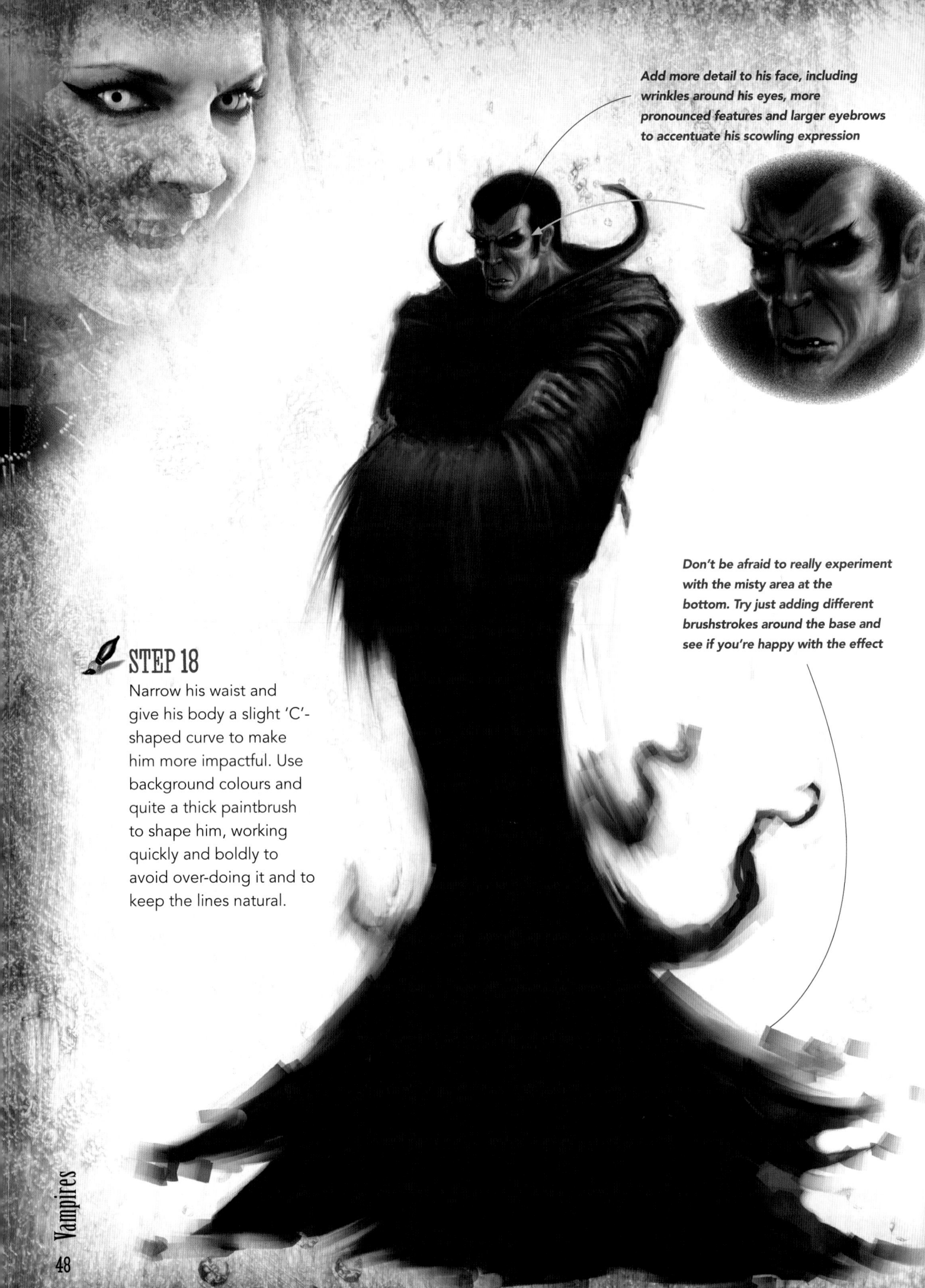

Add more detail to his face, including wrinkles around his eyes, more pronounced features and larger eyebrows to accentuate his scowling expression

Don't be afraid to really experiment with the misty area at the bottom. Try just adding different brushstrokes around the base and see if you're happy with the effect

STEP 18

Narrow his waist and give his body a slight 'C'-shaped curve to make him more impactful. Use background colours and quite a thick paintbrush to shape him, working quickly and boldly to avoid over-doing it and to keep the lines natural.

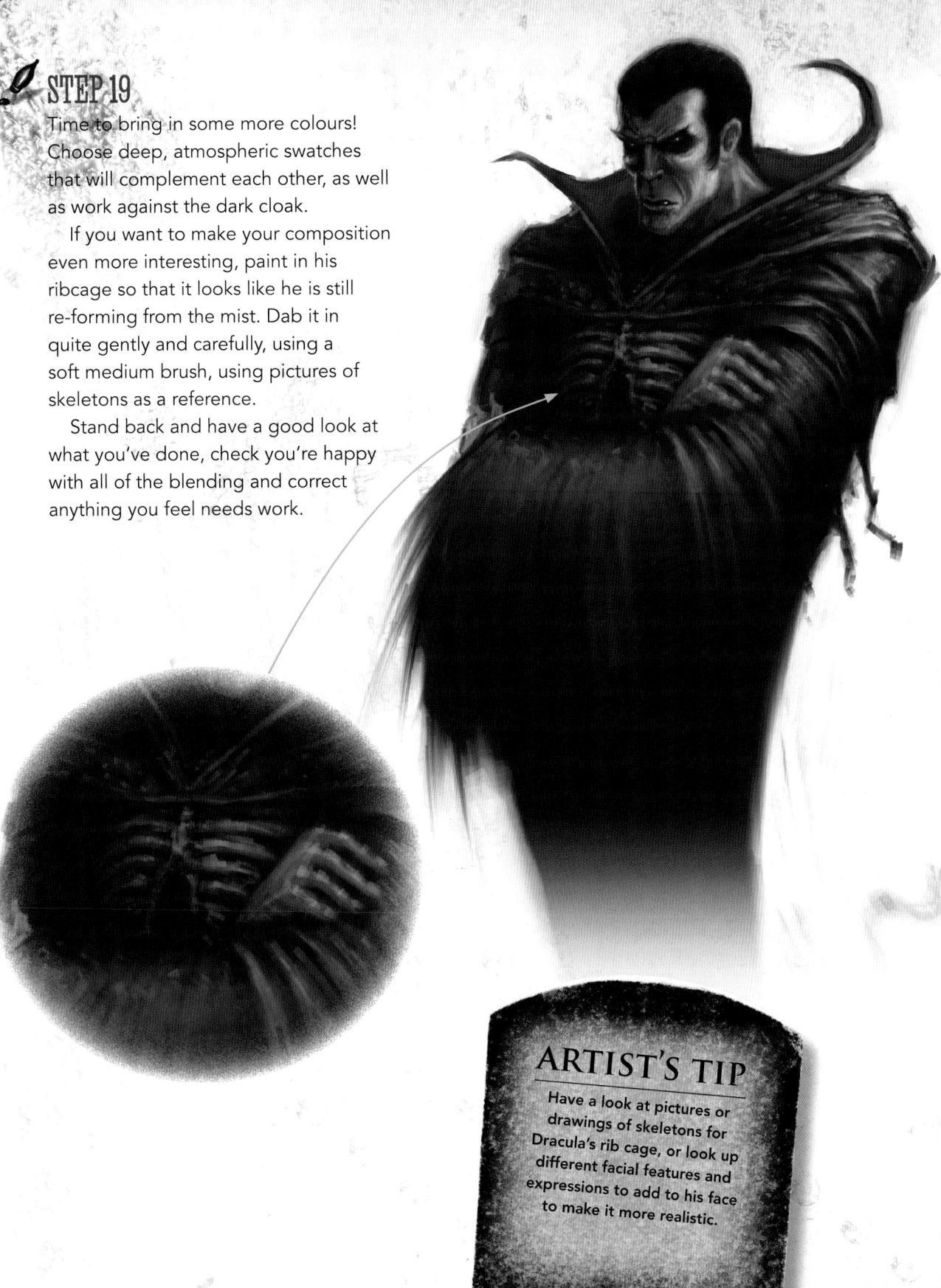

STEP 19

Time to bring in some more colours! Choose deep, atmospheric swatches that will complement each other, as well as work against the dark cloak.

If you want to make your composition even more interesting, paint in his ribcage so that it looks like he is still re-forming from the mist. Dab it in quite gently and carefully, using a soft medium brush, using pictures of skeletons as a reference.

Stand back and have a good look at what you've done, check you're happy with all of the blending and correct anything you feel needs work.

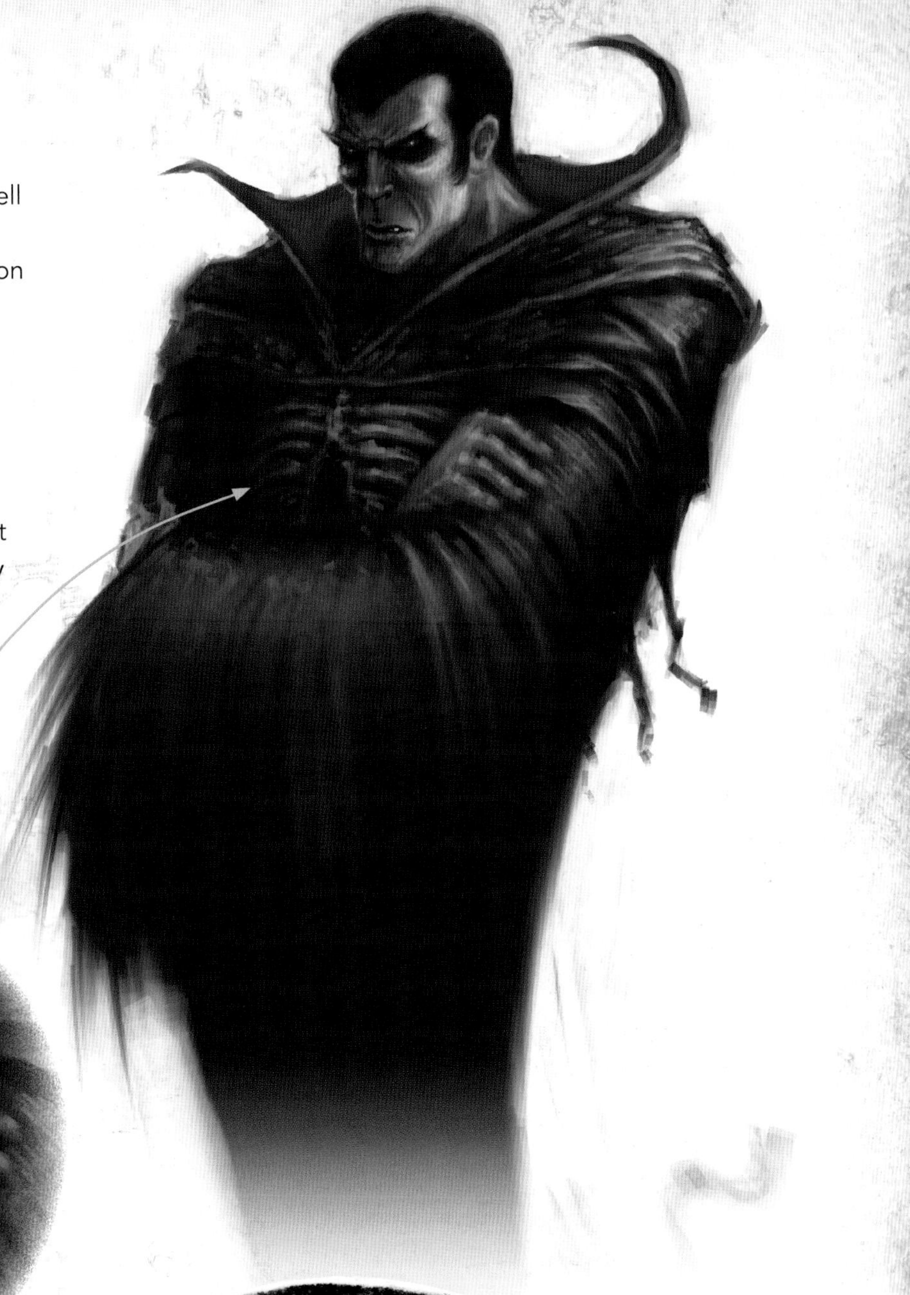

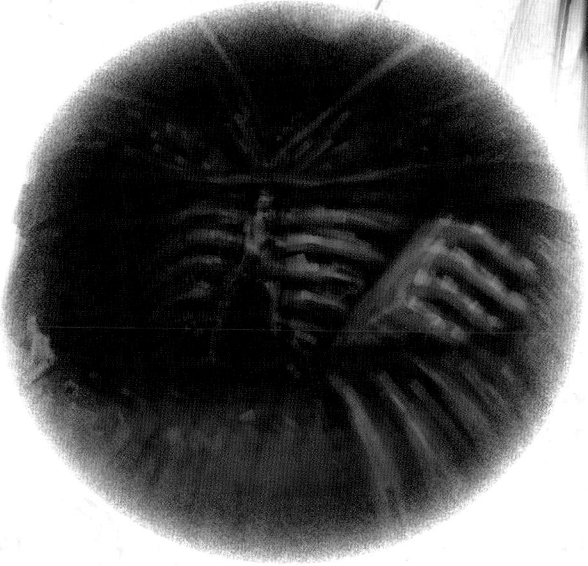

ARTIST'S TIP

Have a look at pictures or drawings of skeletons for Dracula's rib cage, or look up different facial features and expressions to add to his face to make it more realistic.

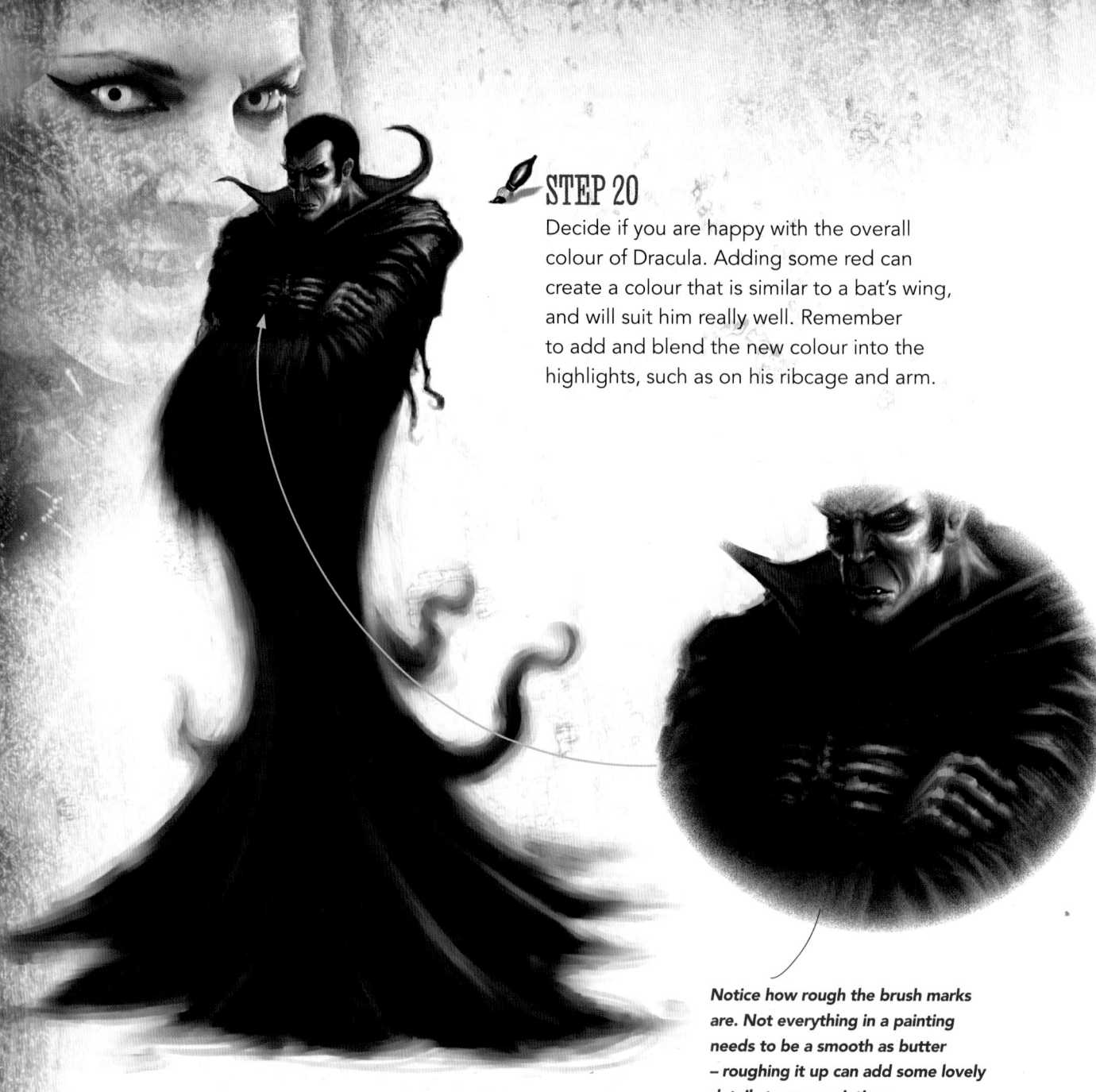

STEP 20

Decide if you are happy with the overall colour of Dracula. Adding some red can create a colour that is similar to a bat's wing, and will suit him really well. Remember to add and blend the new colour into the highlights, such as on his ribcage and arm.

Notice how rough the brush marks are. Not everything in a painting needs to be a smooth as butter – roughing it up can add some lovely details to your paintings

FINAL PIECE

Choose a background wash colour and add this in with a large brush, using gentle strokes over the area you want shaded. Add some final details, such as long hair with additional pencil highlights, and detail on the left side of his face to separate it from the blue wash of the background. For the hair, begin with a large brush mark and then use a smaller brush to add in the highlights. Paint a small necklace in just peeking above his collar. Claws are essential on his hand, along with wrinkles!

Because of the angle, just an indication of Dracula's other hand is enough for your eye and mind to read it, so don't spend too much time perfecting this. The detail should be on his head and shoulders and your eye will be drawn to that. The original, legendary, most fearsome vampire is back!

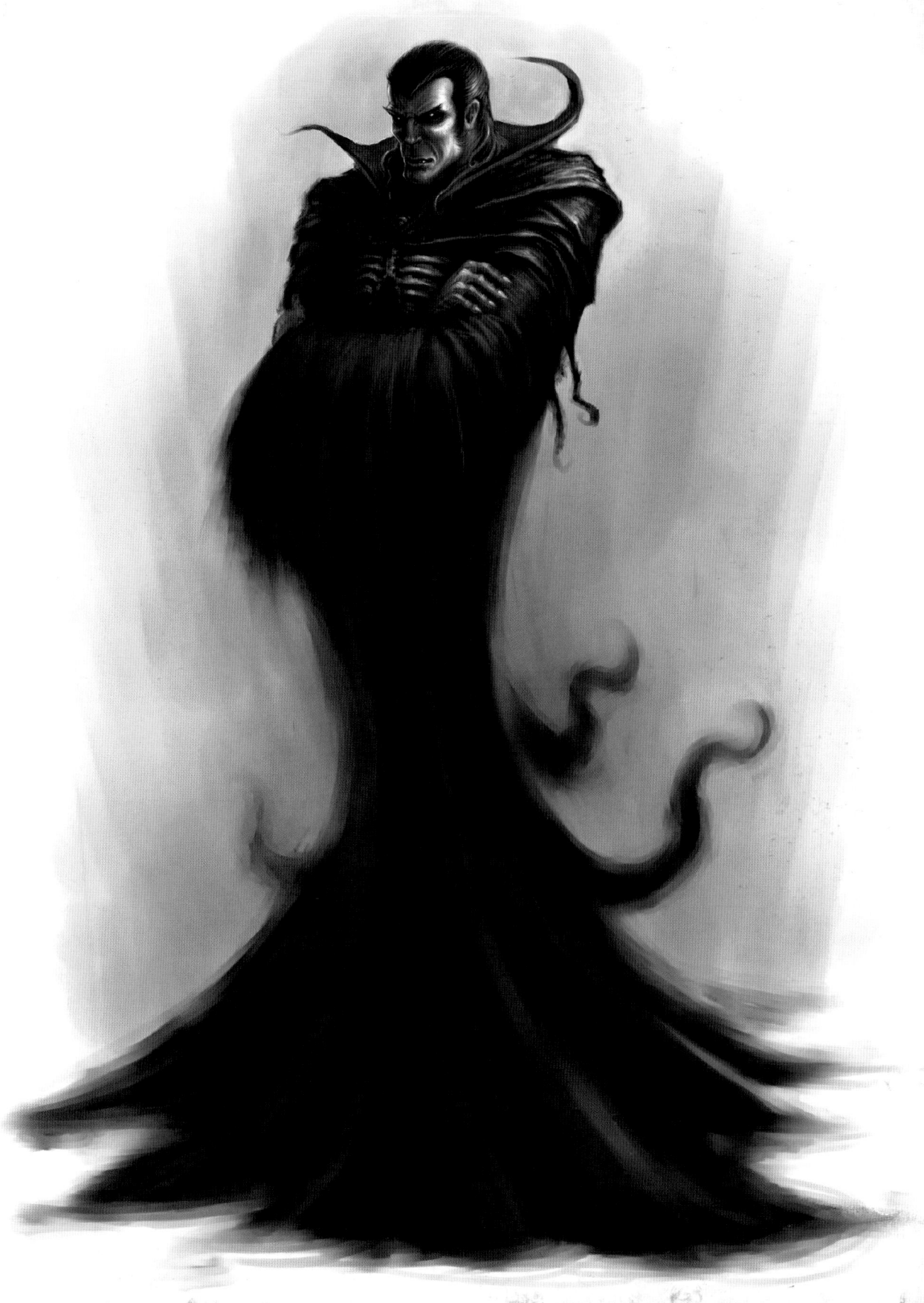

Cheerleader

Britney Bishops, the most popular girl at school, was on her way to the senior prom when her car broke down. Zack, her boyfriend, lifted the bonnet and began to check the engine while Britney smiled to herself happily and checked her makeup. Realising Zack had gone quiet, she decided to get out and check how he was getting on.

As she stepped towards the front of the car she heard a strange snuffling sound. Then the breathing started — heavy breathing that was getting deeper and slower. Daring to look, the scene that met her eyes was one of carnage and bloodshed.

Zack was lying on the floor in bloody pieces and, standing over him on hind legs was what looked like a wolf. It grinned at her with wet, red fangs, and winked. 'Hello Britney' it growled. 'I've got a present for you.' It threw a wet ball-sized object into her chest, knocking her off her feet. Looking down, she saw Zack's lifeless head in her lap, its glazed eyes staring into hers. With tears streaming down her face she started to giggle, threw her head back and laughed out loud. The wolf grinned. 'I want us to be friends, Britney. I want you to be just like me.' He showed his row of shiny fangs and moved towards her, licking his lips. She giggled again, stroked Zack's blood-soaked hair and smiled sweetly as the creature's shadow loomed over her…

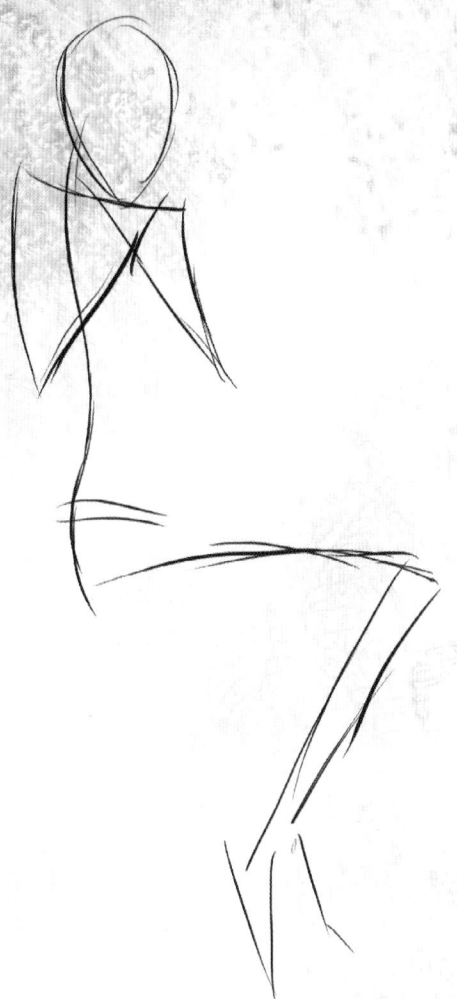

STEP 2

Now start adding some more detail, building on the shapes from under the frame. Tilt her head down to make her look coy but also slightly sinister, and mark your facial lines to help with proportion.

Remember that tilting her head down will mean that we can see more of the top of her head and the ears will be higher

Because this vampire is female, it's important to give her a thinner, more tapered waist than a male character

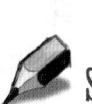

STEP 1

Start with a simple line drawing of the frame and head of your character. Think about the basic shapes that her arms and legs make, and draw this quickly and simply without any detail.

ARTIST'S TIP

Ask a friend to model your character's pose for you so that you can check the perspective. Take photographs from lots of different angles so that you can clearly see what aspects are visible from each viewpoint, and start to build up your very own reference file.

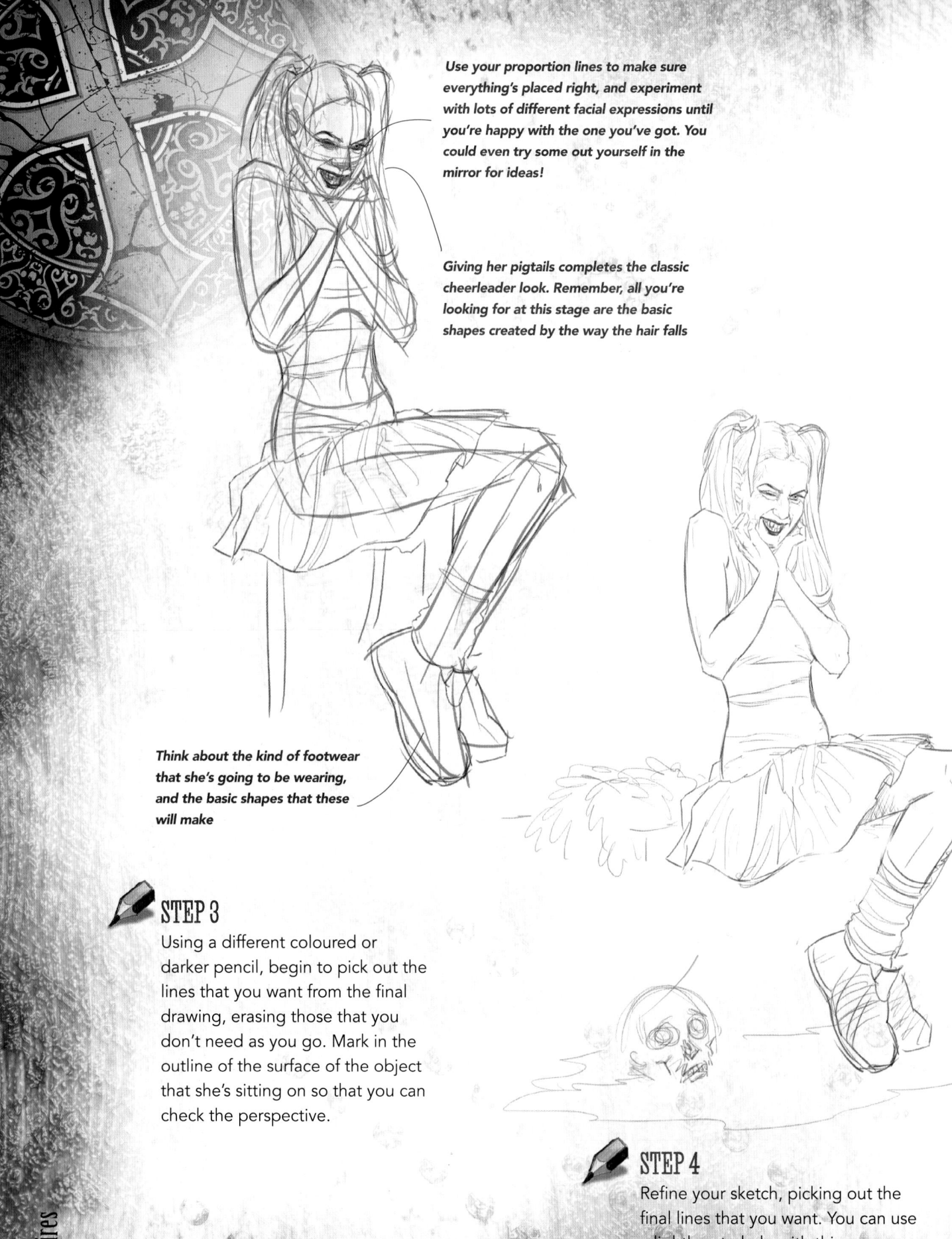

Use your proportion lines to make sure everything's placed right, and experiment with lots of different facial expressions until you're happy with the one you've got. You could even try some out yourself in the mirror for ideas!

Giving her pigtails completes the classic cheerleader look. Remember, all you're looking for at this stage are the basic shapes created by the way the hair falls

Think about the kind of footwear that she's going to be wearing, and the basic shapes that these will make

STEP 3

Using a different coloured or darker pencil, begin to pick out the lines that you want from the final drawing, erasing those that you don't need as you go. Mark in the outline of the surface of the object that she's sitting on so that you can check the perspective.

STEP 4

Refine your sketch, picking out the final lines that you want. You can use a lightbox to help with this process, or a window in daylight will do the trick (see page 70).

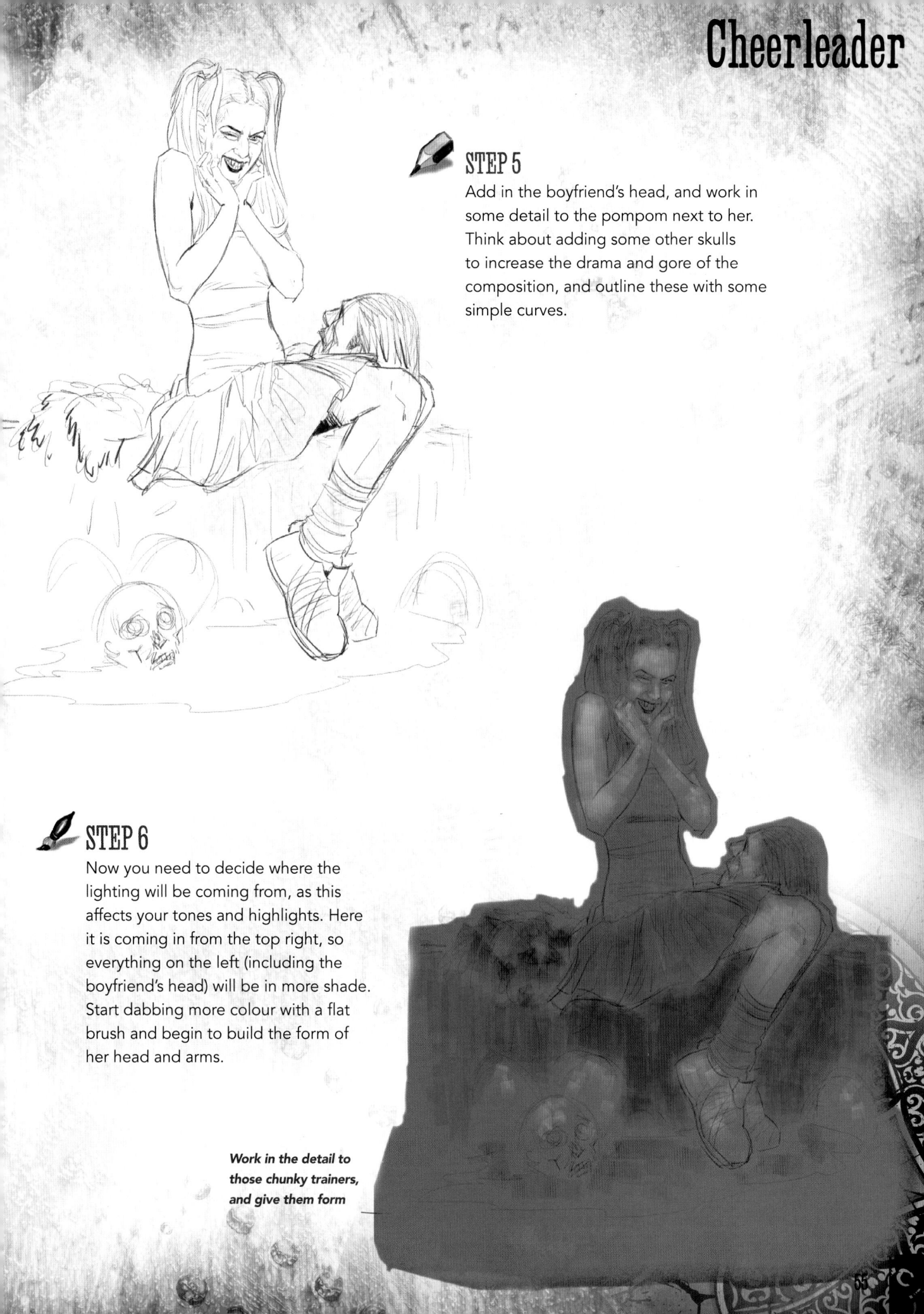

STEP 5

Add in the boyfriend's head, and work in some detail to the pompom next to her. Think about adding some other skulls to increase the drama and gore of the composition, and outline these with some simple curves.

STEP 6

Now you need to decide where the lighting will be coming from, as this affects your tones and highlights. Here it is coming in from the top right, so everything on the left (including the boyfriend's head) will be in more shade. Start dabbing more colour with a flat brush and begin to build the form of her head and arms.

Work in the detail to those chunky trainers, and give them form

STEP 7

Continue adding colour, working particularly now on her skin. Use a slight green edge to work with the background and bring the composition together, with a dirty yellow to accentuate the skin and really give her an unhealthy pallor. Continue blending the skin until you're happy with it, before picking out the highlights when the paint has dried.

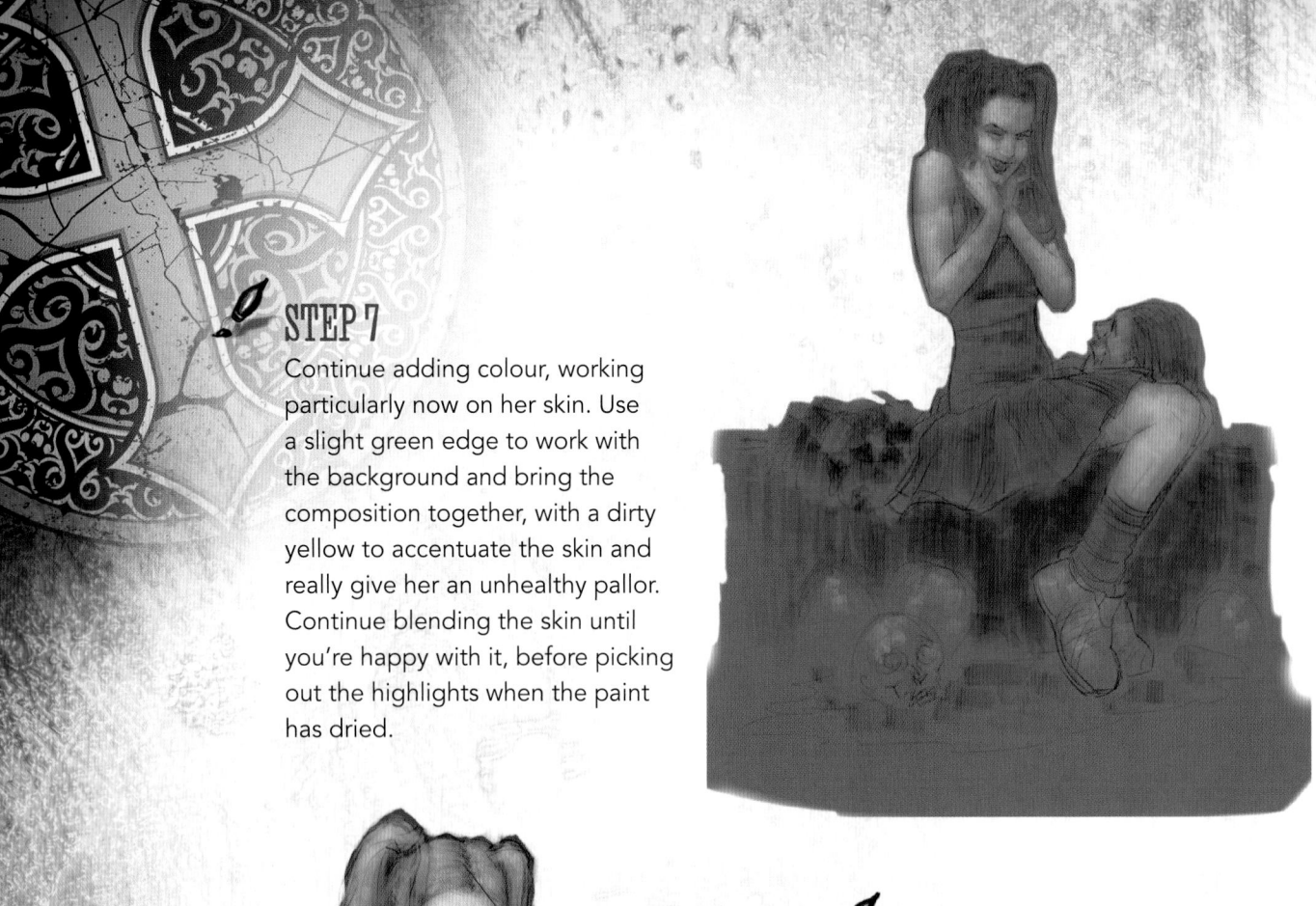

Start picking out the shapes and tones of her skirt, using references if necessary to perfect the lie of the material

Use a small, round oil brush to paint in her lips and start to pick out her hair

STEP 8

You can now see that the highlighting is a little too white, and doesn't look realistic. Rather than stop and correct it now, address it as you work your way around the image as a whole.

ARTIST'S TIP

If you're working digitally it is a good idea to stop and flip your image from time to time. Changing the perspective enables you to see parts of the image that aren't working for some reason. If you're working traditionally, looking at your picture in a mirror will produce the same effect.

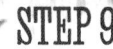

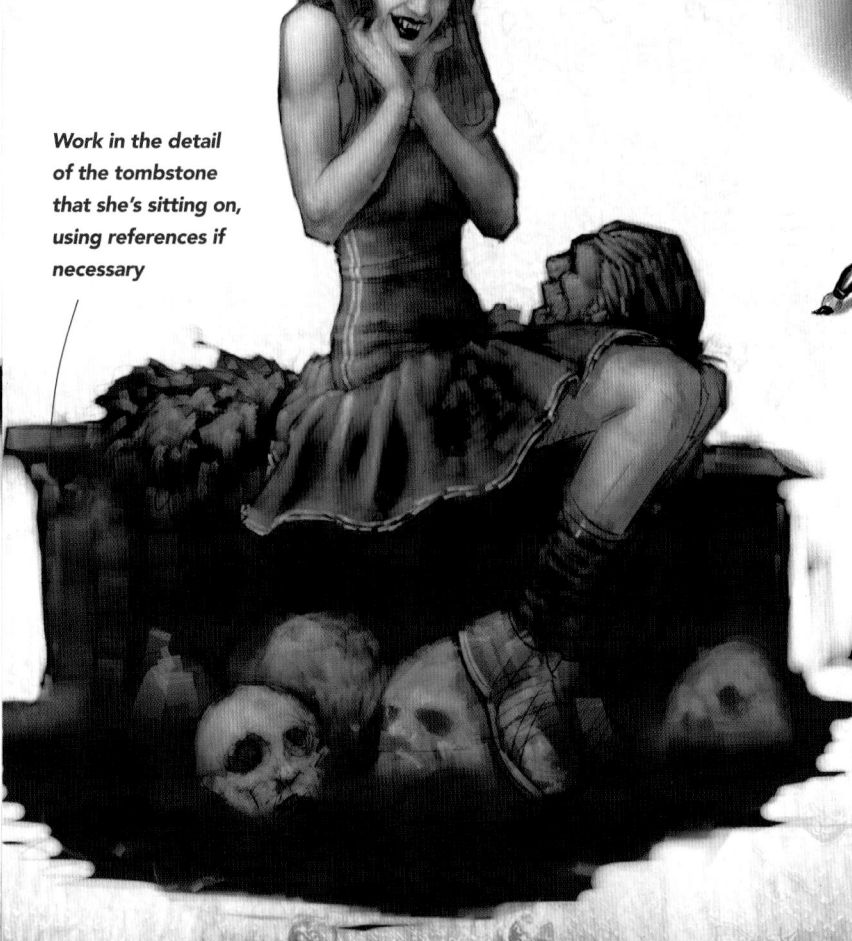

STEP 9

Using a fairly saturated yellow, wash over the skin to give a really sickly tinge to her complexion. This will also help to address the highlighting issue. Pick another analogous, brighter, saturated tone of the red hair, such as orange, and apply that where the light bounces off her head.

STEP 10

Using a small, fine brush, paint in the detail of her iris and pupil. Check the blending of the skin on her face.

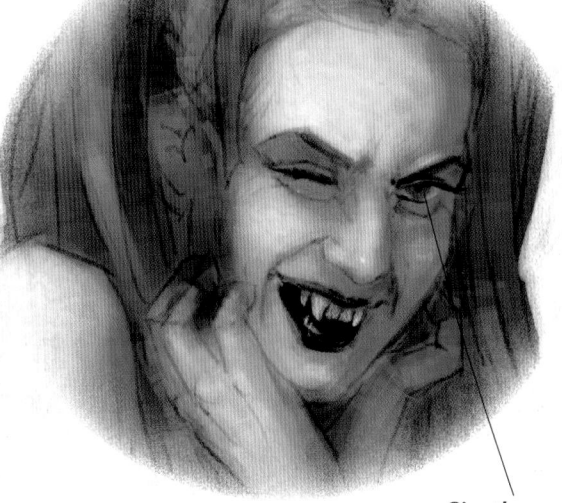

Give the pupil a bright, pin-prick of light using white paint

Work in the detail of the tombstone that she's sitting on, using references if necessary

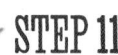
STEP 11

This stage of a project is a good time to stand back and look at it from a distance to check that you're happy with everything. The blue tone of the dead flesh now looks really effective, so increasing the blues in the skin tones and highlights will accentuate this. Check also that you're happy with how the character's details are lying, such as the skirt, hair and top – this is the last opportunity you will get to really change these without it messing up the rest of the image. Use a fine brush to add textures and details, and to make any other changes.

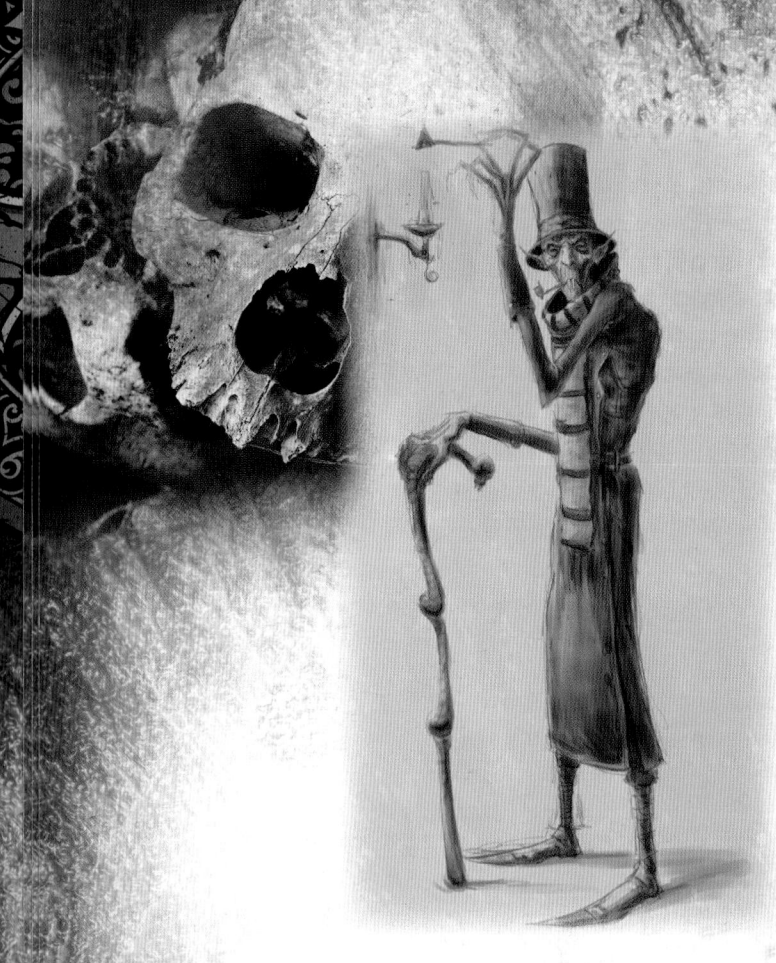

STEP 10

Wash in a grey or green colour on his chin and upper lip to give him the appearance of being unshaven and grubby. Pick a saturated orange to add to his ears, enhancing the colour of the light from the candle.

Choose an opaque paint to work in the light around the candle, and work your way round the whole image blending all of your colour washes, especially on the skin of his hands and face

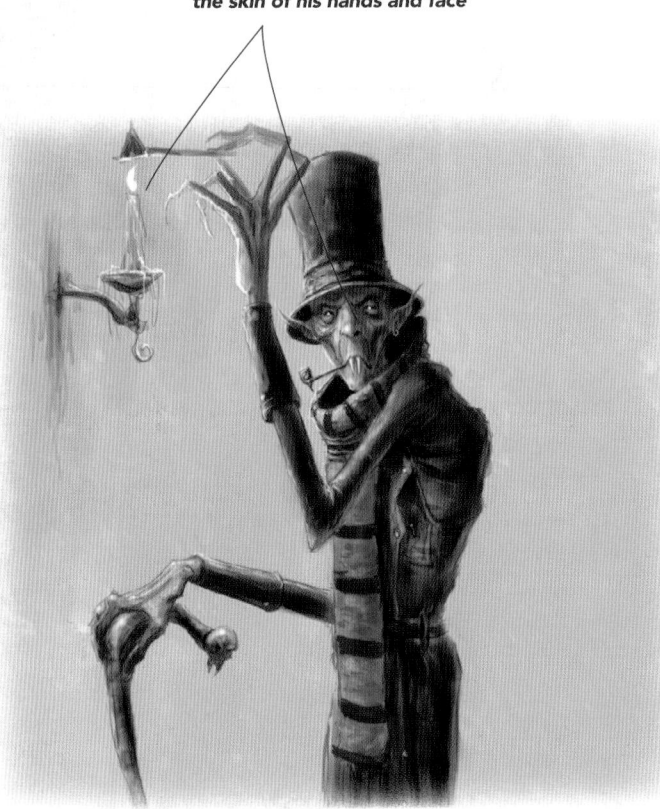

STEP 11

Bring in some more colours now, adding some greys, blues and reds to his coat, and some saturated blues and greens to his scarf. This will really give them depth and texture, and the brightness of the scarf will contrast well with the dreary colours of the rest of the image. Be careful not to overdo the washes otherwise you'll end up with a dirty brown mess!

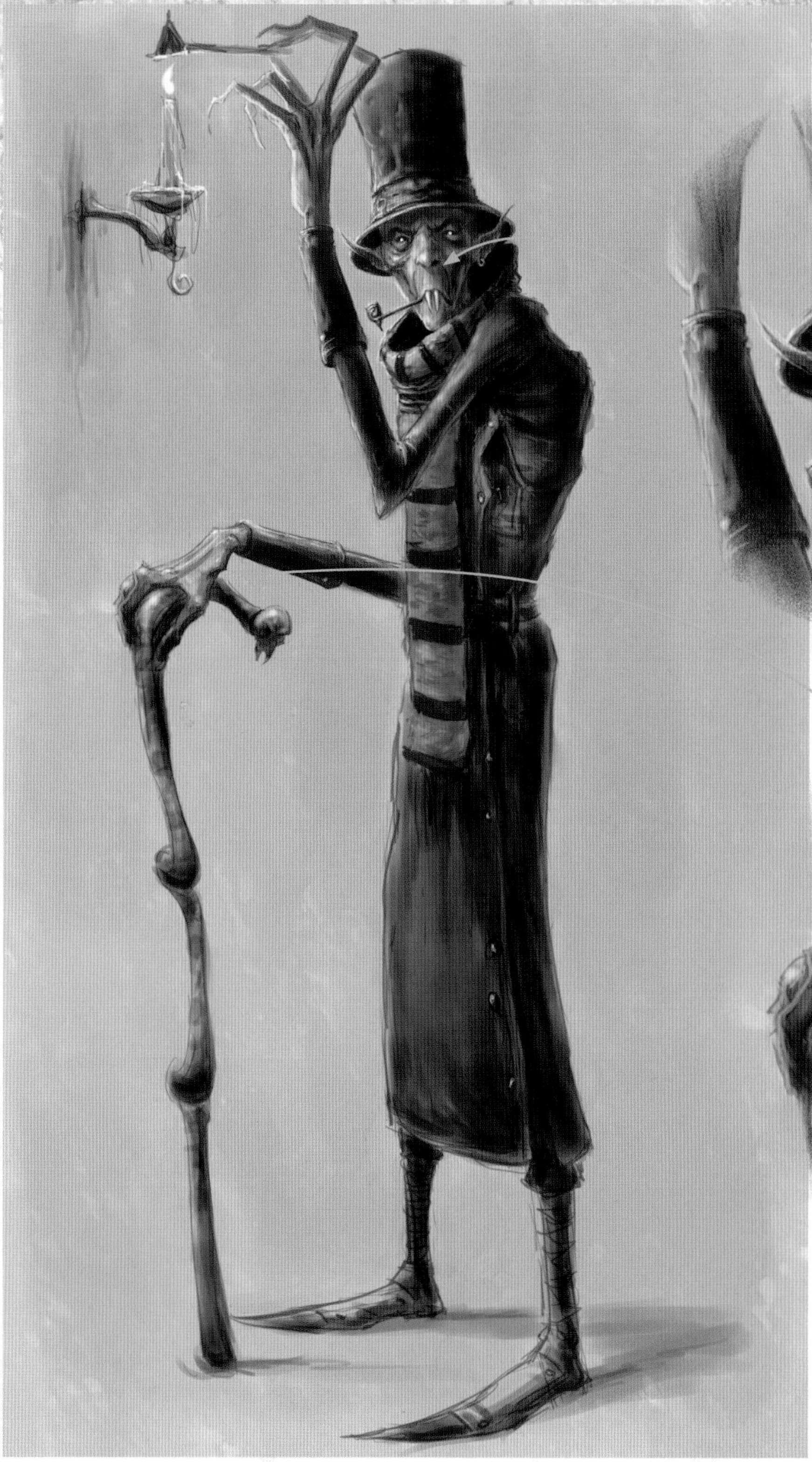

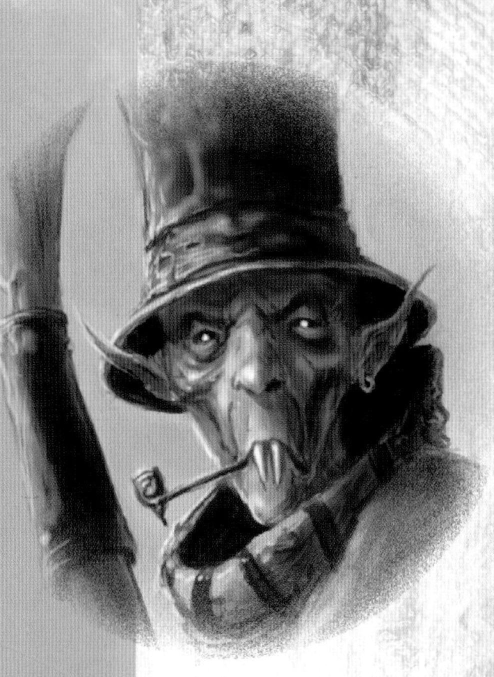

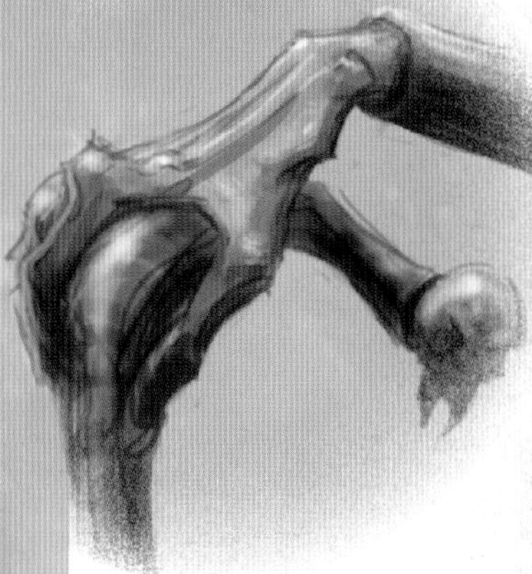

Dr Nosferatu

 ## STEP 12

Check that you're happy with the highlights on his skin areas and work in the detail on his cane. Check also that his legs and feet look realistic – they don't need much detail, but they do need to look suitably dark, skinny and pointy, like the rest of him!

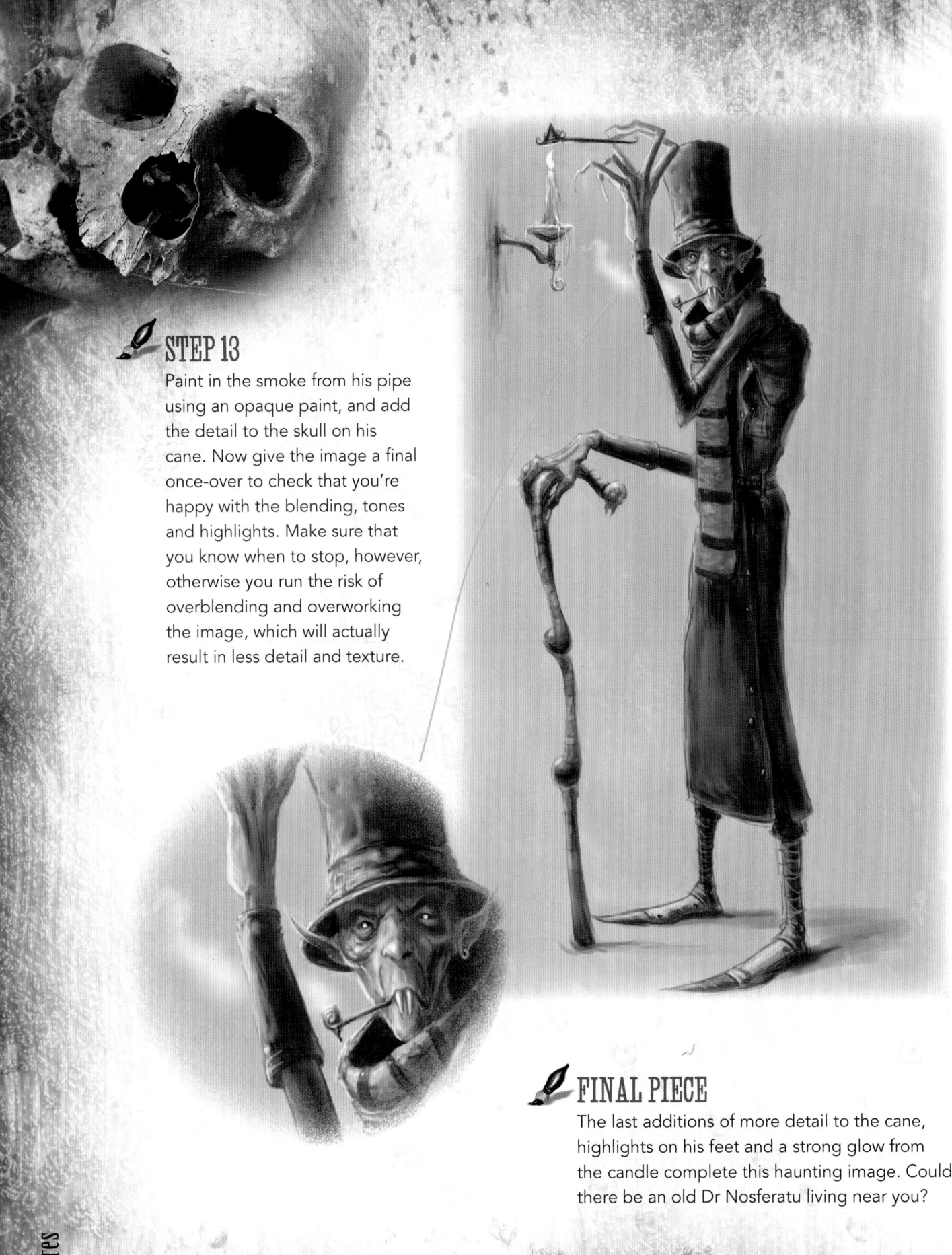

STEP 13

Paint in the smoke from his pipe using an opaque paint, and add the detail to the skull on his cane. Now give the image a final once-over to check that you're happy with the blending, tones and highlights. Make sure that you know when to stop, however, otherwise you run the risk of overblending and overworking the image, which will actually result in less detail and texture.

FINAL PIECE

The last additions of more detail to the cane, highlights on his feet and a strong glow from the candle complete this haunting image. Could there be an old Dr Nosferatu living near you?

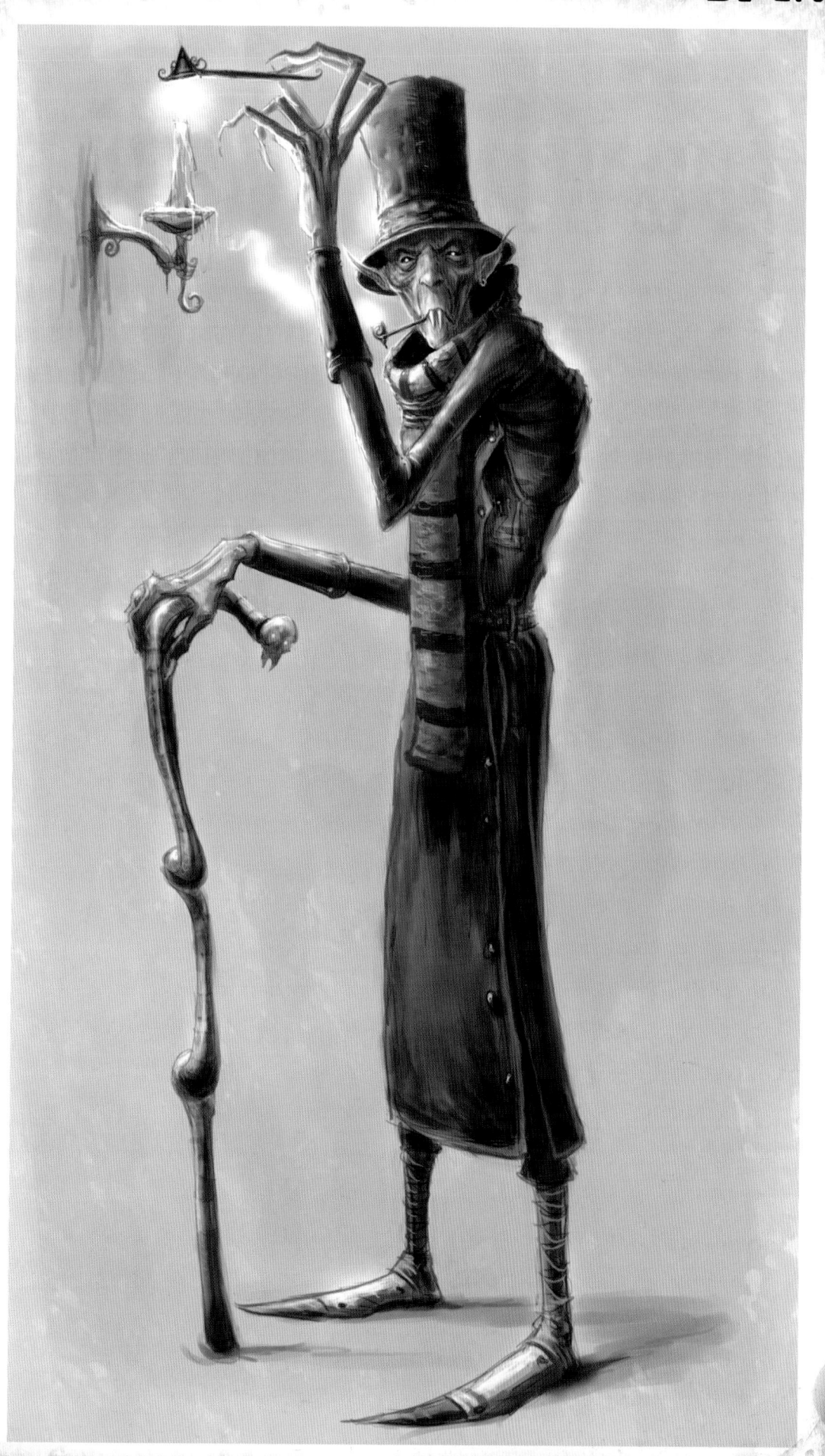

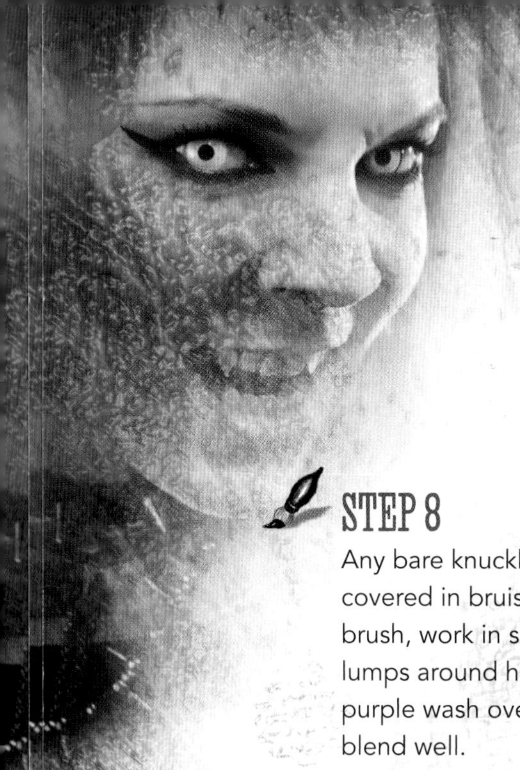

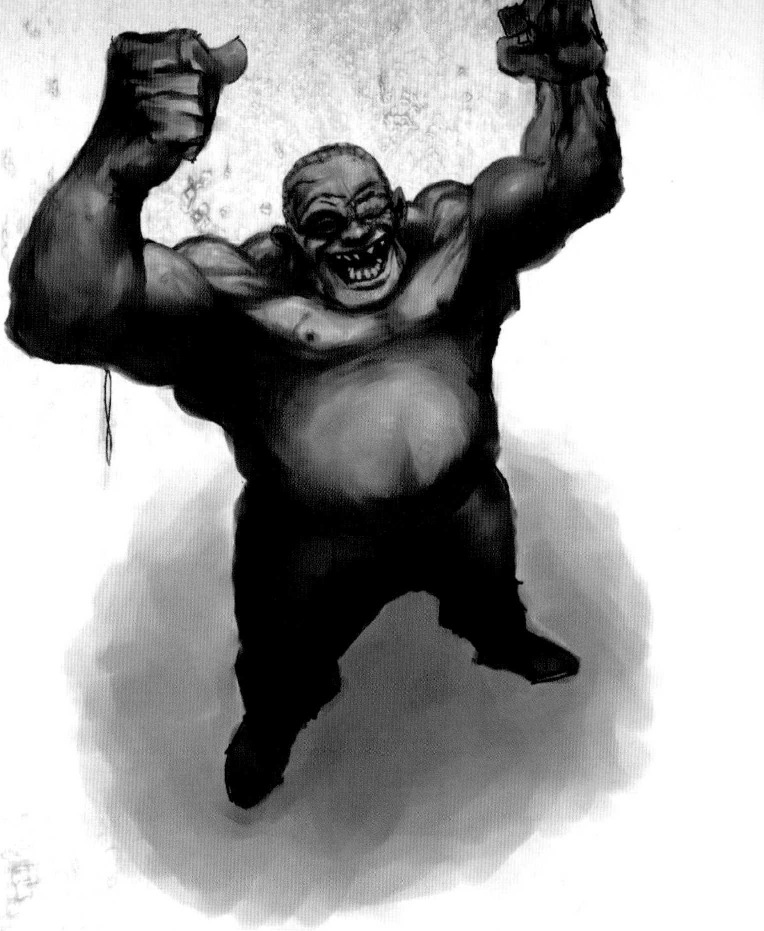

STEP 8

Any bare knuckle brawler will be covered in bruises. Using a fine brush, work in some bruises and lumps around his eyes. Use a light purple wash over these, and then blend well.

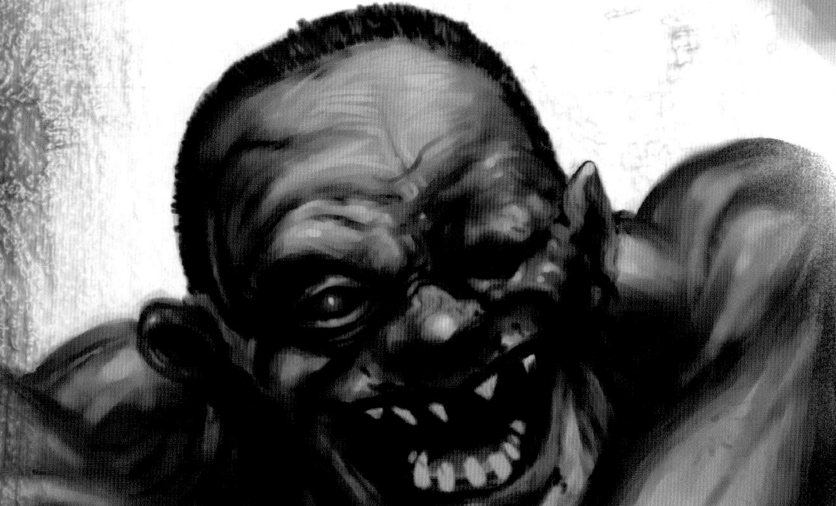

STEP 9

Using pencil or a dark wash on a fine brush, refine the detail and shading on the face. Paint the teeth in, and add some more blood on his chin. Decide on your hair colour and work this in now.

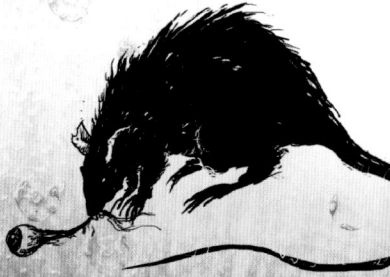

Brawling Vamp

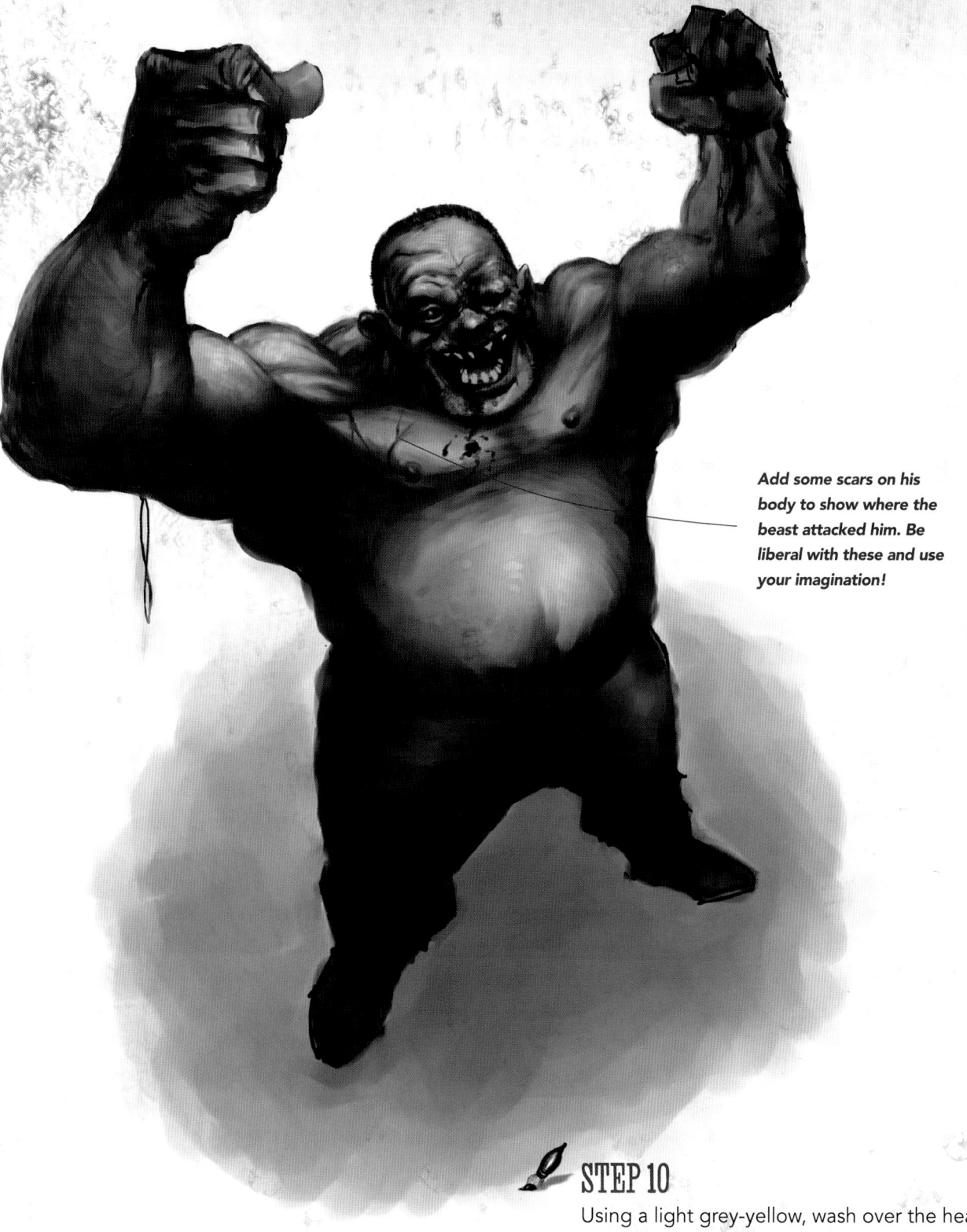

Add some scars on his body to show where the beast attacked him. Be liberal with these and use your imagination!

STEP 10

Using a light grey-yellow, wash over the head, chest and belly areas to show where the light is bouncing. Use a fine brush to refine the forearms, and check you're happy with the tone of the legs.

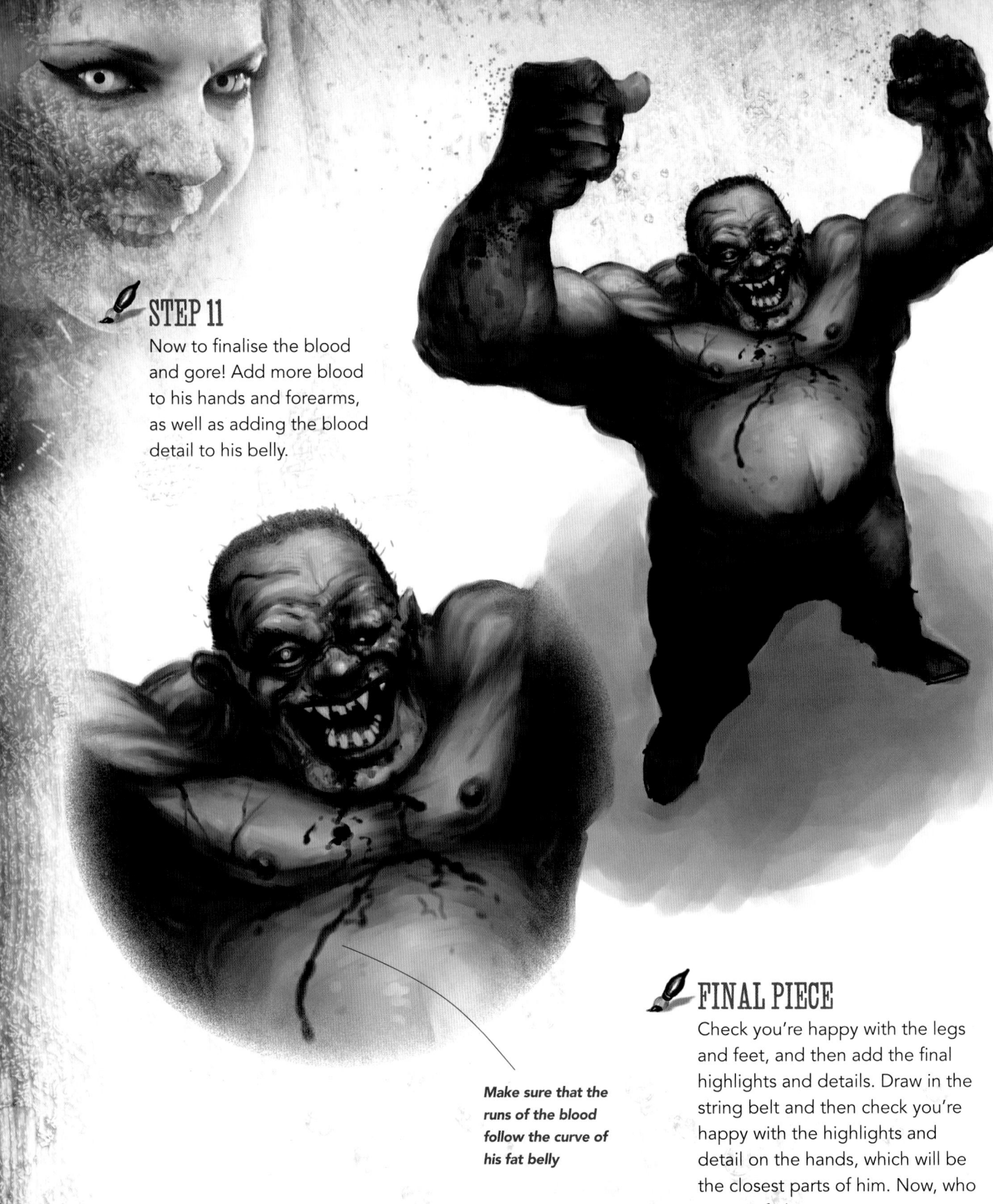

STEP 11

Now to finalise the blood and gore! Add more blood to his hands and forearms, as well as adding the blood detail to his belly.

Make sure that the runs of the blood follow the curve of his fat belly

FINAL PIECE

Check you're happy with the legs and feet, and then add the final highlights and details. Draw in the string belt and then check you're happy with the highlights and detail on the hands, which will be the closest parts of him. Now, who wants a fight?

Brawling Vamp

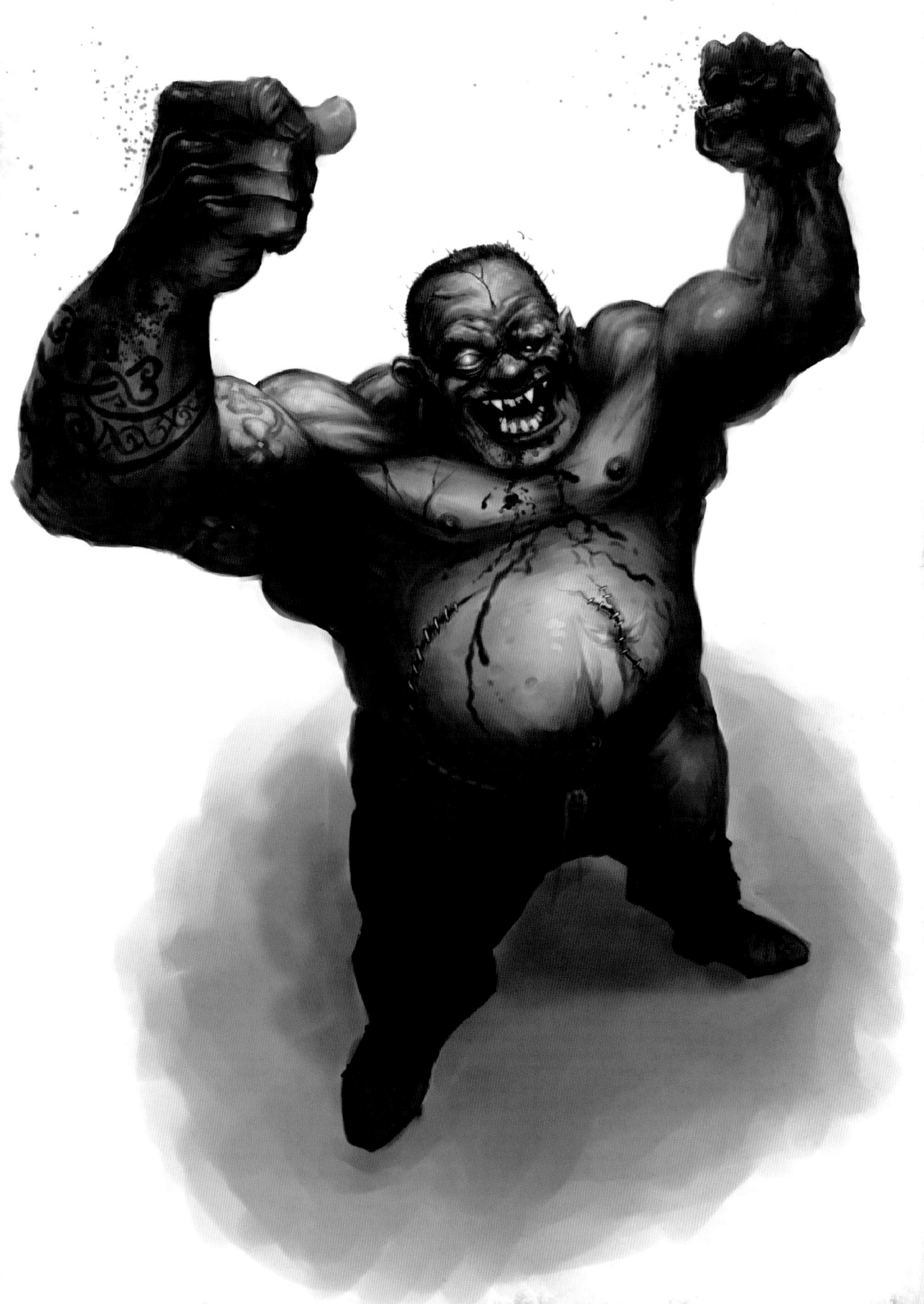

Voodoo Vampire

Dr Jan Von Piercer rushed to the city's main library determined that he would finally find a cure for the cursed disease that killed his wife. For many months he toiled without success, but then Von Piercer changed tactic and searched the library for ancient and dark magical tomes, usually locked away for fear of the knowledge they contained. From one particularly dark, red leather-bound book, inscribed with strange markings, he found what he was looking for.

Through dark magic he could save the entire city in one night, but there was a huge price to pay. His soul must be sacrificed, turning him into one of the living dead, never to be human again, to forever walk the land of the unliving. Willing to make the ultimate sacrifice, it was time for Von Piercer to become one of the undead; it was time to surrender to the magic of voodoo...

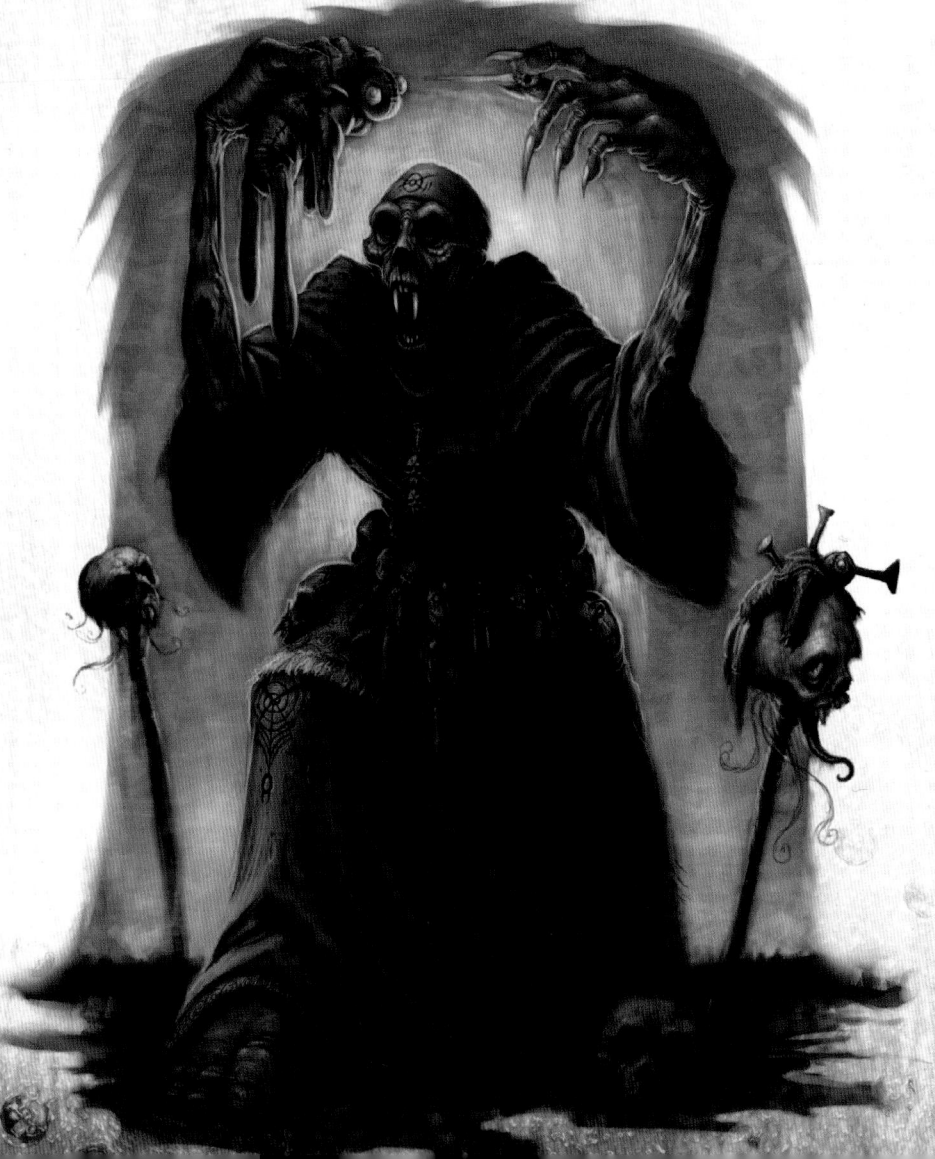

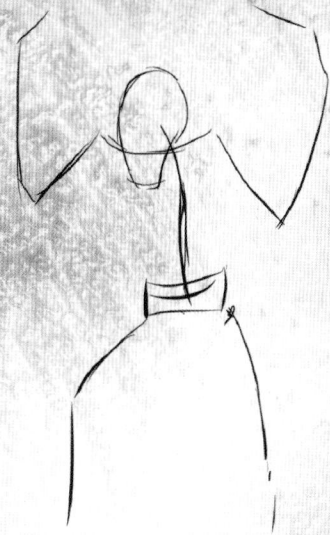

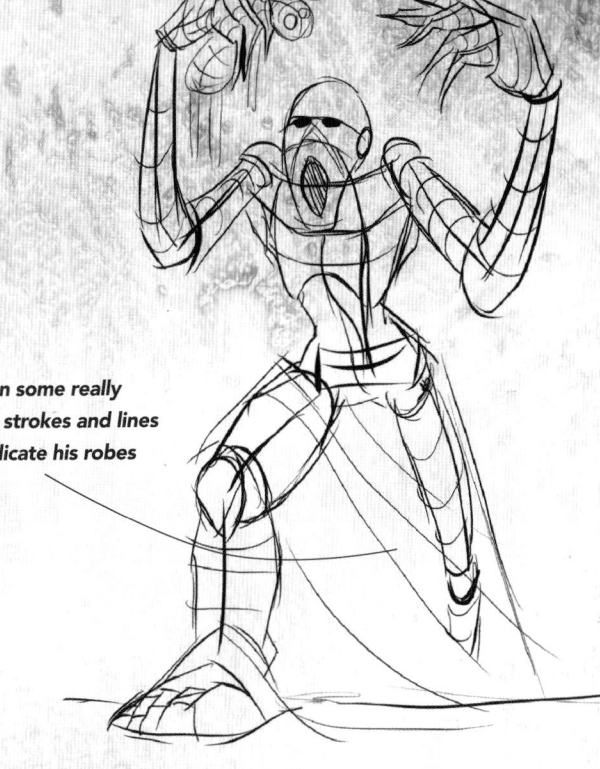

Add in some really quick strokes and lines to indicate his robes

 ## STEP 1

This character is going to be quite ape-like so, using your basic lines for the stick figure, give him a short body with raised, long and gangly arms and a rather long face and lower jaw.

 ## STEP 2

Fill out his form with tubes and lines, and use your basic shapes for his anatomy. It now becomes clear exactly what pose he's in – one leg forward (refresh your mind on foreshortening on page 103!), hands in the air and mouth agape.

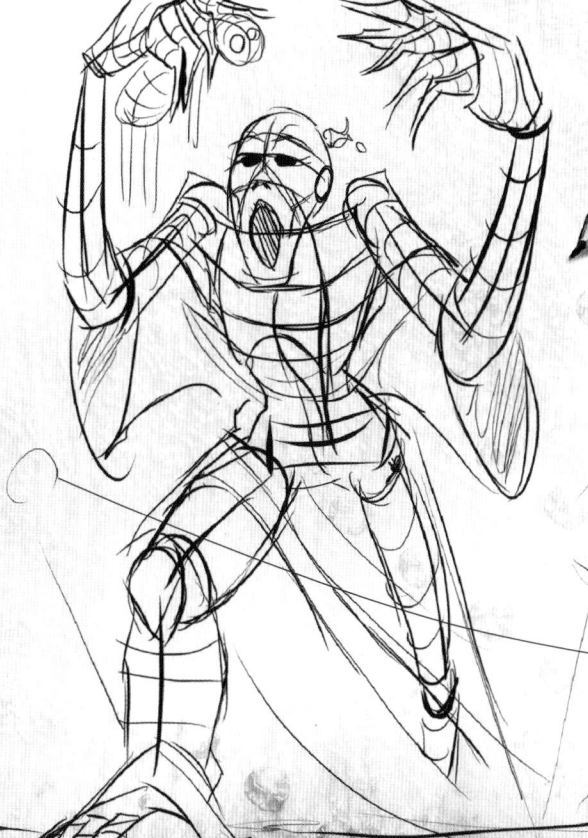

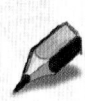 ## STEP 3

Add in a bit more detail now, with a clearer indication for his robes in particular. Begin to think about the background as well, and add in some interesting features to tell the story and provide scale.

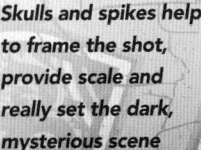

Skulls and spikes help to frame the shot, provide scale and really set the dark, mysterious scene

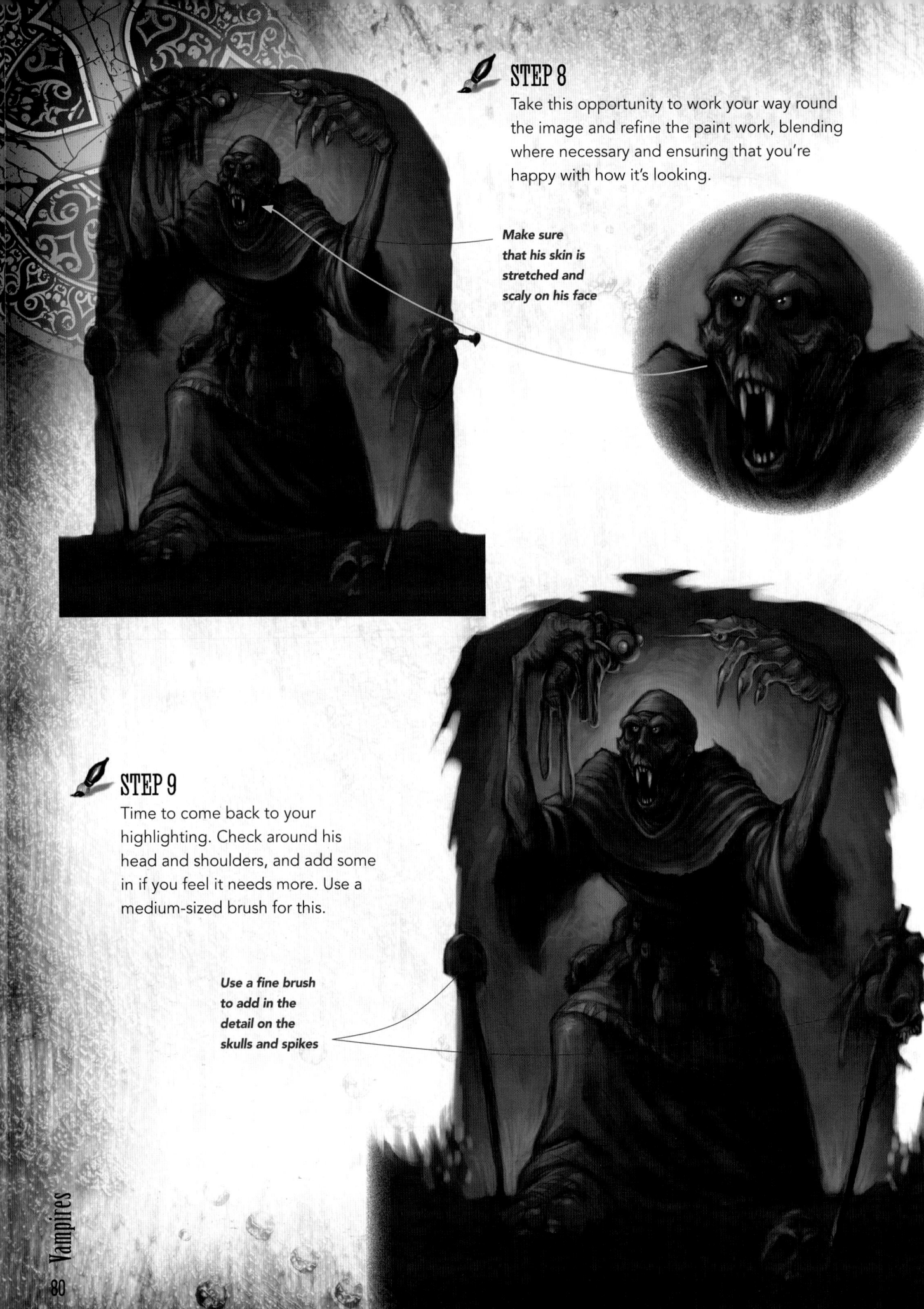

STEP 8

Take this opportunity to work your way round the image and refine the paint work, blending where necessary and ensuring that you're happy with how it's looking.

Make sure that his skin is stretched and scaly on his face

STEP 9

Time to come back to your highlighting. Check around his head and shoulders, and add some in if you feel it needs more. Use a medium-sized brush for this.

Use a fine brush to add in the detail on the skulls and spikes

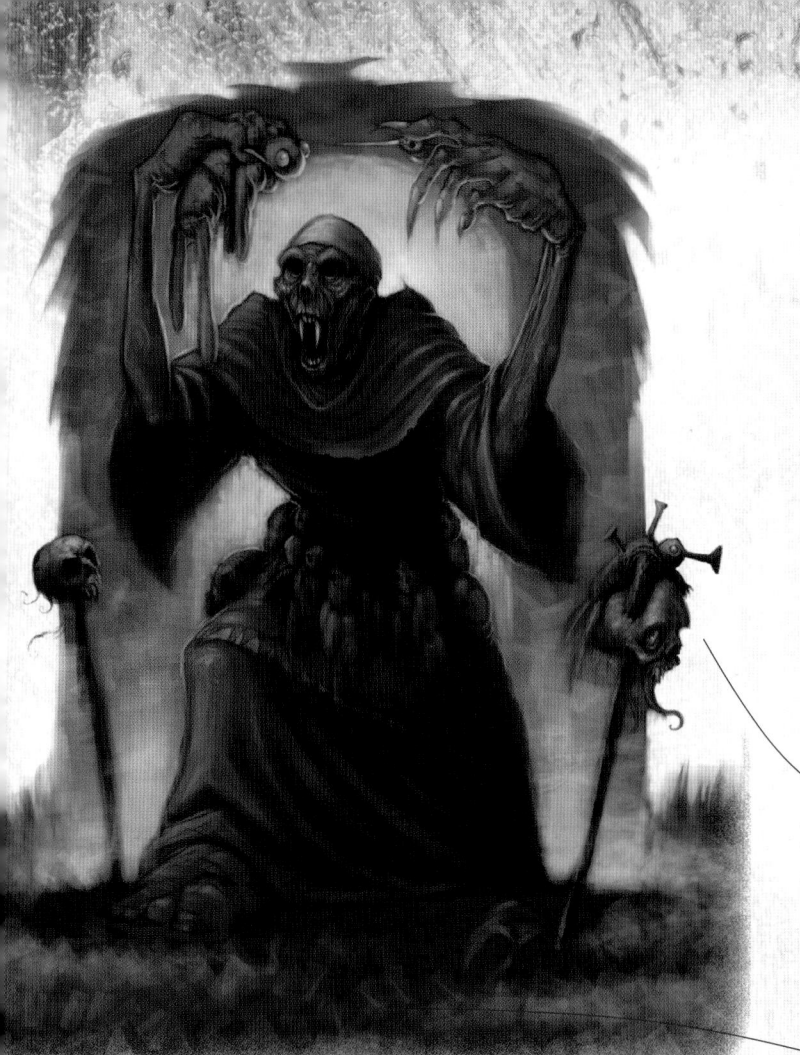

STEP 10

Check that you're happy with the overall colours of the tones and highlights, and intensify any that you feel aren't quite there. Use a medium brush to work in the background light in the doorway. Remember to use different brush strokes to build up texture, before using a flat brush to make the marks on the doorway really stand out.

Using a small, fine brush, continue working in the details on the skulls, making sure that they're really picking up the light from the background

Use a large brush to add in the ground colour, dabbing the bristles onto the paper to achieve texture and depth

STEP 11

Gently wash over a grey-blue on the top of his robe, and orange on the lower half – remember that the lower half will catch more light than the top, which is almost silhouetted by the light in the doorway. Start to define the details of the scabs and scars on his forearms.

Redefine the skull on the floor, and add the little details to the voodoo dolls hanging round his waist

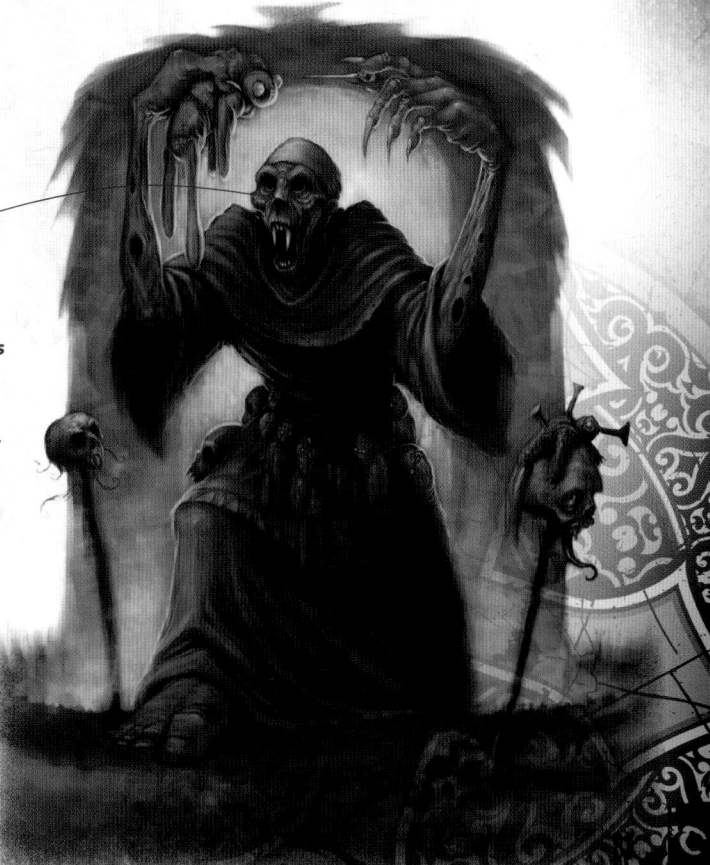

ARTIST'S TIP

If you're using a technique that you're unfamiliar with, such as dabbing, make sure that you practise on a piece of scrap paper before working it into your image.

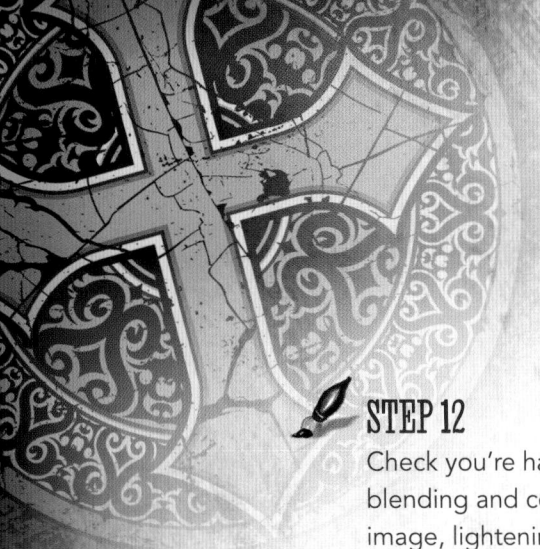

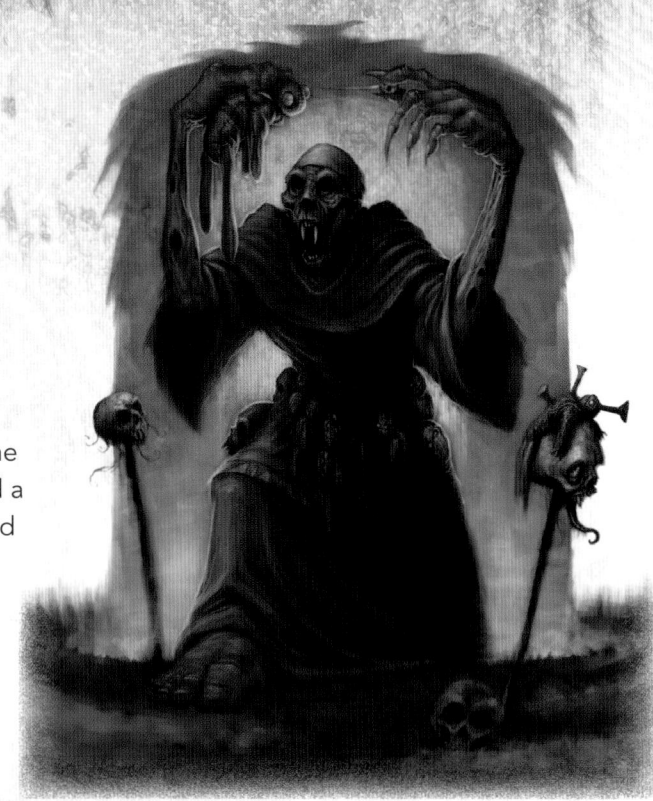

STEP 12

Check you're happy with the blending and contrast all round the image, lightening the background a little if you want to make him stand out a bit more.

STEP 13

We're getting down to the last little details now. Decide on your pattern for the headscarf and work that in with pencil or a fine brush. Why not add some quirky details, such as dirt or a pattern, onto his robe?

FINAL PIECE

Add a swirl design (or whatever takes your fancy) to the skirt and some really scary reddish eyes to the dolls round his waist. Finish him off with a necklace, split his toenail and crack the ground around his feet to complete the look. Check your highlights, and finally make sure that you never, ever catch the plague, otherwise you'll have this vampire to answer to…

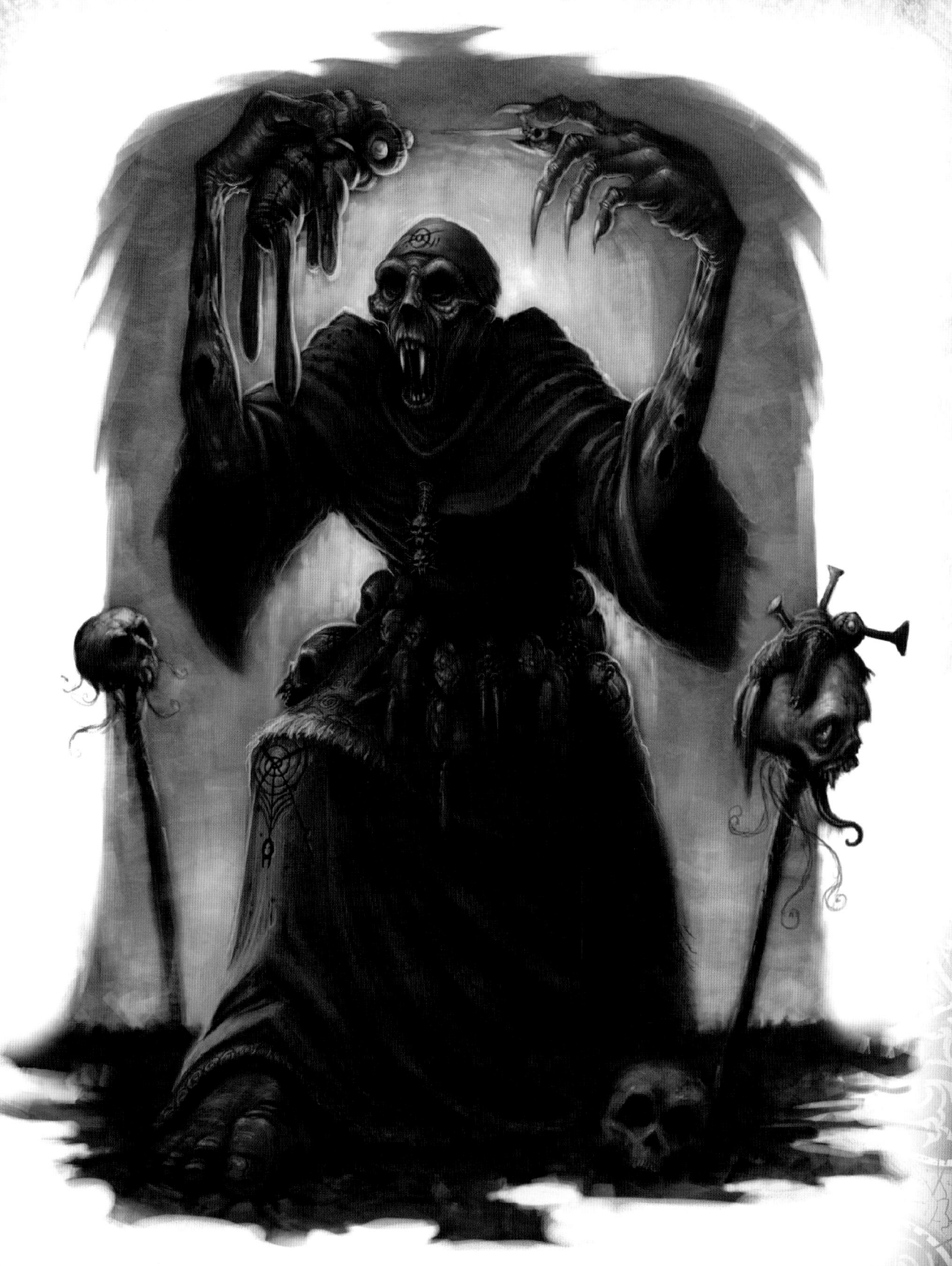

Mistress Vampire

How could Sally, the nicest, sweetest girl in the village escape? Lord Dracula wasn't renowned for being a kind overlord, if ever there was one. Sally realised that fleeing from him would be no good, as he would simply fly after her on his bat-like wings, or send his never-ending supply of slaves, or his wolves, to get her. There was no solution that she could find; no valiant knight willing to earn his stripes in defending her; fear had taken their wits and left her to fend for herself.

Sally realised that her only option was to embrace the fate that lay before her. So, one ordinary morning, she went to the castle and offered her services to Lord Dracula without a flicker of fear or doubt. Sally surrendered her soul the the legendary vampire, and would forever more be his mistress and slave, bringing other helpless victims to him. But one day she will wreak her revenge on the people who abandoned her to this life... oh yes she will...

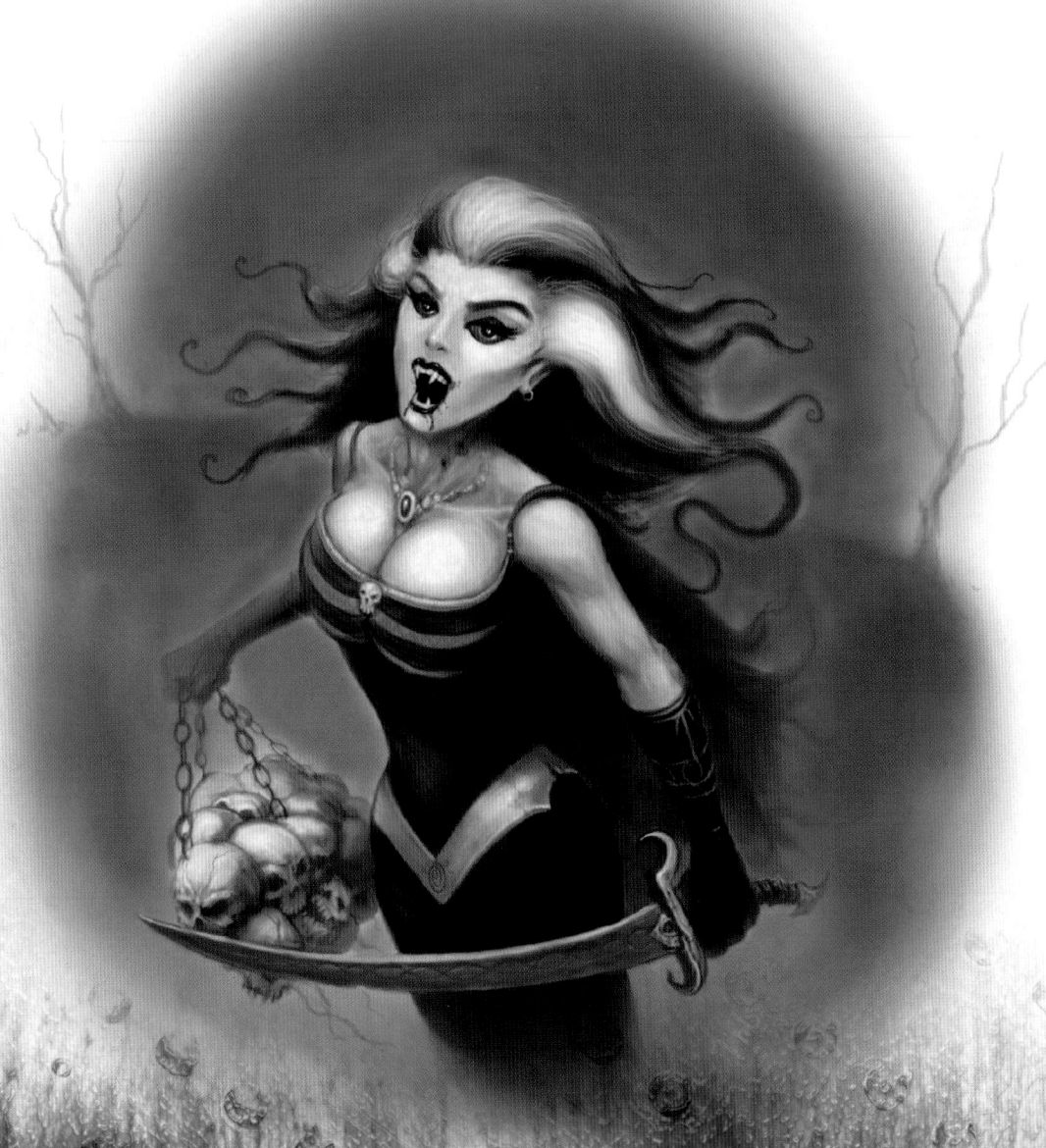

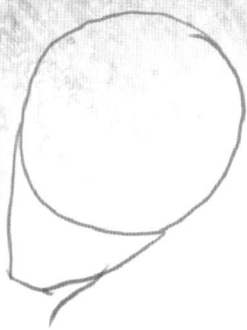

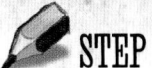

STEP 2

Draw in the crosshairs over the sphere and jaw so you can pinpoint the placement of the eyes nose and mouth. Bear in mind that she will have her mouth agape, to reveal her ultra-sharp, white fangs. Add in the flow of her spine and her collar bone, remembering that the Mistress's left shoulder is going to appear closer to us, so the collar bone should look wider than normal.

STEP 1

We're going to be looking down on the Mistress as she looks up at us, so we need her head tilted back, towards the sky, and her eyes firmly set on us, the target. In this image we won't be drawing or painting below her thighs. Draw in the sphere and jaw shape, with a line to indicate where her neck will follow.

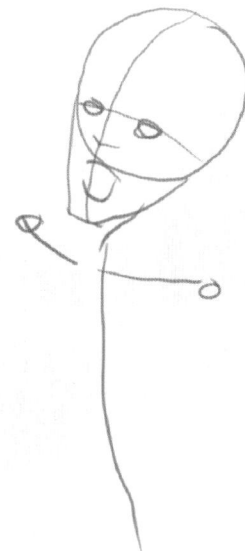

STEP 3

Now draw in her arms, pelvis, tops of her legs and hands, remembering to add her joints as simple circles. Her body will look like it's receding or getting smaller because we're looking down on her from above, so if her body proportions look wrong at the moment, they will make sense eventually!

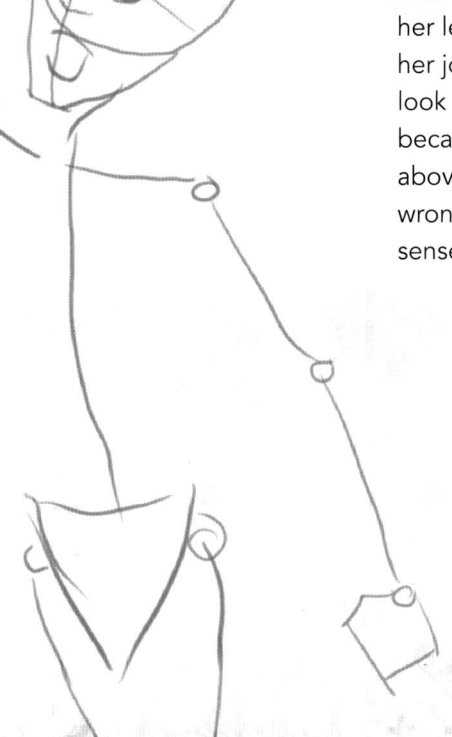

ARTIST'S TIP

If you have any doubt about perspective and proportion from different angles, do lots of research on the internet, in books, and with real life people making sure you see exactly what they look like from different angles, including from above and below.

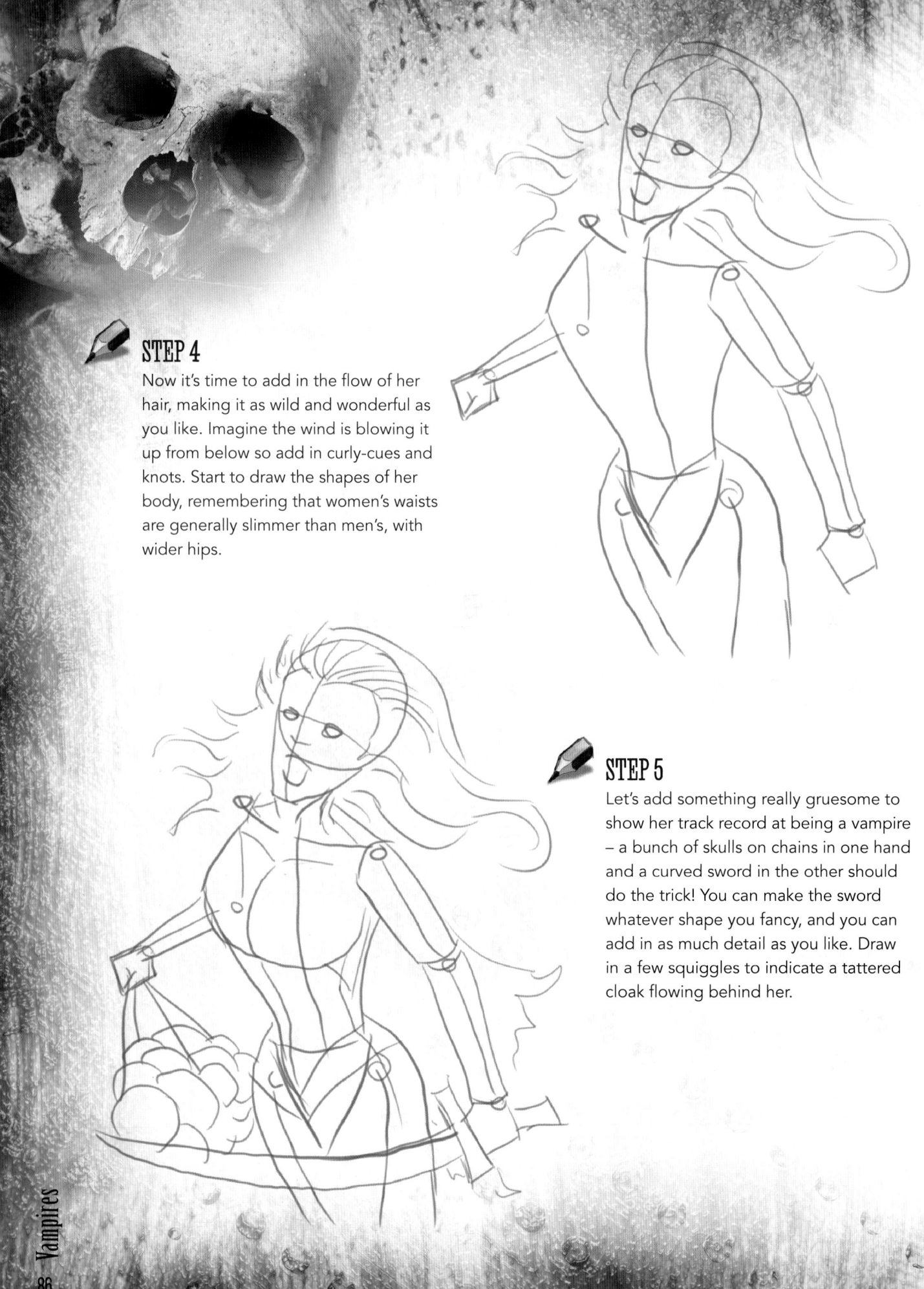

STEP 4

Now it's time to add in the flow of her hair, making it as wild and wonderful as you like. Imagine the wind is blowing it up from below so add in curly-cues and knots. Start to draw the shapes of her body, remembering that women's waists are generally slimmer than men's, with wider hips.

STEP 5

Let's add something really gruesome to show her track record at being a vampire – a bunch of skulls on chains in one hand and a curved sword in the other should do the trick! You can make the sword whatever shape you fancy, and you can add in as much detail as you like. Draw in a few squiggles to indicate a tattered cloak flowing behind her.

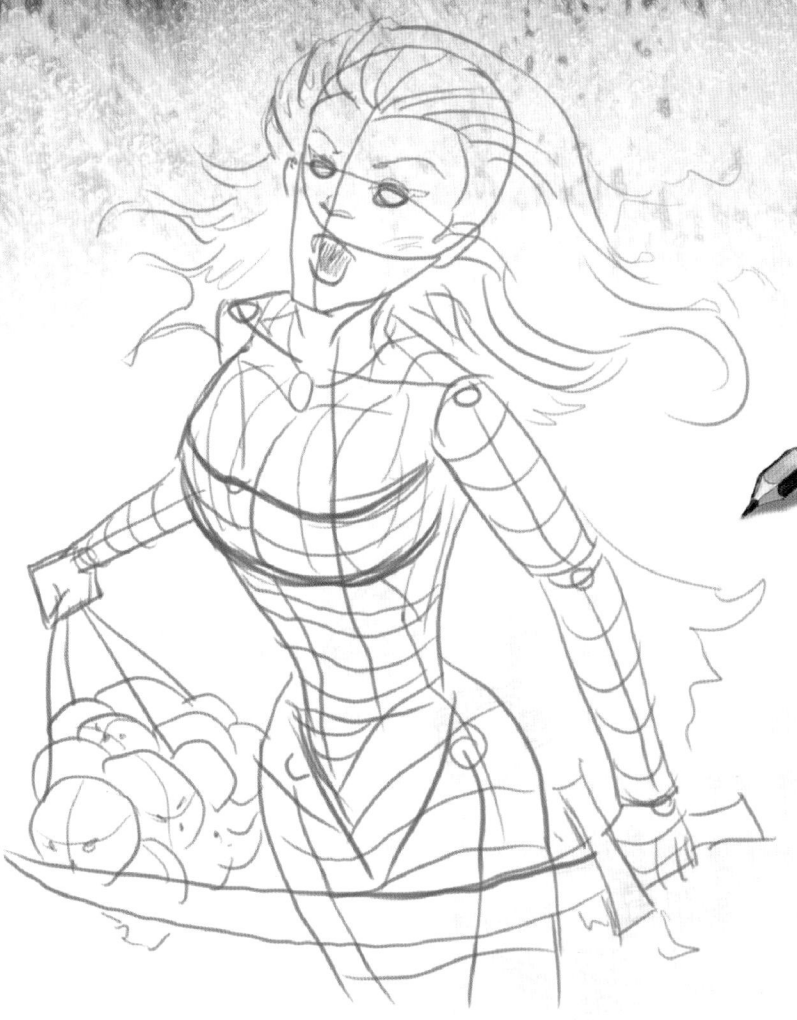

STEP 6

Drawing in the form lines should help you to shape any areas that you might be struggling with, such as her breasts and hips.

STEP 7

Once you're happy with her form you can progress to the final sketch. Really work into her hair and make sure that you get it flowing nicely – it's really difficult to get in loads of detail at the paint stage without a strong sketch to work from. Add some grey streaks to her hair to make it really unusual.

It's all in the detail: a skull on her dress, the chains in her hand and ornate sword just add to the story

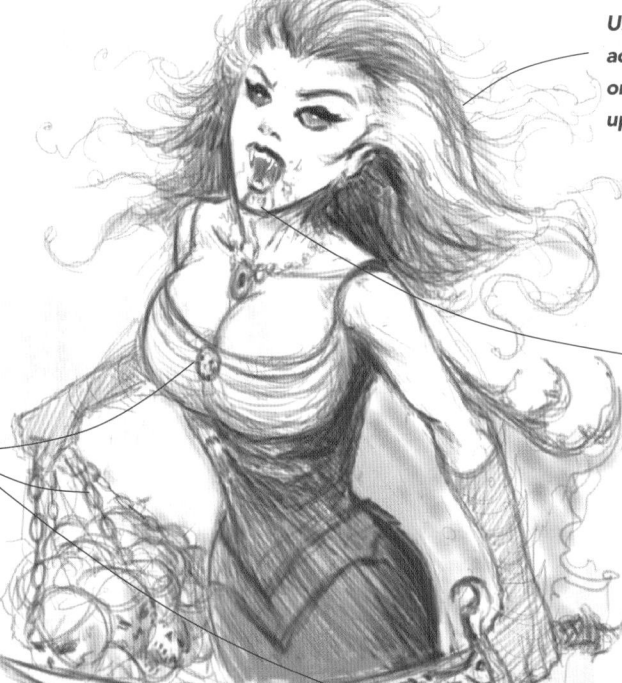

Use quick flicking actions with the stylus or pencil to help build up the hair

Some splattered blood on her lips and chin are a good reminder of her latest victim... and a warning to the next!

Features such as evil, red eyes can be added at this stage, but you can also paint over them later if you're not happy with them

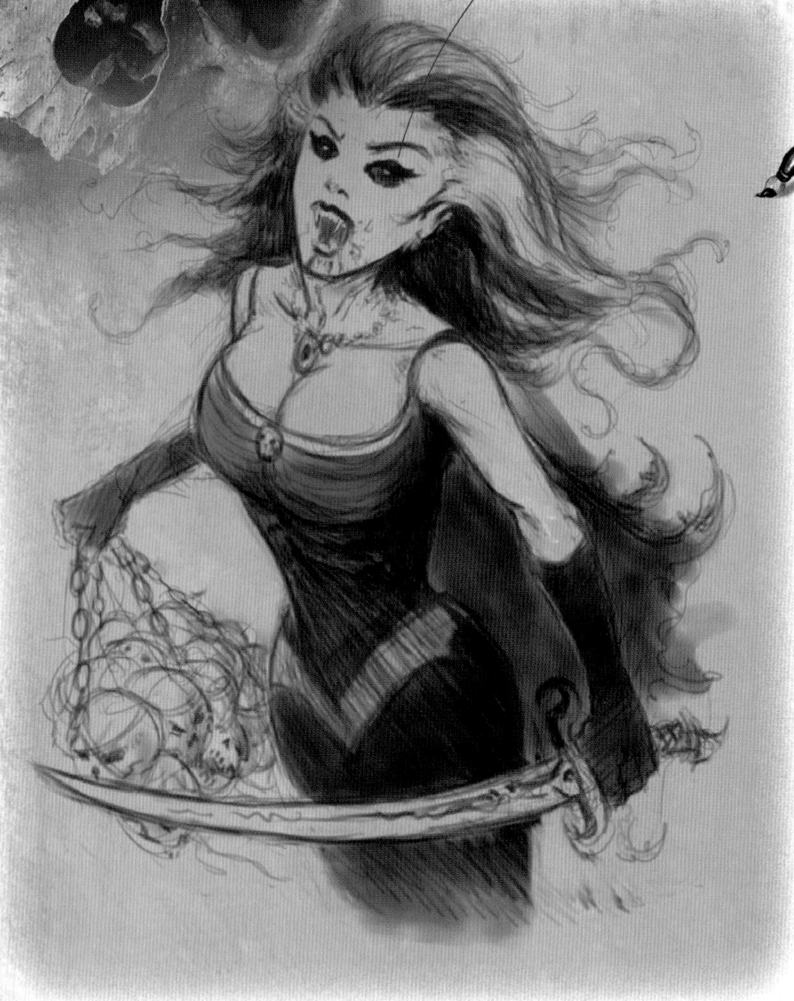

STEP 8

Wash over with a light brown base colour, and allow it to dry before adding more washes. Alternatively, if you're working digitally, use multiply layers. Select some basic colours for the rest of the Mistress, including pale green for her flesh (remember she's one of the undead!), grey/blue with a yellow trim for her dress, and a red cloak to really set it all off.

STEP 9

Using a medium brush, wash in some shadows under her cheekbones, selecting darker tones of those in her face. Remember that she's a seductive mistress and temptress, so give her some eye shadow.

Add a basic wash on the sword – you can select the final colour later!

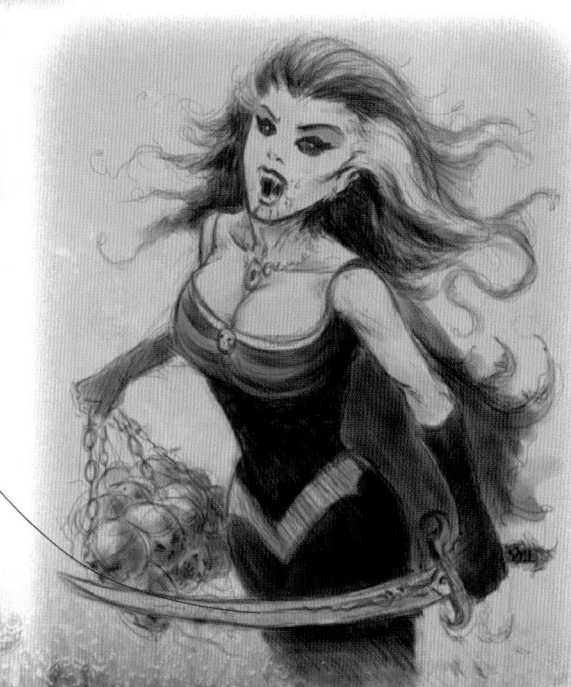

Slowly refine her eyes so that the pin points are looking towards us, the viewer

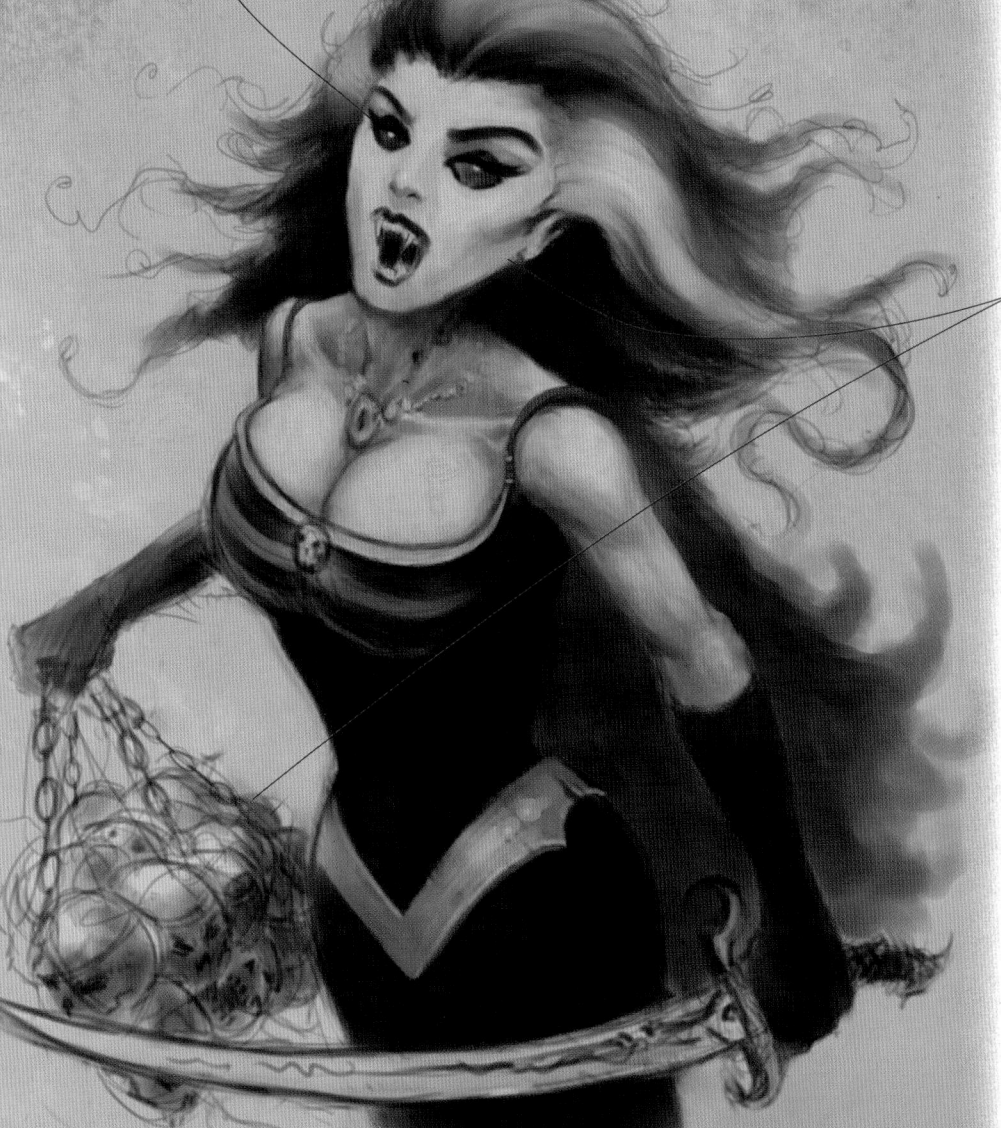

Use a fine brush to refine the details such as the hair behind her neck and head, and the skulls

STEP 10

Select a base wash colour to start building up the tone of her hair. Yellow might seem an odd choice, but it will work out later! The light is going to be coming from above her, but straight in front, so she needs some shadows under her chin.

ARTIST'S TIP

Use a hard (HB) pencil for the sketching, with softer leads for the shade. Subtle, delicate strokes will build up a nice texture and depth in the work, without the need to press down hard.

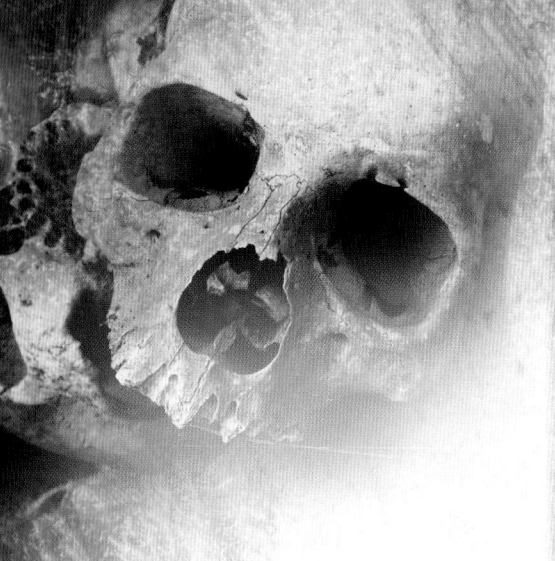

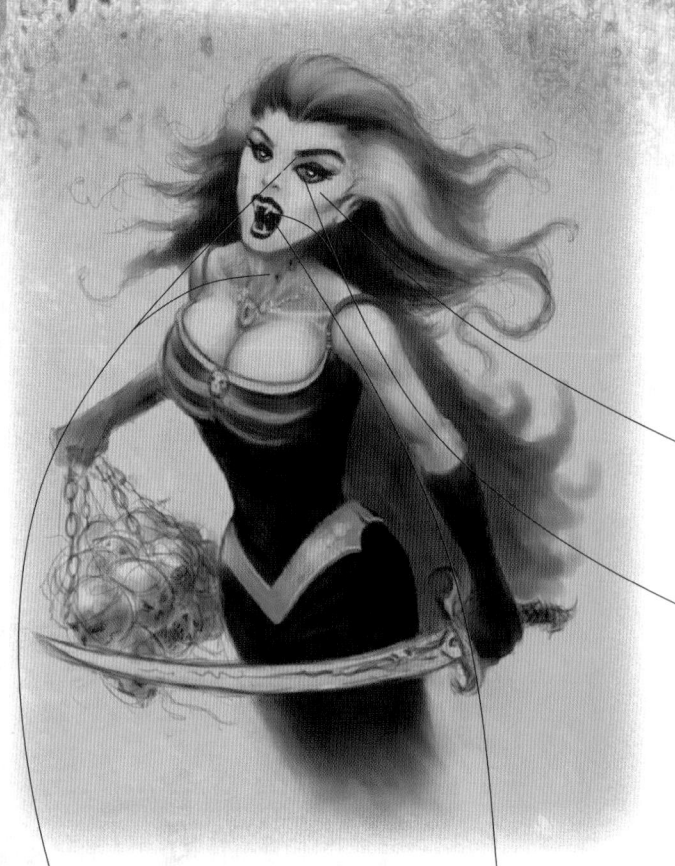

Blend her flesh gently, especially around her neck and face – we want her to be as smooth and faultless as porcelain

Take a fine brush or pencil and pick out the light in her eyes and refine her teeth

STEP 11

Start checking on the blending and softness in the image now, working out any pencil lines and ensuring that the blending is as subtle as possible.

Use a pencil to add in some highlights on her eye shadow and belt area, along with the bite marks on her neck

Fill her mouth with an abyss-like opaque dark red/brown. This will help to contrast with her pale face and draw the reader in to the main part of the image

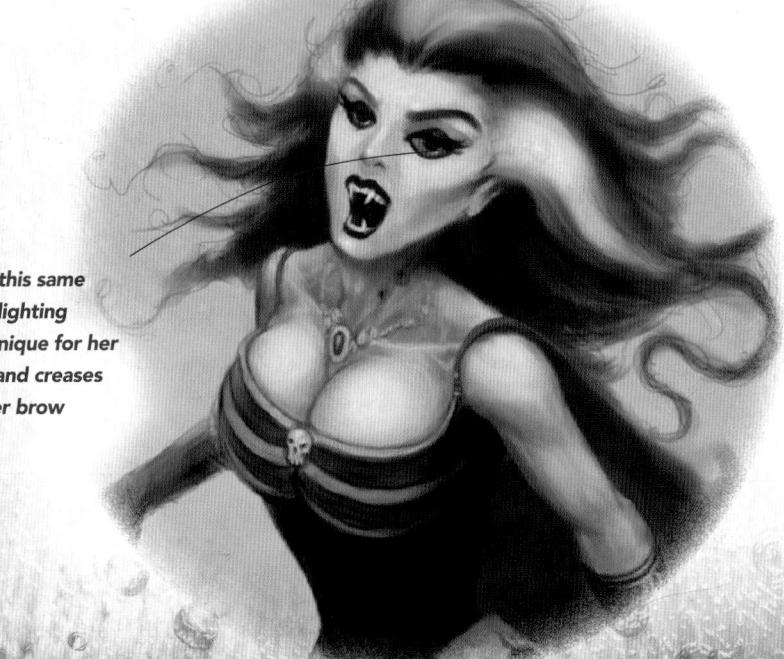

Use this same highlighting technique for her lips and creases in her brow

STEP 12

Very gently, paint in a little orange wash over her nose, then add a pinpoint of a highlight using a pale yellow/green on a very fine brush. Highlight the skull on her dress in the same way, and paint in small details.

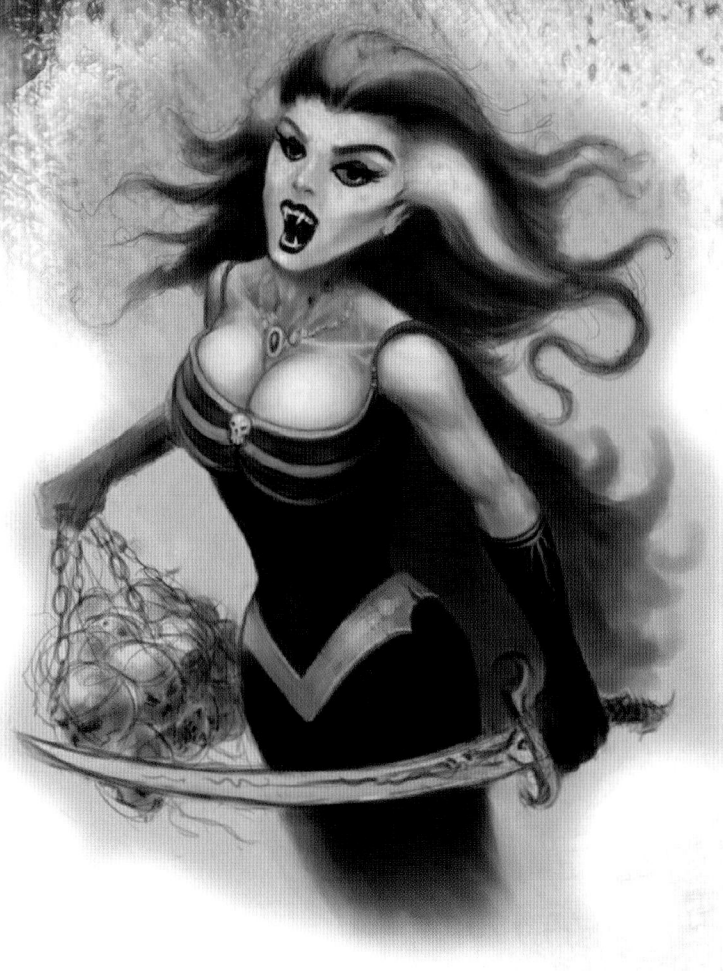

STEP 13

We don't want a huge amount of detail in the dress as it will detract from her face, but we also don't want it to be a flat and featureless blue. Very gently paint in some subtle highlights on her dress using a lighter and slightly greyer blue. Using a fine brush, work on the decoration of her necklace as you go, keeping this simple.

STEP 14

Take a step back and assess the work, going back over any areas that you feel need a bit more refinement. Add in any small details that you want. Decide which colours you would like the blade on the sword to have and add these in. Yellow is best for a golden metal, or a grey/green or blue for steel-like metal. Highlight the skulls using a pale green and paint some decoration onto your sword.

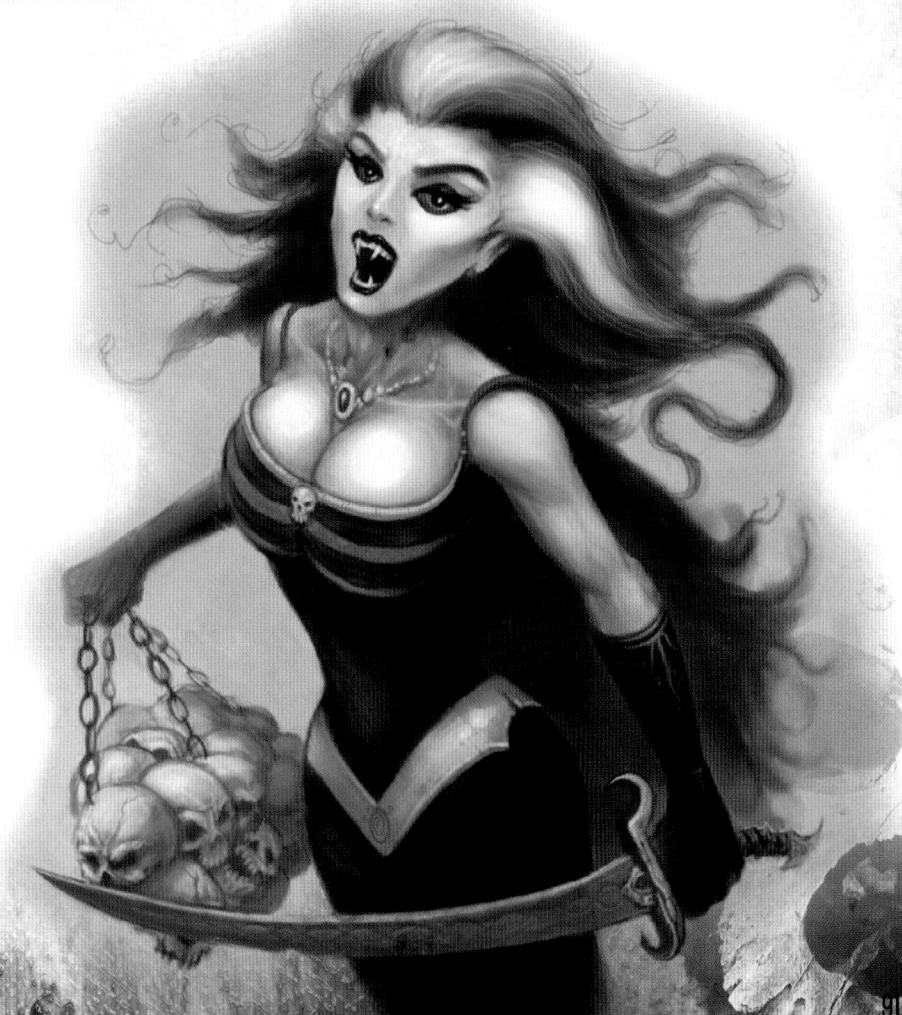

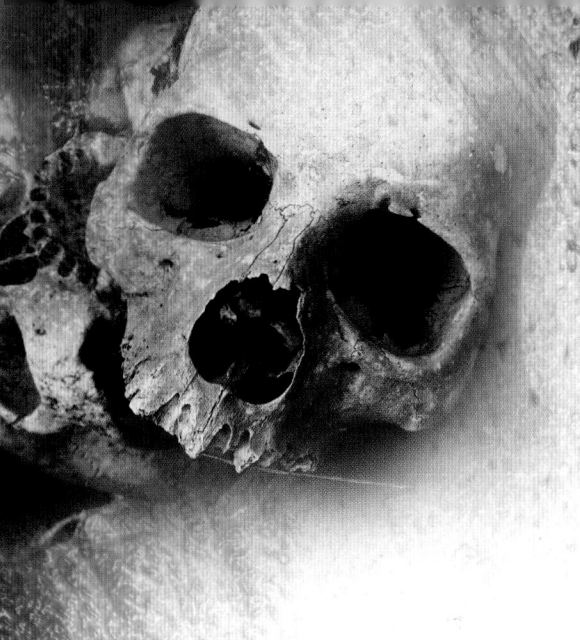

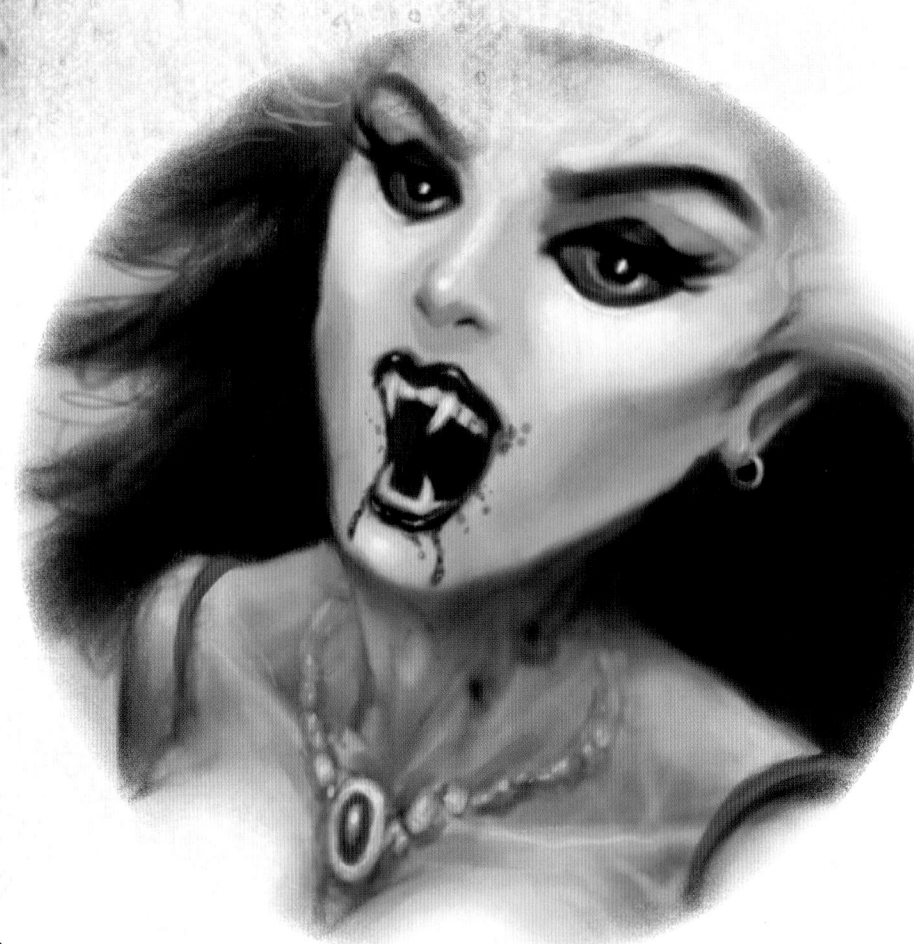

 STEP 15

Let's add that splatter of blood around her mouth!
Paint on a normal layer with a red/brown and highlight with yellow using a pencil or fine brush. Make sure the blood is flowing around the form of her lower lip and jaw otherwise it might look odd. Add a few dots of red to appear as if the blood has 'spattered' slightly after she bit into her victim's neck.

 FINAL PIECE

If you want to give your character an interesting background, now's the time to do it. Try adding a creepy wood and/or a graveyard behind her, or simply a bold colour such as red, like here. Whatever you decide to do, begin by washing in your base colours around her. Add in your textures to the background, ensuring that the most intense colour is at the focal point of the image. Now she's ready to receive her latest instructions from Dracula, so watch out boys! I do hope you haven't crossed her...

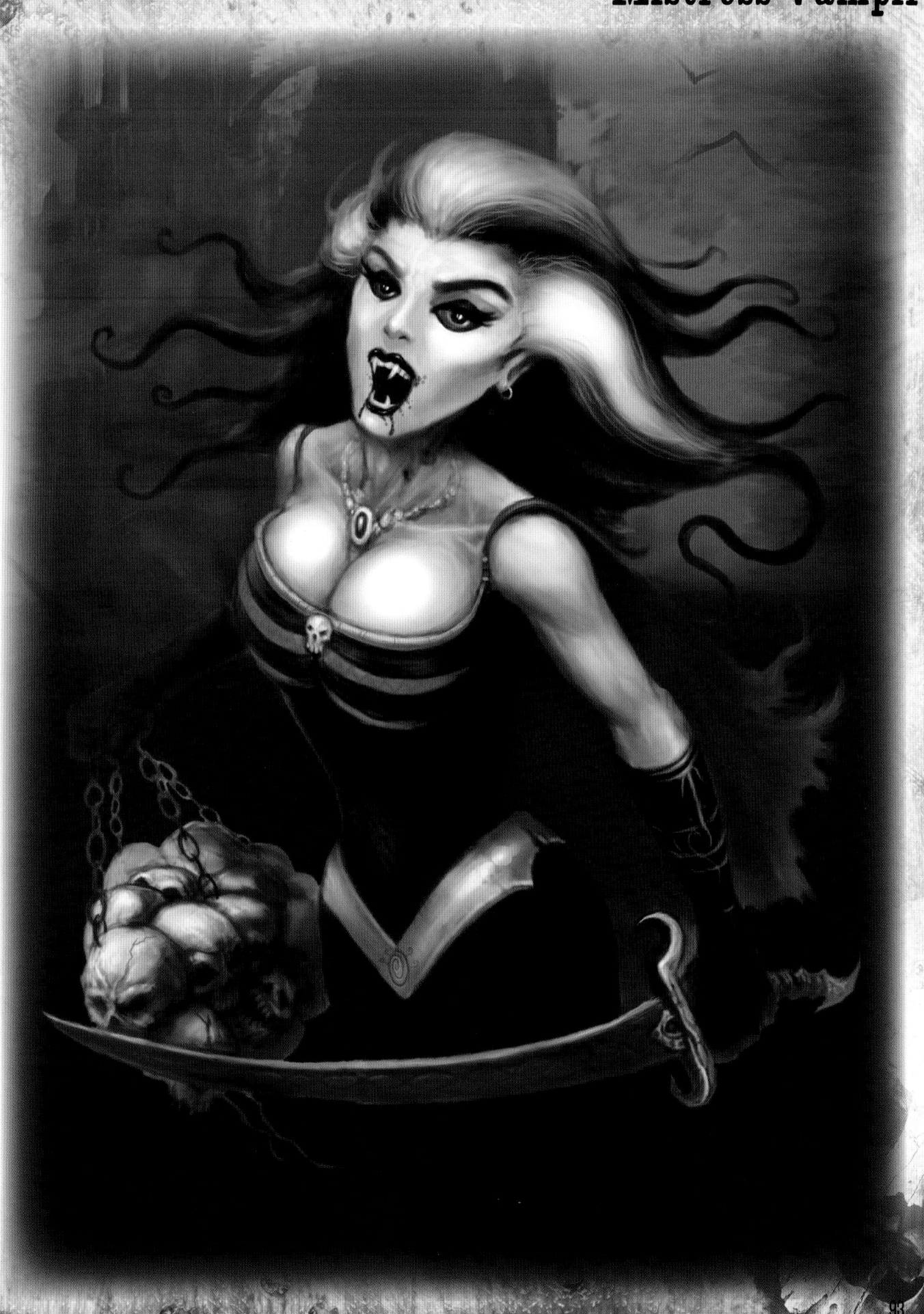

Lupine Vampire

Henry Wolfe bent down in front of the furnace and reached inside, his brow glistening. Finding the treasure, he heaved himself up, raised his hand closely to his face and uncurled his fingers to reveal a small golden key. The head was moulded into the shape of a howling wolf, the shaft decorated with twisting runes that ran all the way down to the teeth. He stabbed the two fangs sharply into his neck, before wrenching them out and throwing the key across the room into the darkness.

Henry began to writhe and shake violently, his arms and legs flinging themselves about, gnashing his jaws and frothing from the mouth as his teeth cracked and stretched into sharp glistening fangs. His face contorted and he yelped like a dog. His eyes were turning a burning deep red, while large, thick veins appeared on his neck. His muscles grew, as did a layer of thick, wiry hair. His hands and legs stretched, each finger ending in a dirty razor sharp claw, and the transformation was complete.

Even standing slightly hunched over, Henry was almost twice as big as he was before. He smiled to himself, bearing his wicked fangs. 'Time for revenge sweet Britney Bishops!' He growled under his breath.

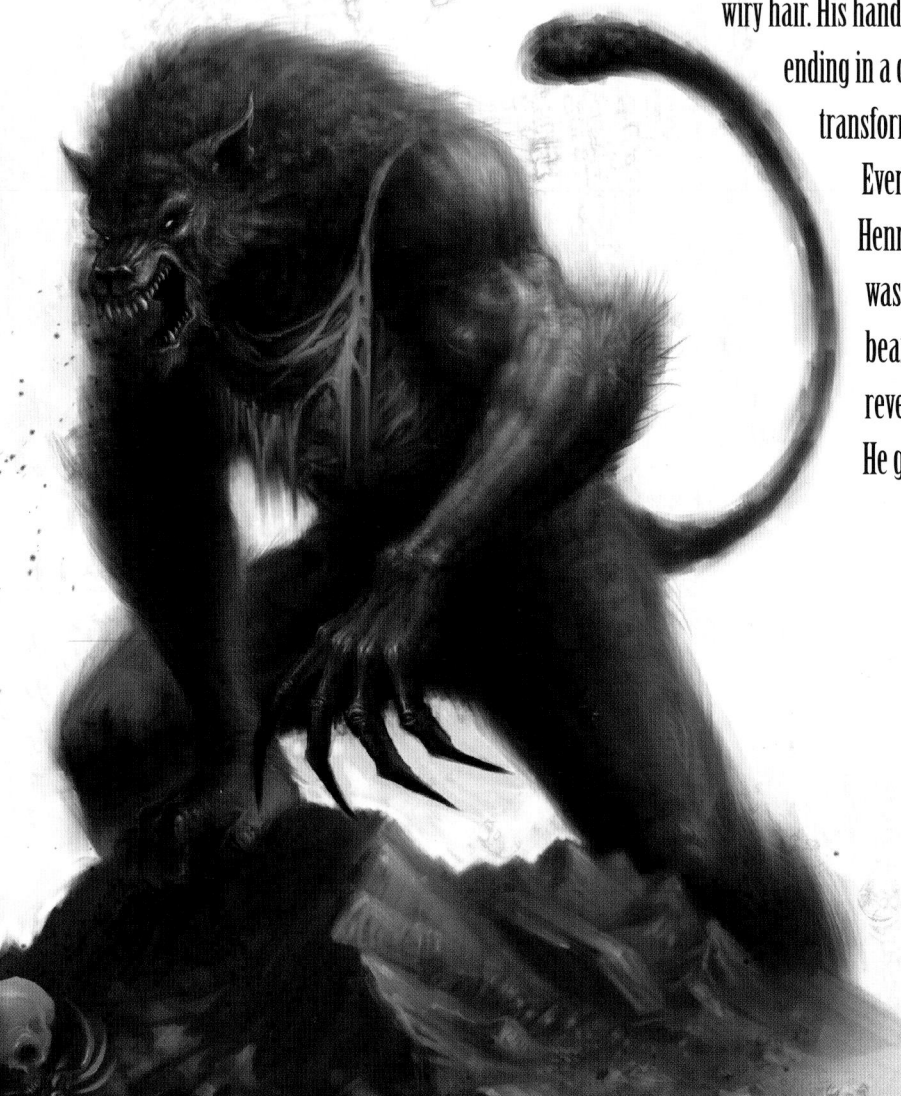

Lupine Vampire

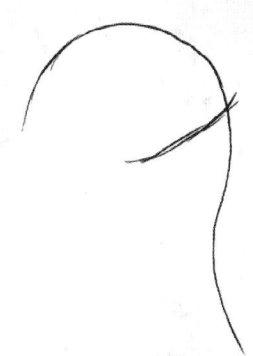

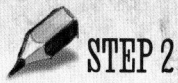

STEP 2

You can see how this line has now provided the basis for the Lupine's upper body framework. Build the form of the body on to this, using lines and the usual basic shapes.

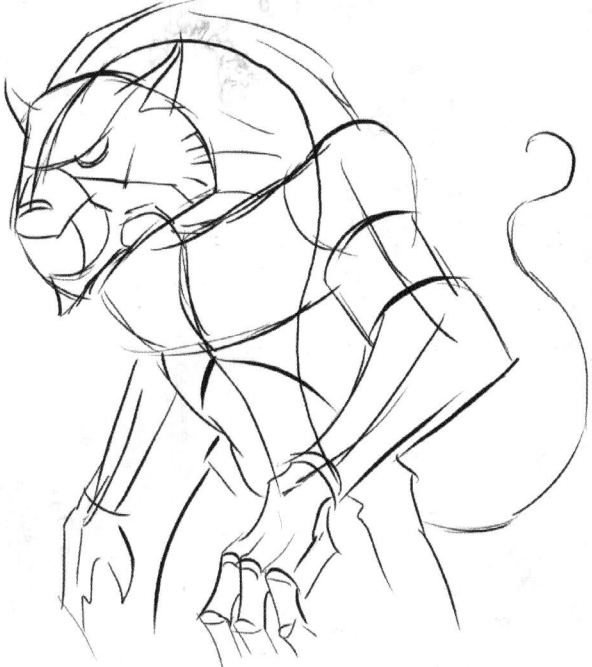

STEP 1

The Lupine Vampire, though tall, is a hunched creature of the night. This basic 'f' outline represents his over-arching neck and shoulders.

STEP 3

Start to add some more of the beast's features, such as the mane and straining muscles. Outline the basic shape and placement of the tail, but don't worry if you're not entirely happy with it at this stage – we can refine it or even change it altogether later.

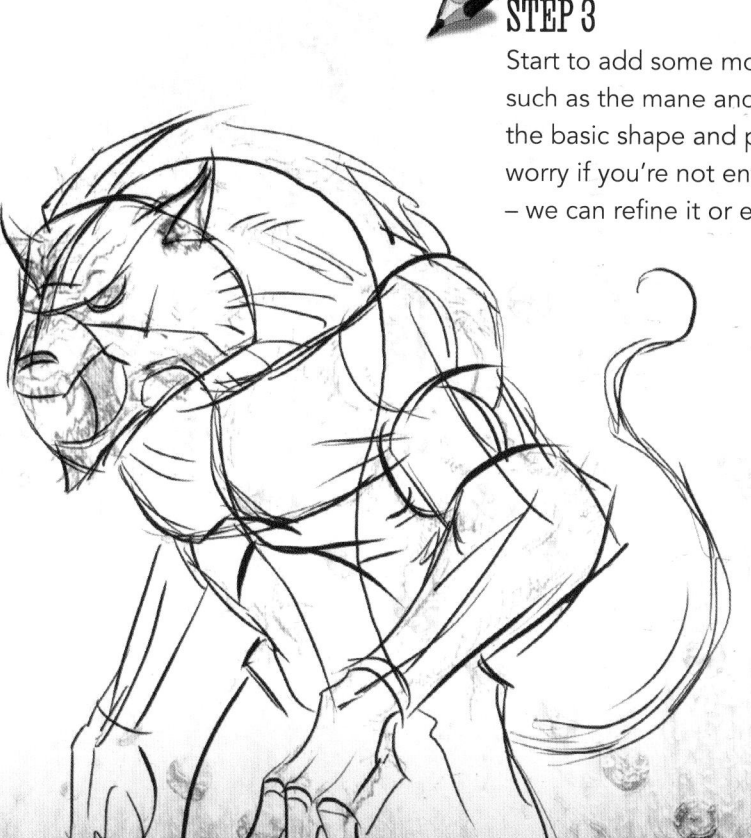

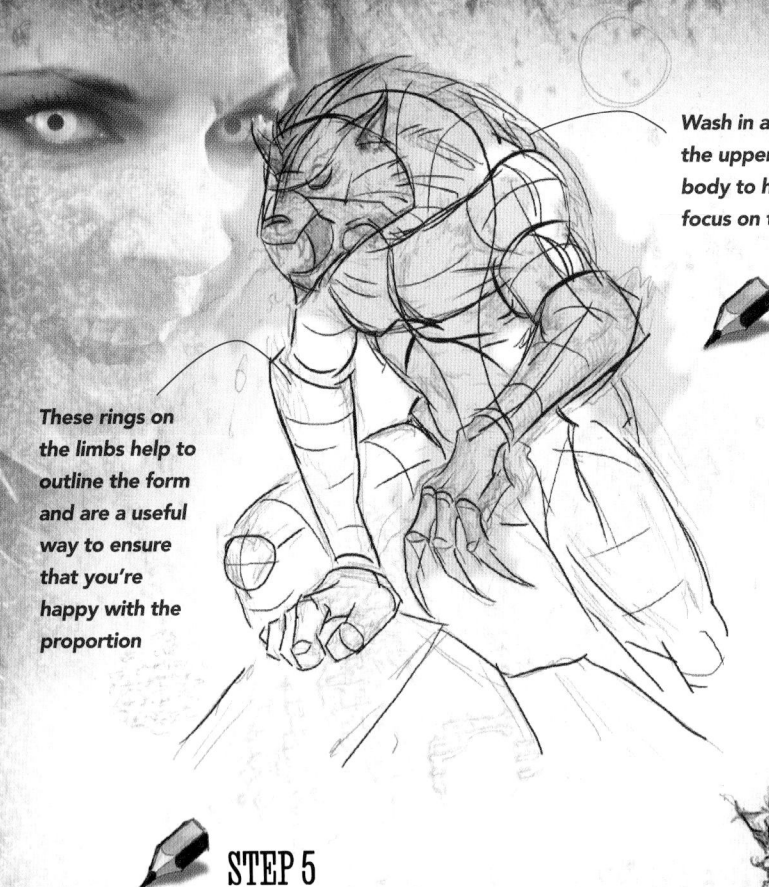

Wash in a little grey on the upper part of the body to help you to focus on the lower part

These rings on the limbs help to outline the form and are a useful way to ensure that you're happy with the proportion

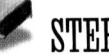 **STEP 4**

If you're happy with the basic outline of the upper body and pose, start working in the legs and arms. Having the character leaning on this rock accentuates his hunch, and also makes him more menacing, looking as though he's ready to pounce on his next victim.

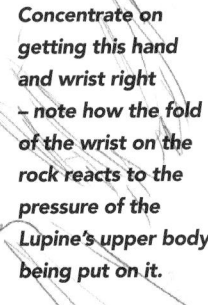 **STEP 5**

Continue working on your sketch, selecting and building up the lines you want to keep and gradually adding more detail and tone. Remember to erase the lines that you don't want so that you keep the image as clean as possible.

Concentrate on getting this hand and wrist right – note how the fold of the wrist on the rock reacts to the pressure of the Lupine's upper body being put on it.

 STEP 6

Start to wash out the grey on the upper part of the torso as you refine your sketch. Add in some tighter detail around the ears, eyes and mouth. The face is a vital part of this creature's story – the rest of the body has its roots in the human figure, but facially it is almost entirely canine.

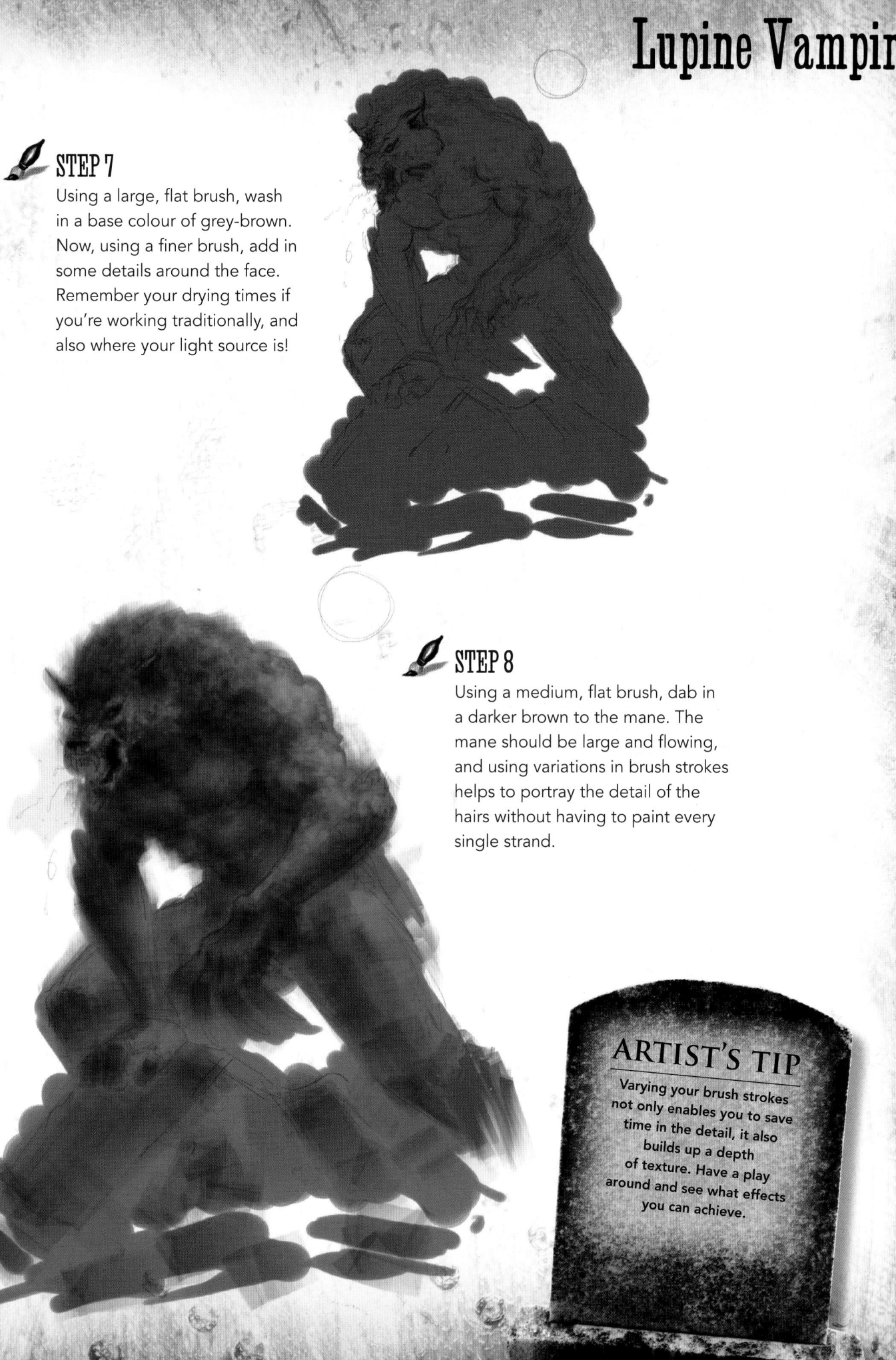

STEP 7

Using a large, flat brush, wash in a base colour of grey-brown. Now, using a finer brush, add in some details around the face. Remember your drying times if you're working traditionally, and also where your light source is!

STEP 8

Using a medium, flat brush, dab in a darker brown to the mane. The mane should be large and flowing, and using variations in brush strokes helps to portray the detail of the hairs without having to paint every single strand.

ARTIST'S TIP

Varying your brush strokes not only enables you to save time in the detail, it also builds up a depth of texture. Have a play around and see what effects you can achieve.

STEP 9

Using a fine brush, start adding some rough highlights to the areas that are catching the light. When these are dry, gently wash over with an orange colour – his hands and face will be predominantly red from all of the blood, and adding this orange wash provides the basis for this.

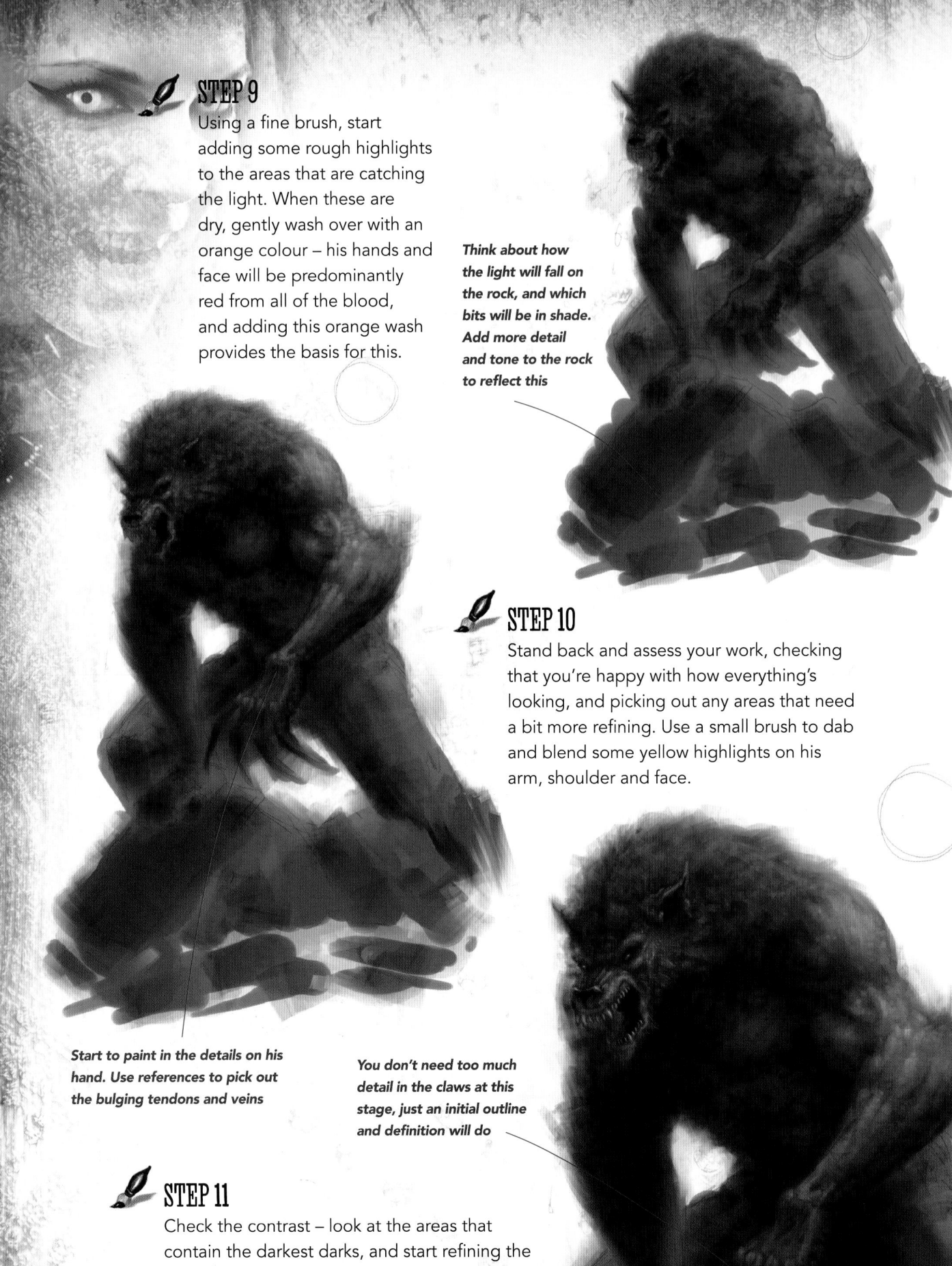

Think about how the light will fall on the rock, and which bits will be in shade. Add more detail and tone to the rock to reflect this

STEP 10

Stand back and assess your work, checking that you're happy with how everything's looking, and picking out any areas that need a bit more refining. Use a small brush to dab and blend some yellow highlights on his arm, shoulder and face.

Start to paint in the details on his hand. Use references to pick out the bulging tendons and veins

You don't need too much detail in the claws at this stage, just an initial outline and definition will do

STEP 11

Check the contrast – look at the areas that contain the darkest darks, and start refining the highlighting on the points of interest, such as the face, hand and forearm.

Lupine Vampire

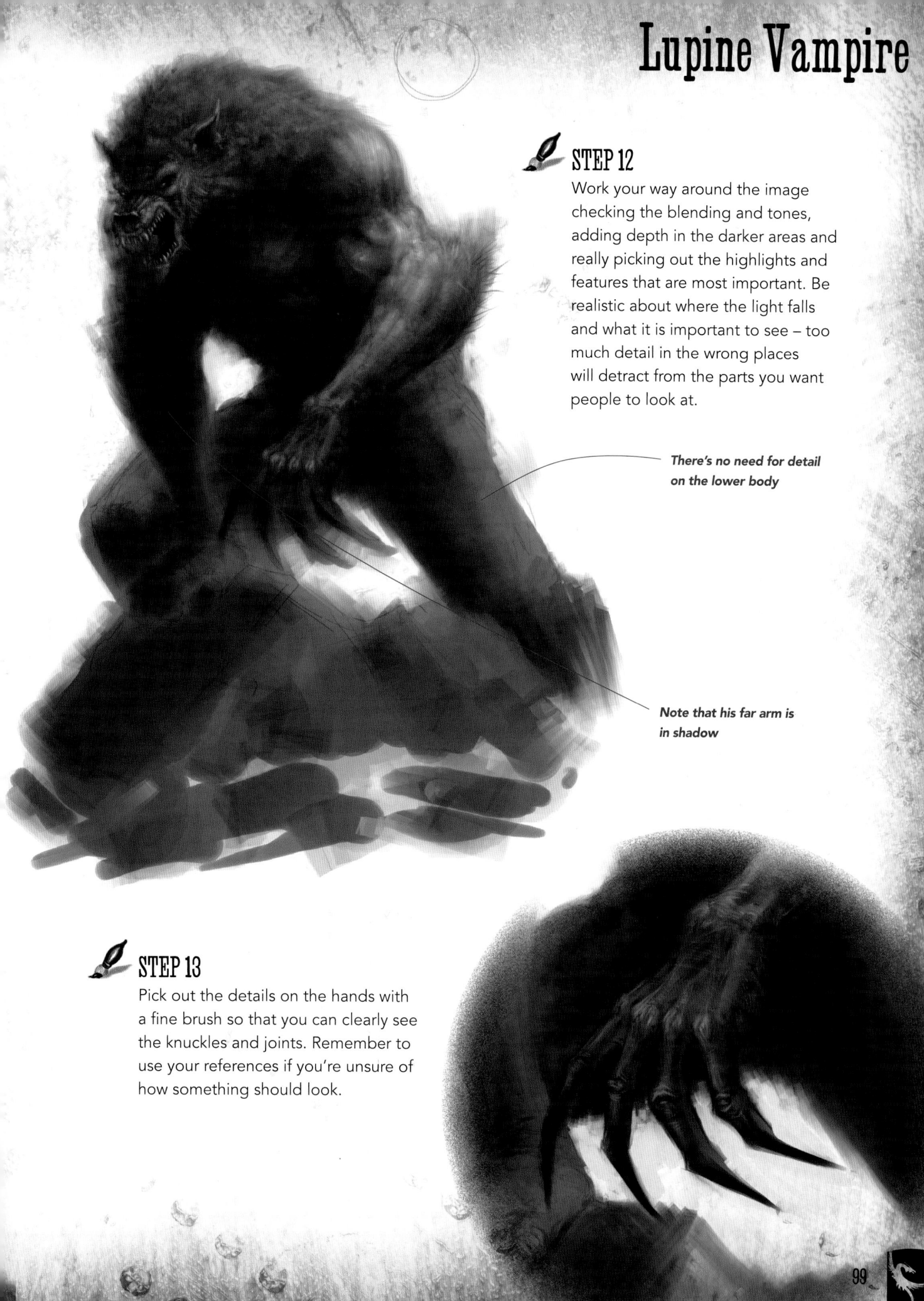

STEP 12

Work your way around the image checking the blending and tones, adding depth in the darker areas and really picking out the highlights and features that are most important. Be realistic about where the light falls and what it is important to see – too much detail in the wrong places will detract from the parts you want people to look at.

There's no need for detail on the lower body

Note that his far arm is in shadow

STEP 13

Pick out the details on the hands with a fine brush so that you can clearly see the knuckles and joints. Remember to use your references if you're unsure of how something should look.

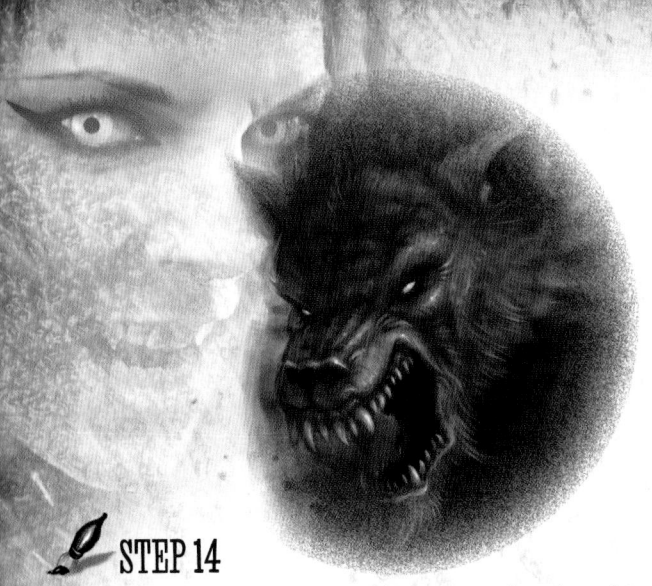

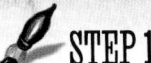
STEP 15

Where would the Lupine Vampire be without lots of torn clothing? Use a medium brush to start adding it in, and a fine brush for the detail of the creases and folds. Have a look at different references to ensure that you get them looking as realistic as possible.

STEP 14

Use a fine brush to work in some details to his teeth. Load it with an opaque white for his eyes to add depth. Splatter red dots on the paper using a large, flat brush to give the effect of globs coming from the mouth.

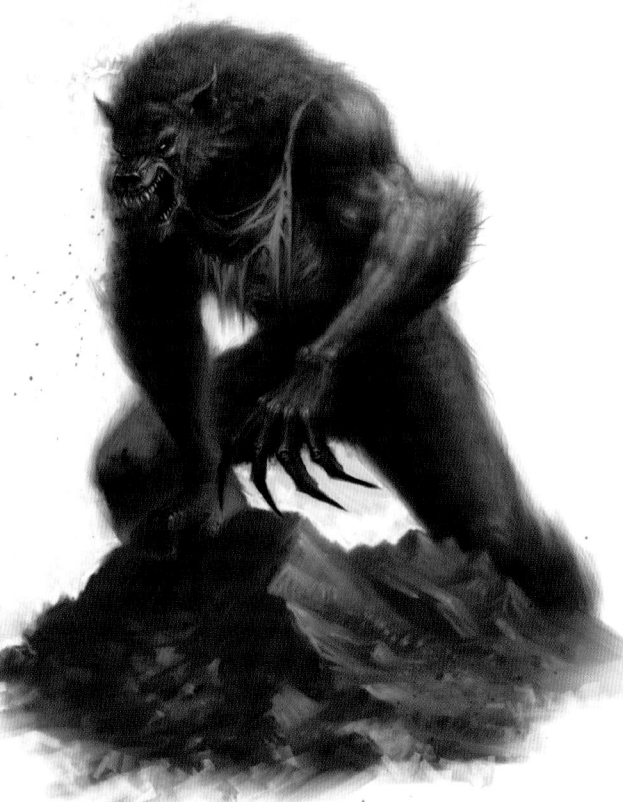

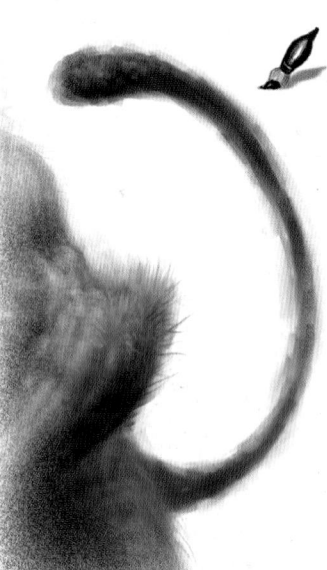

STEP 16

And now to return to that tail. Think about how tails on dogs react to what the body is doing – having it in a huge loop behind the vampire helps to accentuate his menacing forward pose.

ARTIST'S TIP

Always practise your splattering on a clean sheet of paper first. Try different flicking techniques but, more importantly, practise with different amounts of paint on the brush – more paint and water will result in lots of larger blobs, while less paint and water will result in lots of small, fine blobs.

FINAL PIECE

As a final touch, and to leave your viewer in no doubt about the Lupine Vampire's sheer size, quickly add in some skulls and ribs around the rock to provide some scale. Can anyone smell blood?

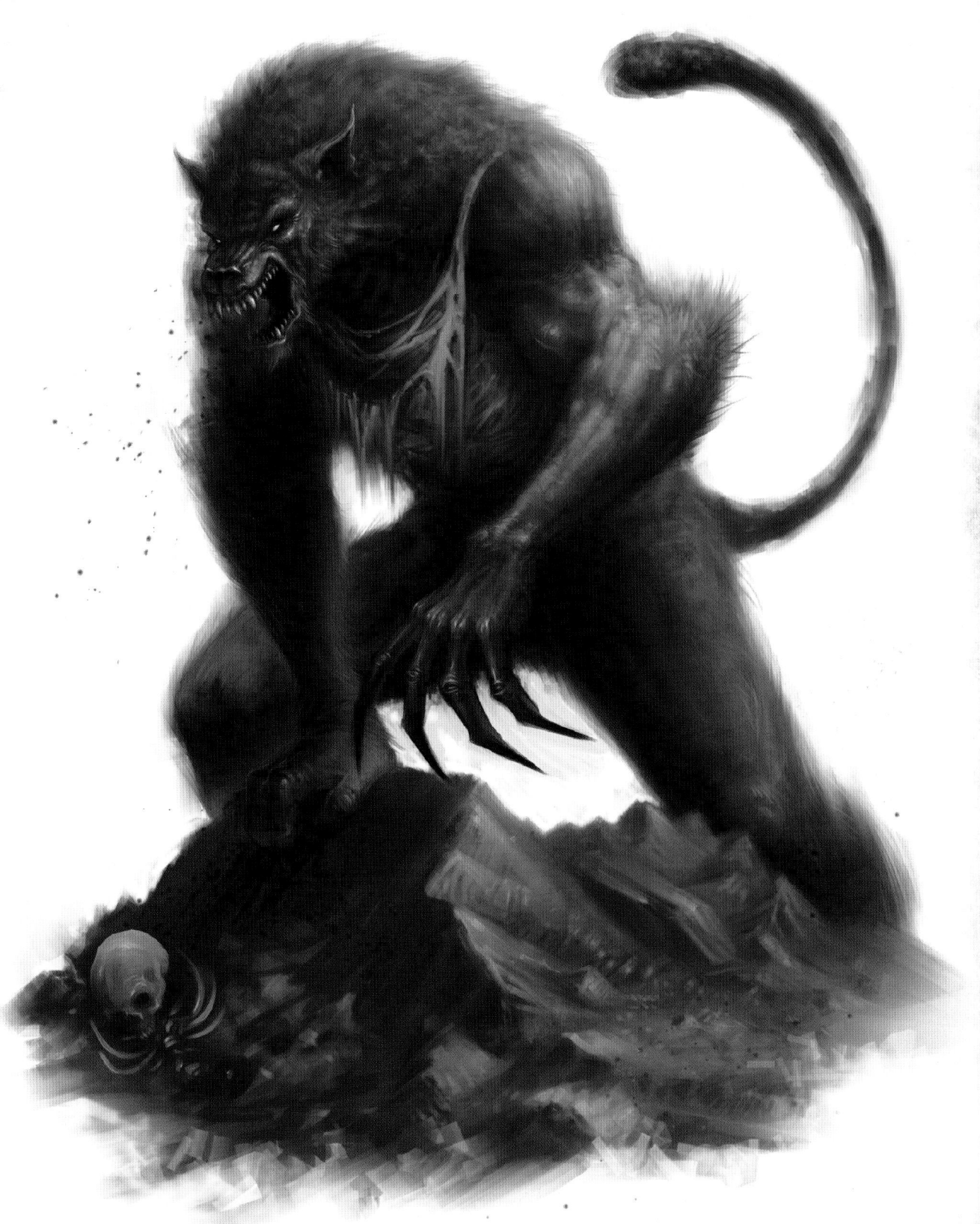

Spring Heeled Jack

Jack Junior Trubblestone was quite terrifying to look at. His disfigured face was just plain scary, and his feet were completely different to any living creature on earth. But it was his heels that made him really different. They had a special extension that could flex and spring him high into the air, and they also enabled him to have a soft landing when he returned to the ground.

In spite of his rather clumsy appearance, Jack Junior was surprisingly nimble and agile. As he grew into his teenage years he discovered that he could spy on the people of London from the rooftops. He would jump up and skitter from one rooftop to the next, observing the ant-like actions of the people below.

Jack Junior despised everyone — but especially his father. One dark, misty night he decided to follow him, spying on him silently from the cold, dew-covered tiles of the roofs above. He watched his father bully, beat and terrify the locals all night long. His blood started to boil. He leapt down from his vantage point, landing softly beside his father. Shocked, his father fell backwards onto his rump with a wet thud. His eyes were wide with fear as he looked up into his son's face. 'Son, what, what are you doing?' His father cried. 'Time to die, Daddy,' hissed Jack Junior, slowly moving in for the kill.

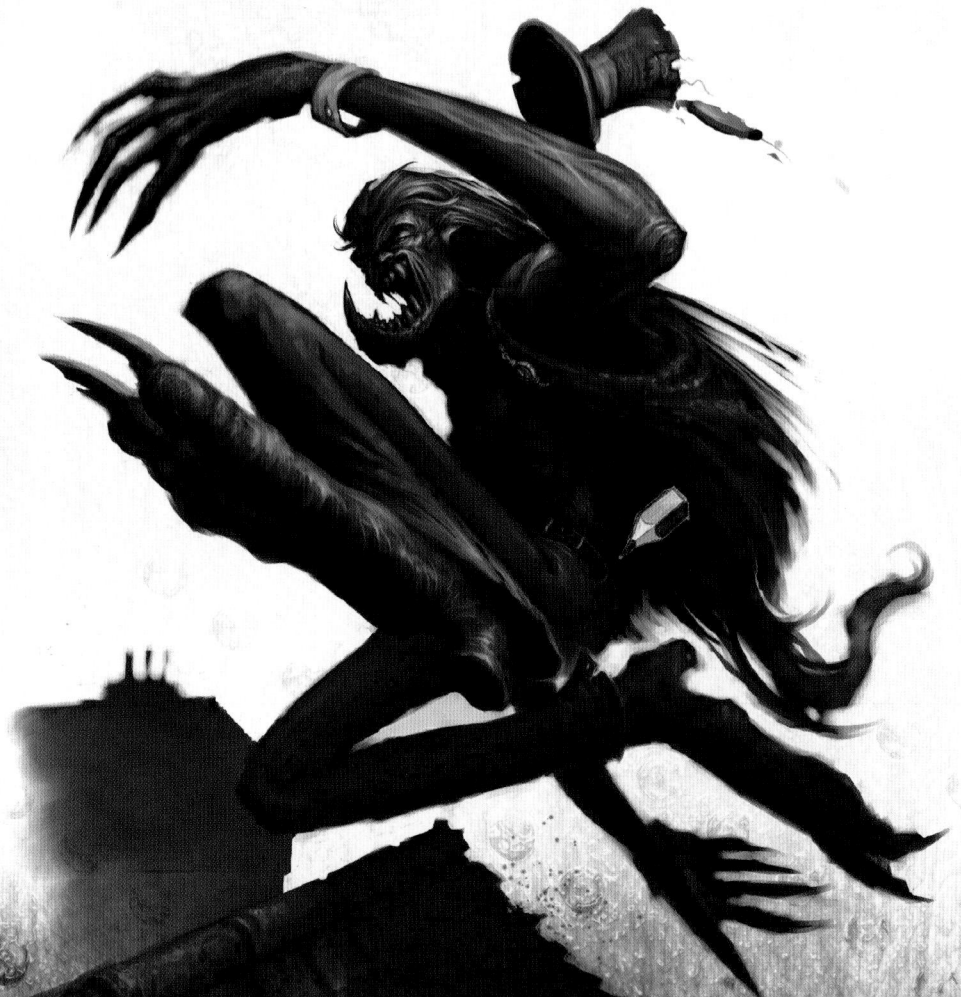

STEP 1

This guy jumps, and he jumps high on to the rooftops. An action pose is the only way with such a dynamic character, and showing him from below is a really good way to demonstrate that he's in the air or flying. We will be using quite a lot of foreshortening for his long limbs. Start by doing a rough outline to indicate where the arms, legs and spine will be.

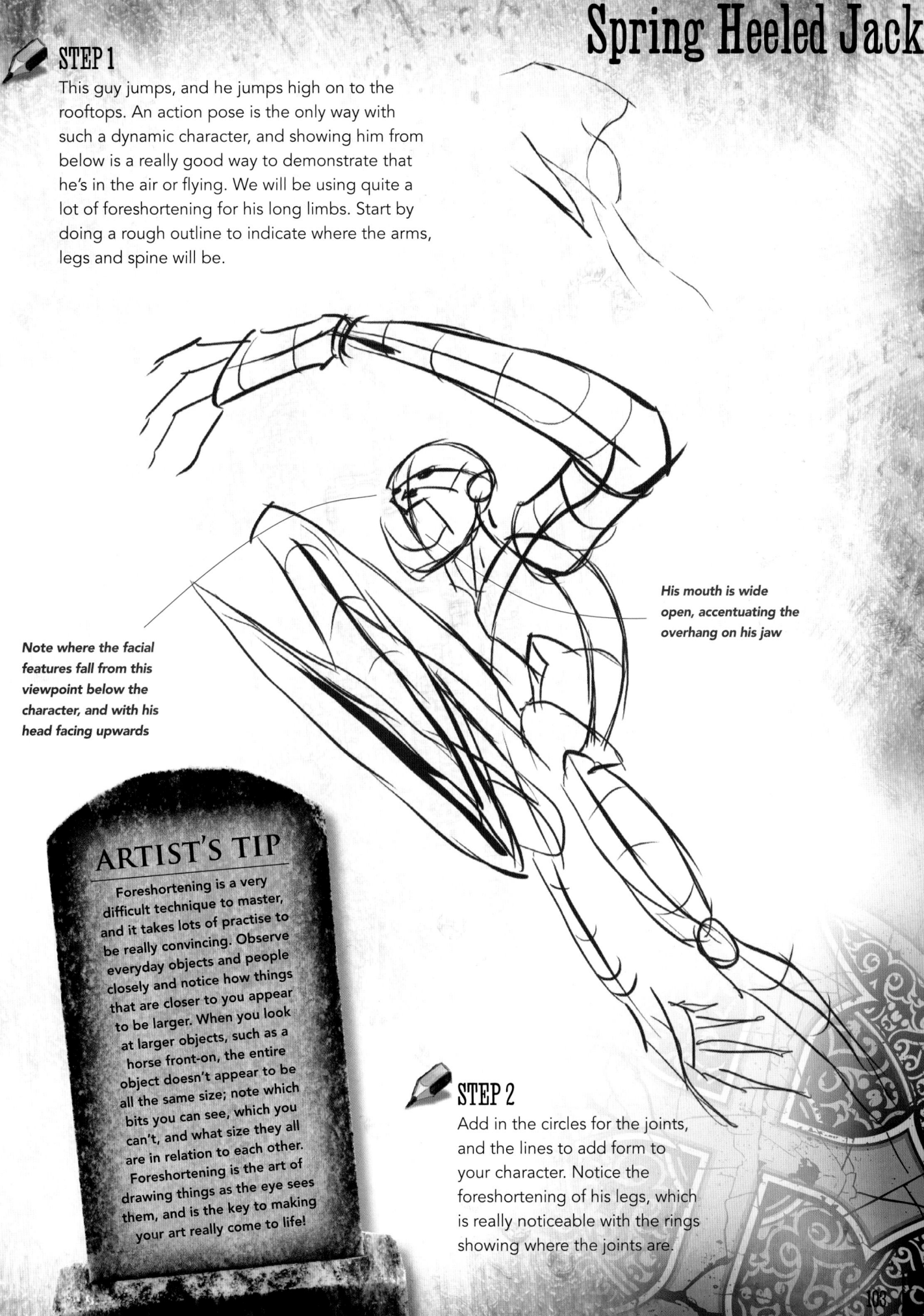

His mouth is wide open, accentuating the overhang on his jaw

Note where the facial features fall from this viewpoint below the character, and with his head facing upwards

ARTIST'S TIP

Foreshortening is a very difficult technique to master, and it takes lots of practise to be really convincing. Observe everyday objects and people closely and notice how things that are closer to you appear to be larger. When you look at larger objects, such as a horse front-on, the entire object doesn't appear to be all the same size; note which bits you can see, which you can't, and what size they all are in relation to each other. Foreshortening is the art of drawing things as the eye sees them, and is the key to making your art really come to life!

STEP 2

Add in the circles for the joints, and the lines to add form to your character. Notice the foreshortening of his legs, which is really noticeable with the rings showing where the joints are.

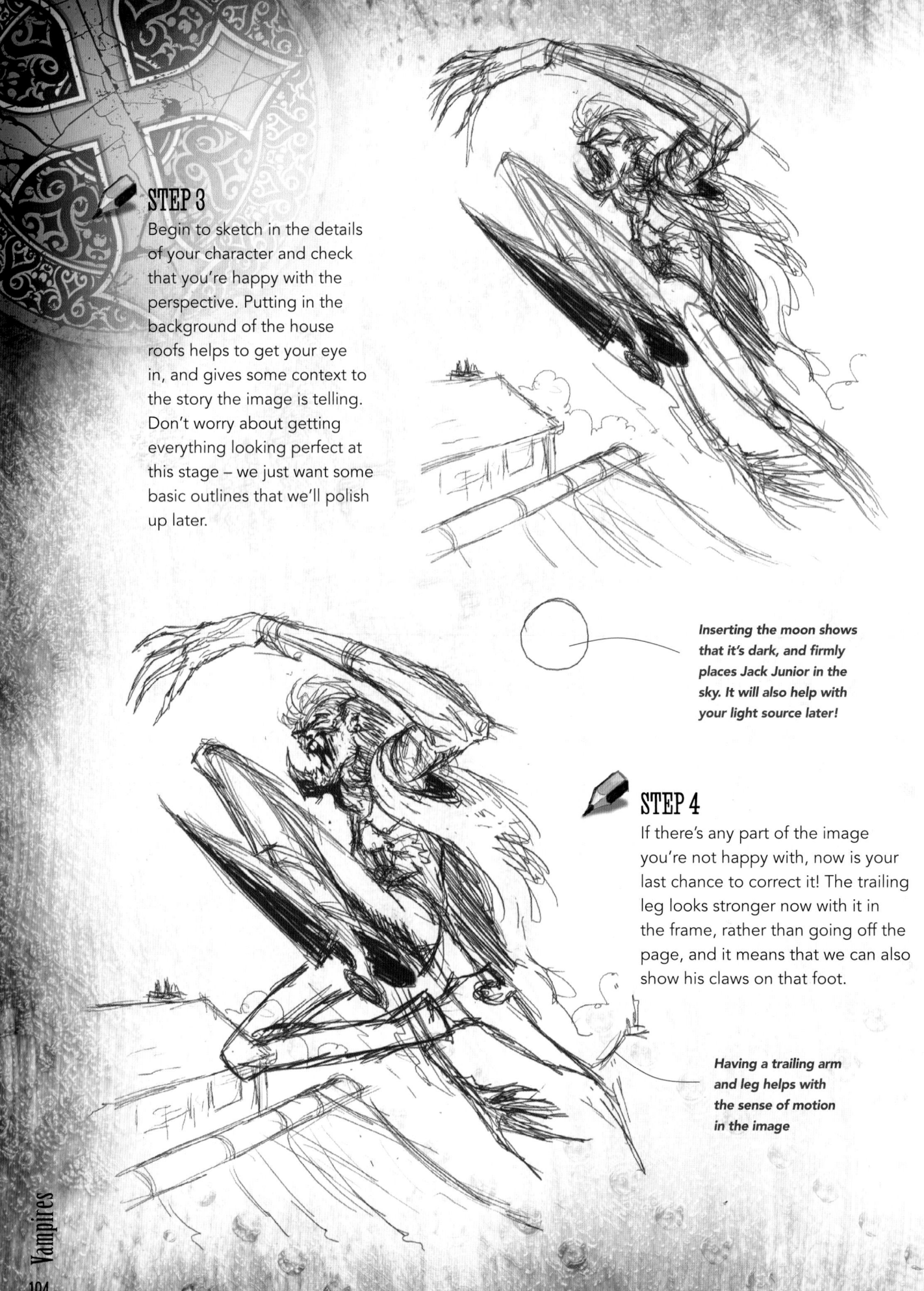

STEP 3

Begin to sketch in the details of your character and check that you're happy with the perspective. Putting in the background of the house roofs helps to get your eye in, and gives some context to the story the image is telling. Don't worry about getting everything looking perfect at this stage – we just want some basic outlines that we'll polish up later.

Inserting the moon shows that it's dark, and firmly places Jack Junior in the sky. It will also help with your light source later!

STEP 4

If there's any part of the image you're not happy with, now is your last chance to correct it! The trailing leg looks stronger now with it in the frame, rather than going off the page, and it means that we can also show his claws on that foot.

Having a trailing arm and leg helps with the sense of motion in the image

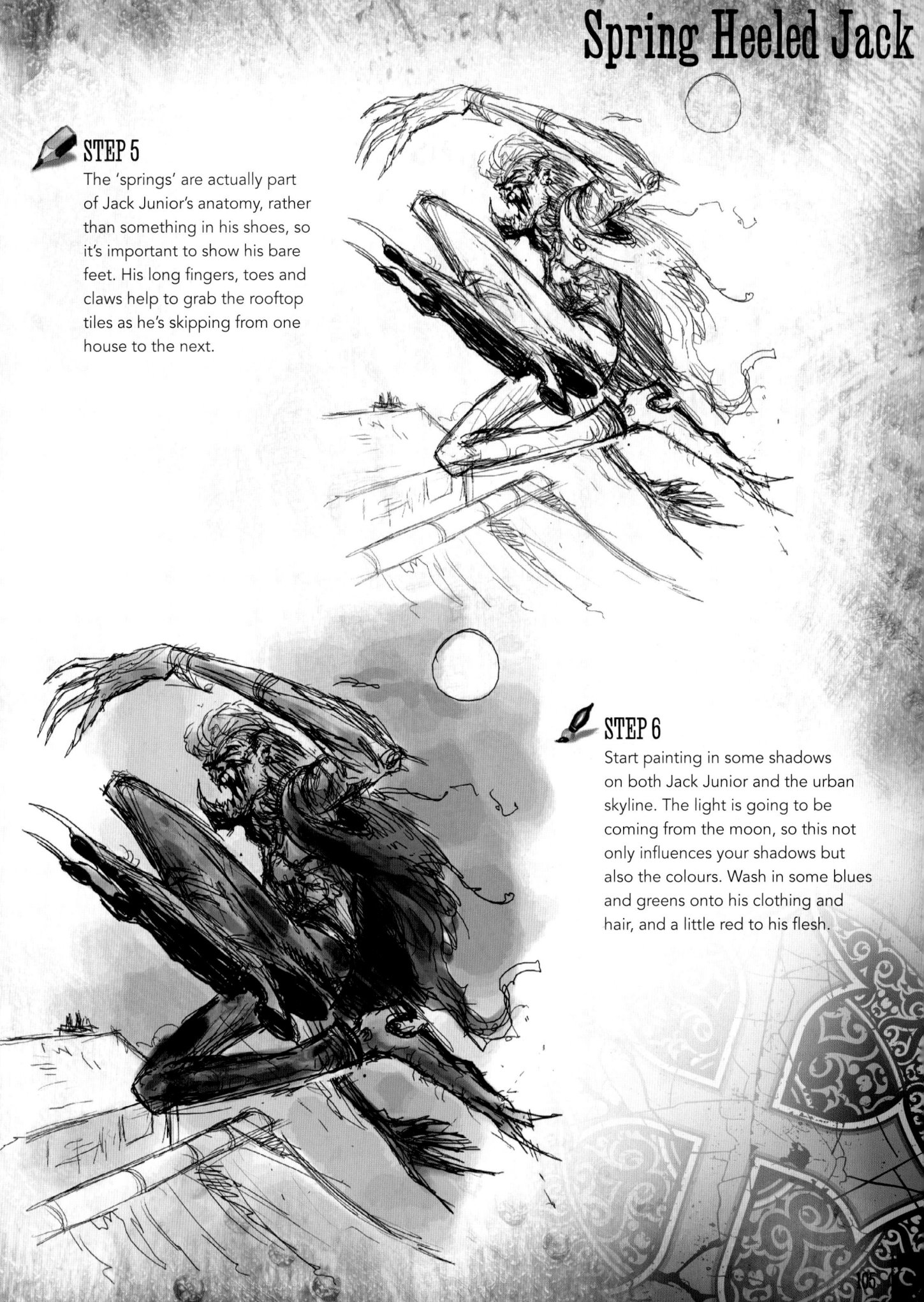

STEP 5

The 'springs' are actually part of Jack Junior's anatomy, rather than something in his shoes, so it's important to show his bare feet. His long fingers, toes and claws help to grab the rooftop tiles as he's skipping from one house to the next.

STEP 6

Start painting in some shadows on both Jack Junior and the urban skyline. The light is going to be coming from the moon, so this not only influences your shadows but also the colours. Wash in some blues and greens onto his clothing and hair, and a little red to his flesh.

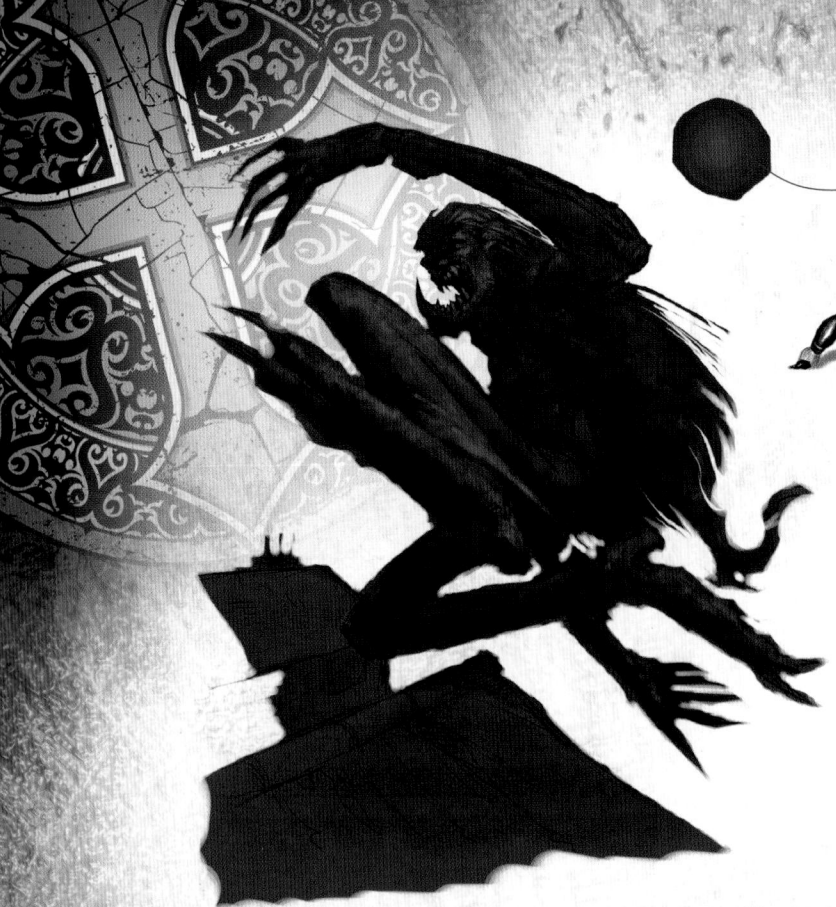

STEP 7

Using a large, flat brush, start to dab in some lighting and highlights. Remember to use lighter shades of your base colours for the areas that are catching the light.

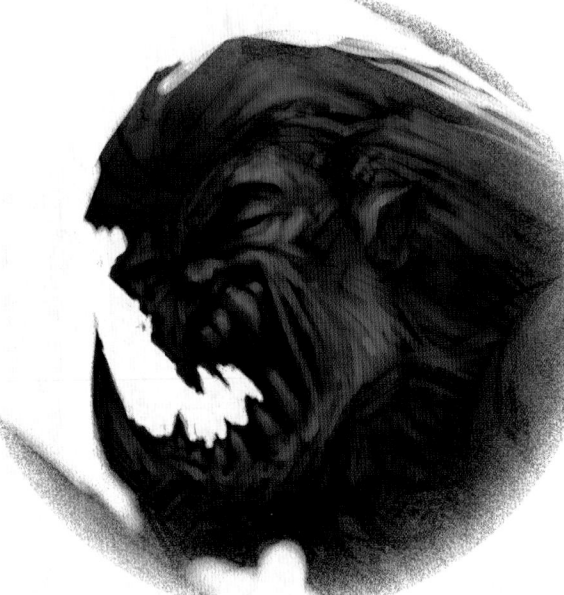

STEP 8

Time to do some fine tuning on those highlights. Use some saturated flesh colours and, using a fine brush, pick out the highlights and details on his face and neck.

STEP 9

Using a fine brush, work your way around the image blending out any remaining pencil marks. Check that you have identified all of the areas of Jack Junior that will be bouncing the light, including the feet, fur on his cloak, his hair and face. Gently highlight these with a fine brush that has very little water on it.

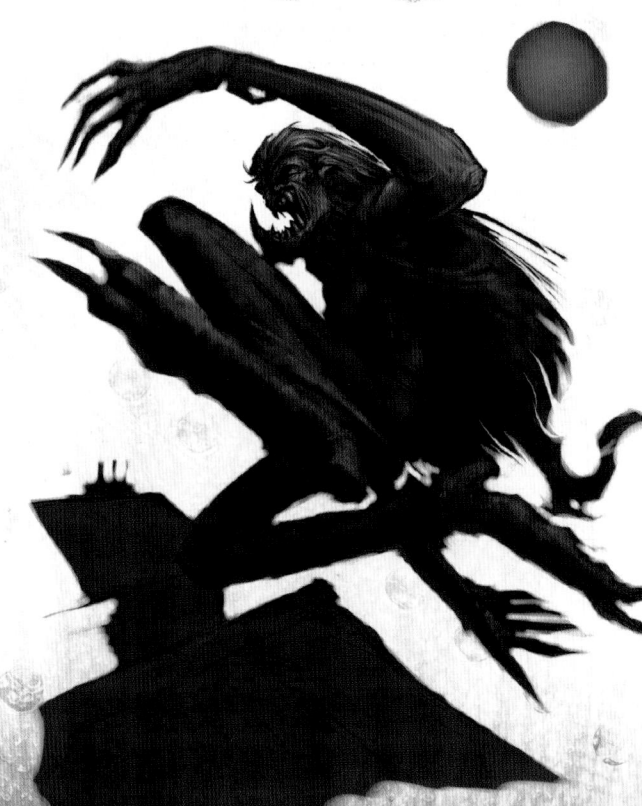

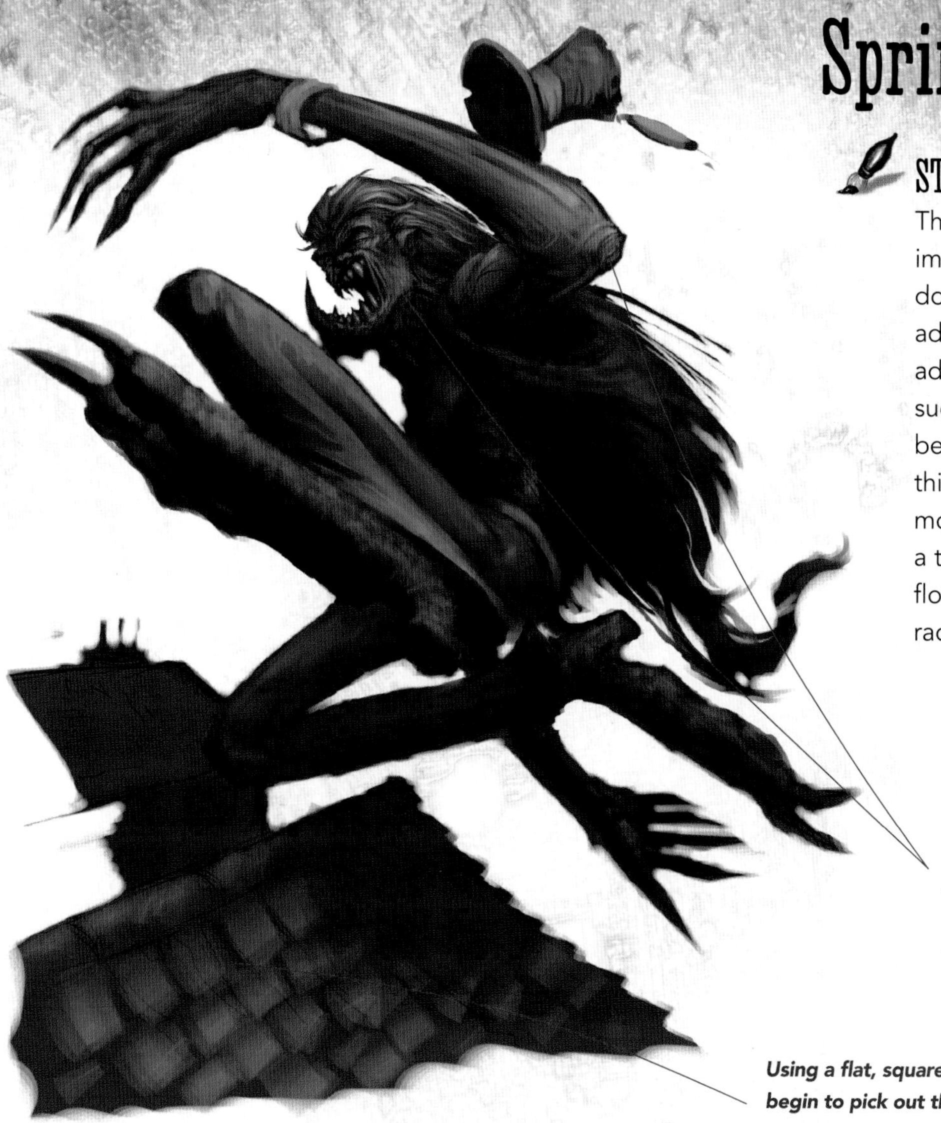

Spring Heeled Jack

STEP 10

The key parts of the image have to be tied down before you start adding the colour, but additional elements, such as the moon, can be changed if you don't think they're working. The moon here has become a tatty top hat that has flown off as Jack Junior raced across the rooftops.

Add in saturated flesh tones to the exposed skin, such as the face and elbow, until you're happy

Using a flat, square brush, begin to pick out the shapes of the roof tiles

STEP 11

Check the highlights and colour of the base of the foot, which is the central part of the image. You don't just want it to be black, so try adding in some gentle red lighting with some orange highlights for added interest.

Using a fine brush, pick out the interesting details that will help to define his face

Return to the tiled roof to block in the shaded areas

ARTIST'S TIP

Getting skin tones right can be really difficult and time consuming, so don't be afraid to stop, have a break and let the paint dry before going back later with fresh eyes. You don't want to ruin your image by overworking an area or getting too much paint and water on it.

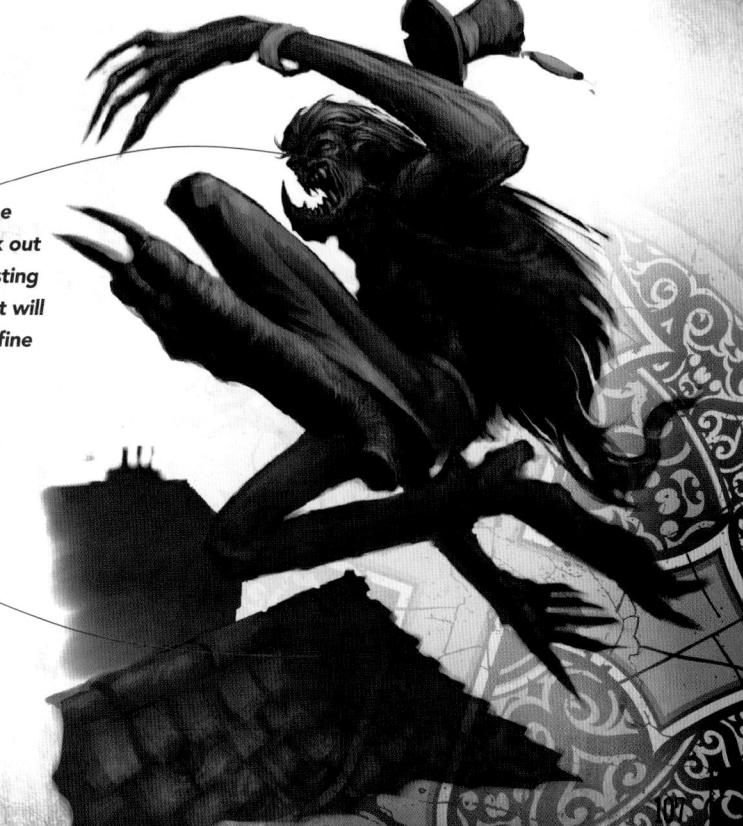

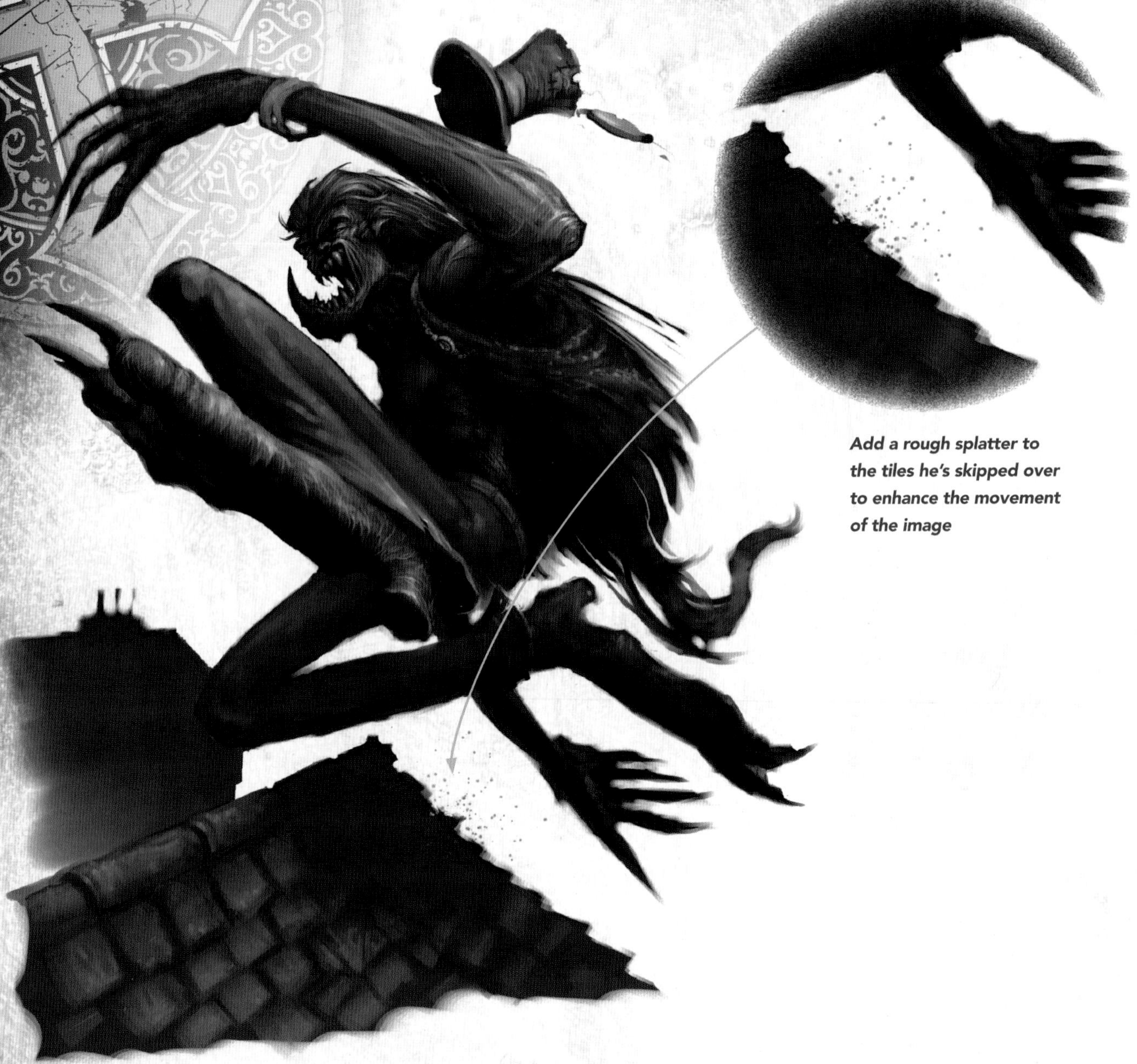

Add a rough splatter to the tiles he's skipped over to enhance the movement of the image

 ## STEP 12

Run your eye over the whole image and check that you're happy with the blending, shading and highlights, remembering to be disciplined about when to stop! When you're happy, add the finishing touches to Jack Junior using a really fine brush to pick out the detail on areas such as the fur cloak, belt straps and a bit more detail on the main foot.

 ## FINAL PIECE

Finally, add in the last highlights on his face, the detail on his pocket watch and trousers, and tidy up his belt. And there is the ugly, awkward spectacle that is the Spring Heeled Jack. Now, where did I leave my daddy?

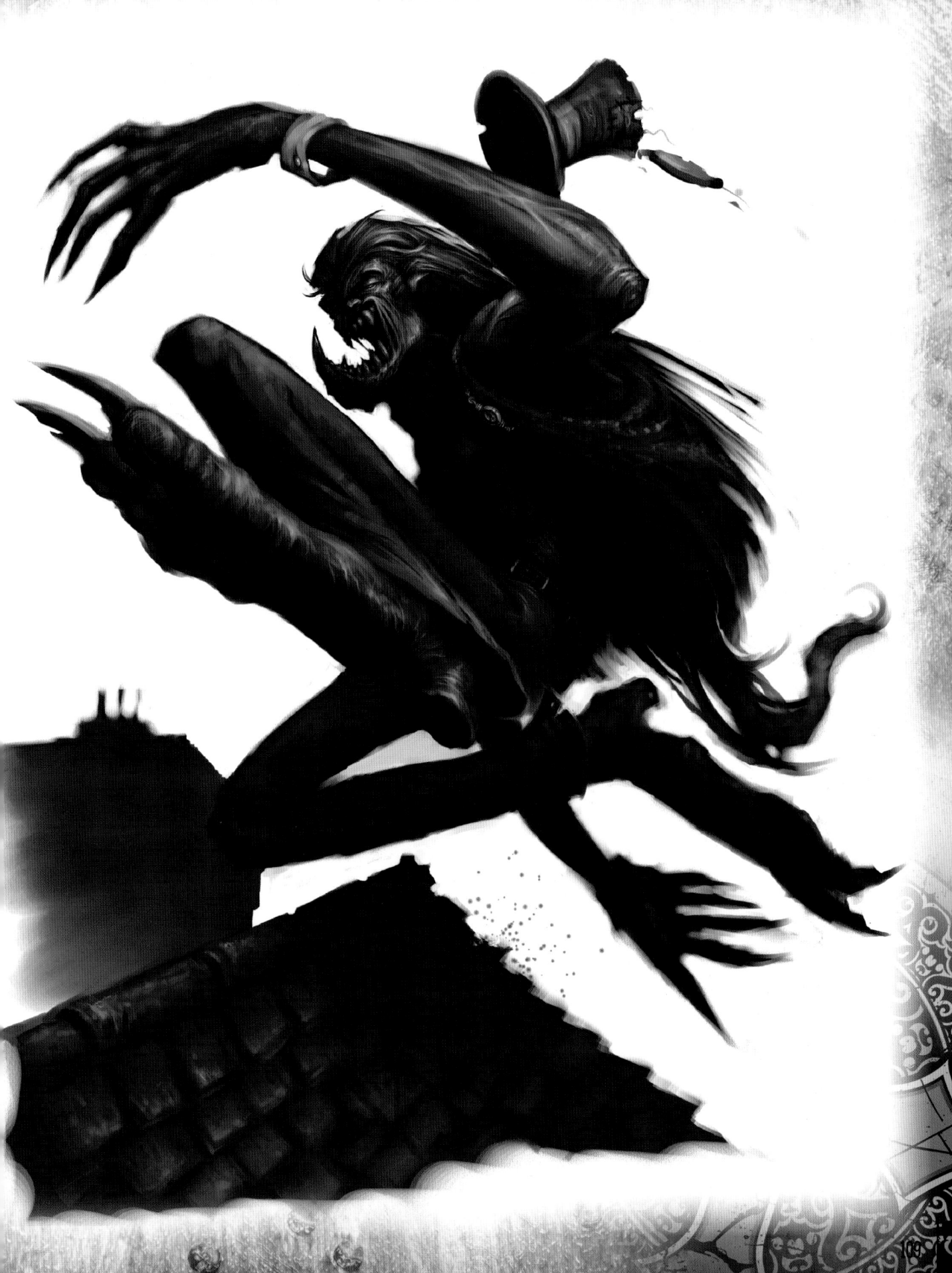

Bat Vampire

Henry couldn't take his eyes of the silhouetted castle on top of the hill in Transylvania, where he was staying on a school trip. He skittered off into the shadows, away from the rest of the group and went to have a closer look. He loped his way up to the castle, through tangled bushes, thorns and foul smelling mud to the cliff's edge and the giant arched doorway of the castle.

The next thing he knew, he was waking up in a strange room. He gently opened his eyes, but everything seemed black. He tried to move, but it hurt his head too much, and his neck was really sore, especially down his left side. He tried to speak, but all he could hear were clicking sounds. He tried again, but heard only the clicking sounds.

The darkness was clearing and he was beginning to see around him. He could see the tiny spider sitting in its web. He could see the tiny drops of water hanging off the moss in the cracks of the brick floor. He could also now see that he was lying in a coffin, and had massive wings extending uncomfortably behind him. It was then that the penny dropped and he realised what had happened to him...

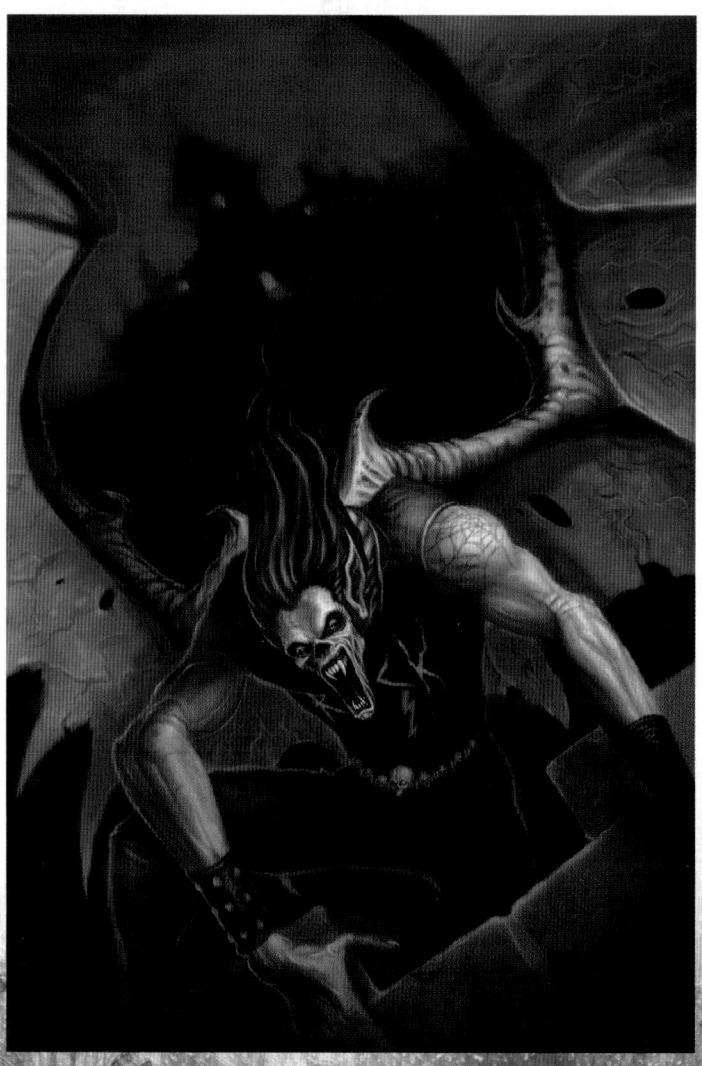

Bat Vampire

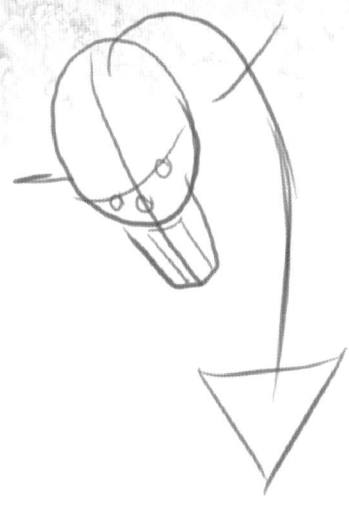

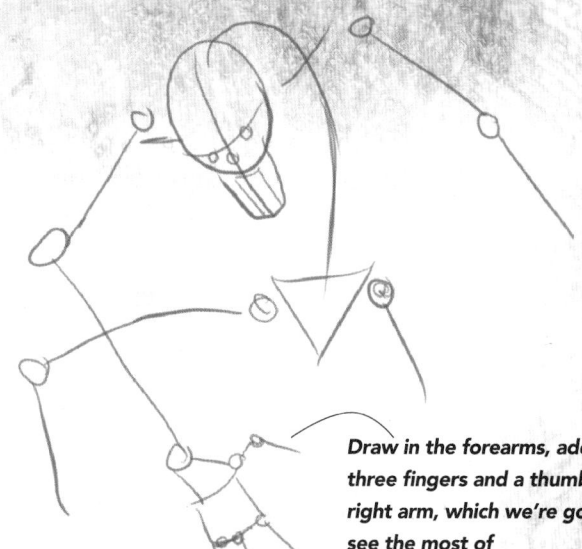

Draw in the forearms, adding three fingers and a thumb to his right arm, which we're going to see the most of

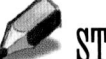

STEP 1

Henry's going to be leaning forward towards us, wings open as he crawls over a wall as if he's in the process of wrenching himself up. Draw in the sphere for his head, extended jaw and his bent/curved spine. Now indicate where his eyes, nose and mouth will be, draw in the lines for his collar bones and the triangle for his pelvis.

STEP 2

Now draw in his upper arms, with circles indicating the joints, and add in the lines for his legs. His right leg will be raised so that you can see the knee joint, while the other leg will mostly be hidden behind the wall, so you don't need to worry about that.

Remember that Henry is hunched over towards us, so you can see the top of his shoulders above his head

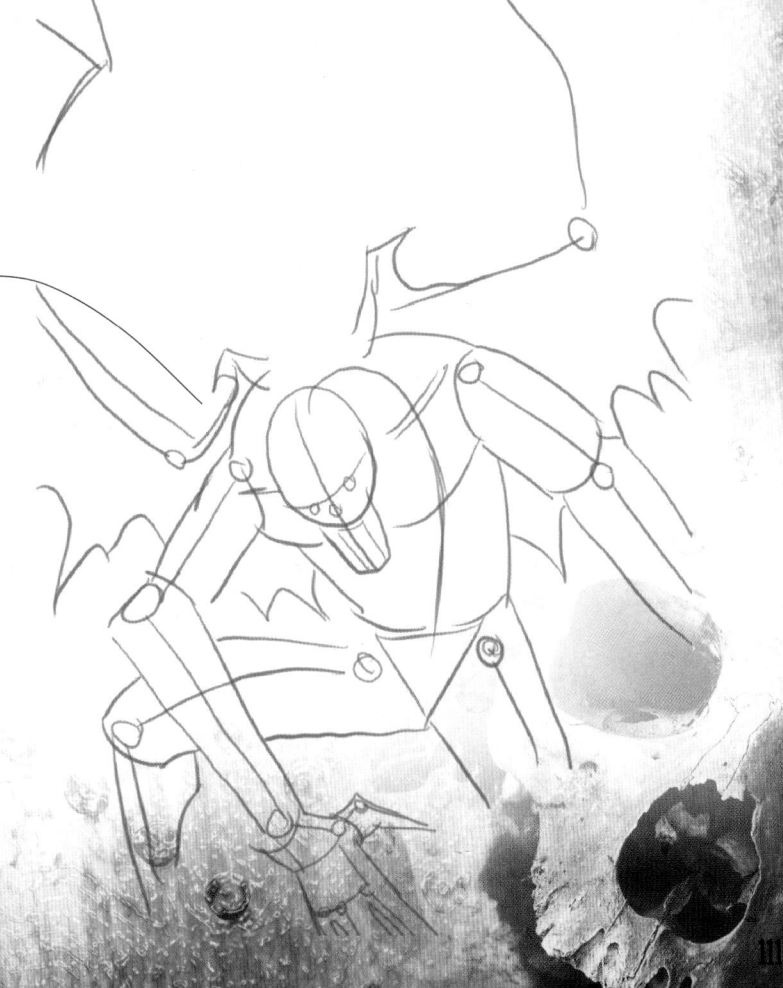

STEP 3

We want his wings raised up and behind him, so draw the lines in remembering to add the joints. Now start to fill in the shapes over his entire body, which will give you something to build from when it comes to the final sketch.

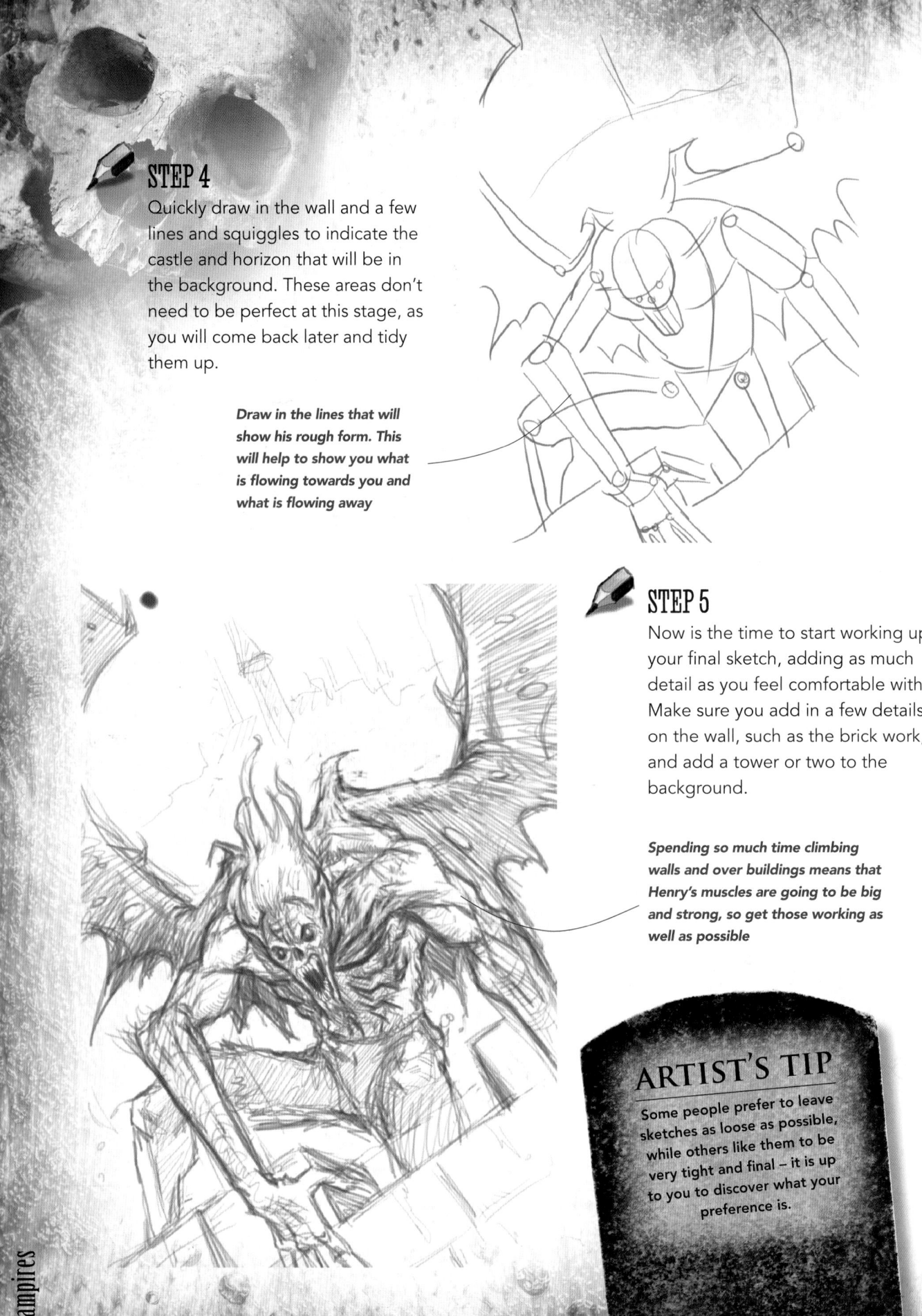

STEP 4

Quickly draw in the wall and a few lines and squiggles to indicate the castle and horizon that will be in the background. These areas don't need to be perfect at this stage, as you will come back later and tidy them up.

Draw in the lines that will show his rough form. This will help to show you what is flowing towards you and what is flowing away

STEP 5

Now is the time to start working up your final sketch, adding as much detail as you feel comfortable with. Make sure you add in a few details on the wall, such as the brick work, and add a tower or two to the background.

Spending so much time climbing walls and over buildings means that Henry's muscles are going to be big and strong, so get those working as well as possible

ARTIST'S TIP

Some people prefer to leave sketches as loose as possible, while others like them to be very tight and final – it is up to you to discover what your preference is.

STEP 6

Using a large, flat brush, wash over the background with a light brown or sepia colour.

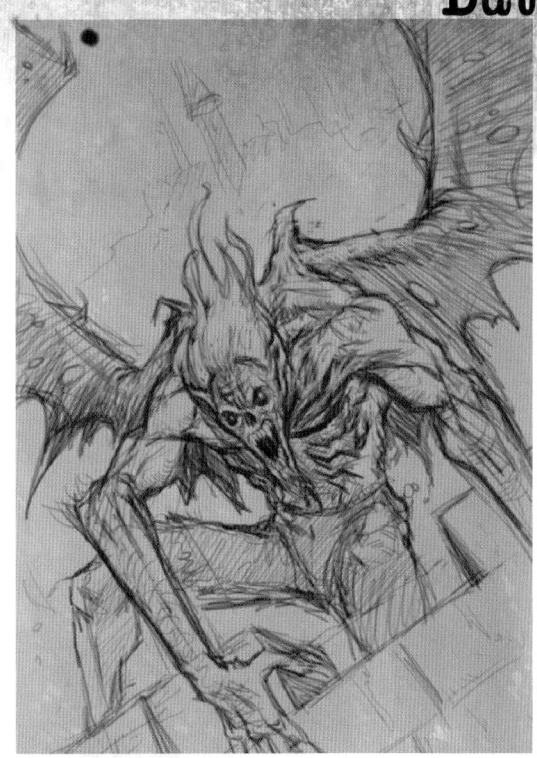

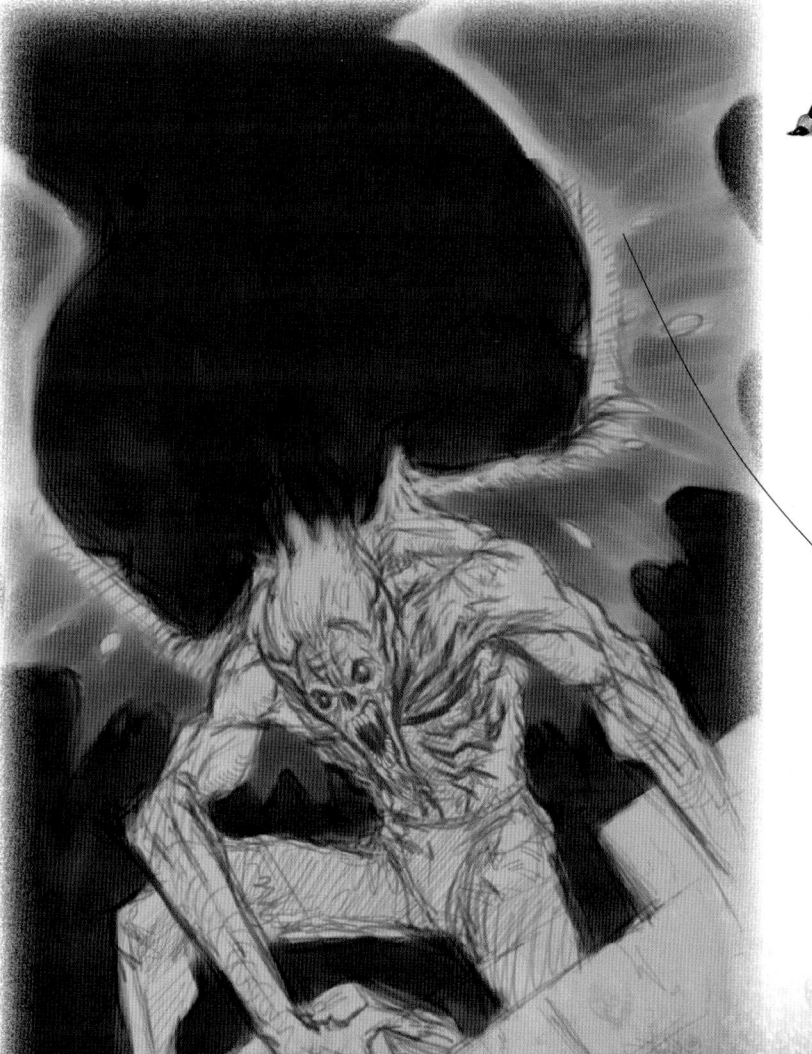

STEP 7

Making sure that your initial wash is dry, use another large, flat brush to wash in a deep red over the background cityscape area. Don't worry too much about getting a nice smooth finish, or if you go over the lines as we can fix this later.

Start to blend in an orange colour for the wings, remembering your analogous colour combinations (see page 34)

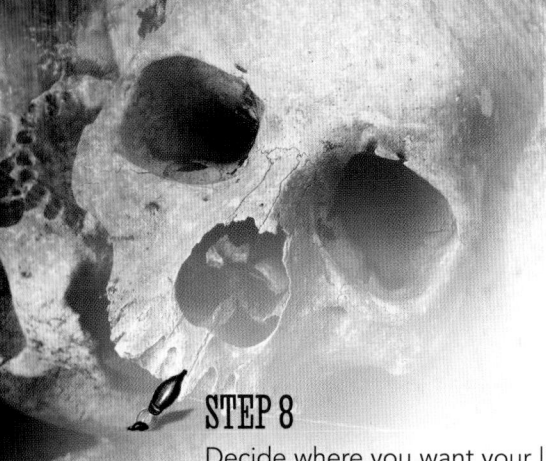

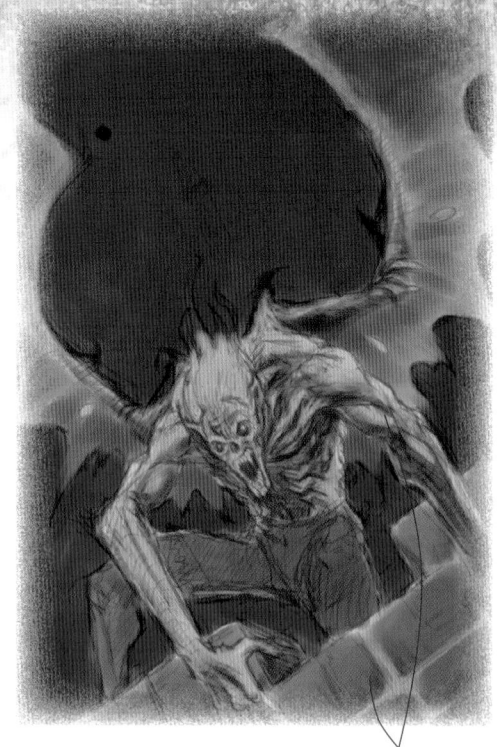

STEP 8

Decide where you want your light to be coming from – here it is coming from the right of the picture, but you can change this if you wish. Now pick a darker colour from the initial brown texture wash and begin to add in some tone and shading. Selecting the colours in this way will give you some really effective deep tones.

Lightly wash a slightly green-grey colour onto his flesh and the wall

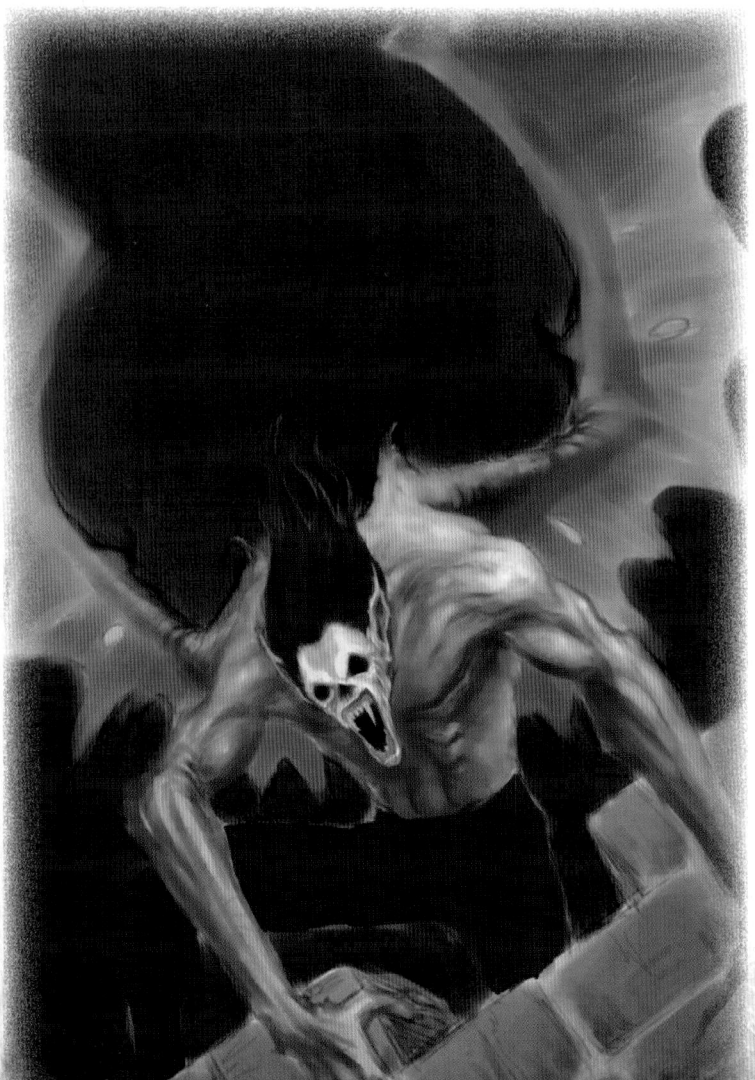

STEP 9

Start to work your way around the image, blending in the colours on his flesh. Using a fine brush, pick out some highlights on his skin with a grey/yellow.

Bat Vampire

STEP 10

Stand back and check that you're happy with how the image is working. Flip the image (or look at it in the mirror) and see if any glaring errors jump out at you. Keep blending his flesh and start to paint in details on his face. His face will be brighter and lighter than the rest of him, so that the viewer's eye is drawn to it in all its freaky glory.

Keep painting in those highlights, especially around the area where his wings connect to his shoulders and the light is really bouncing

STEP 11

Let's have fun with his clothing! Using a dark brown paint start working in his top, making sure that you leave his super-strong arms exposed. Add some grey for his belt buckles and studs on his wristbands. Use a medium-fine brush to add in some lighter brown in the folds of the cloth around his shoulder area.

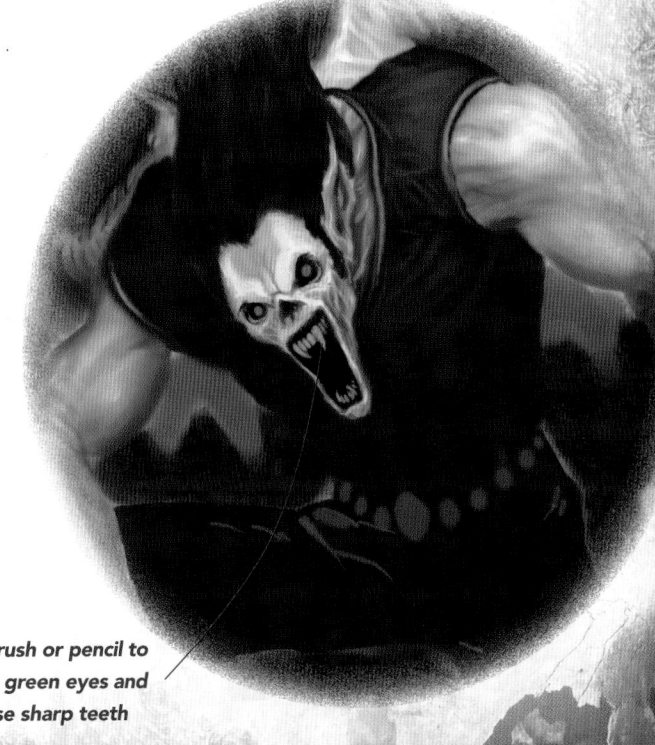

Use a small brush or pencil to paint in some green eyes and pin point those sharp teeth

ARTIST'S TIP

Check your reference sources to make sure that you've got the clothing working realistically. It will make your picture all the more appealing for the effort.

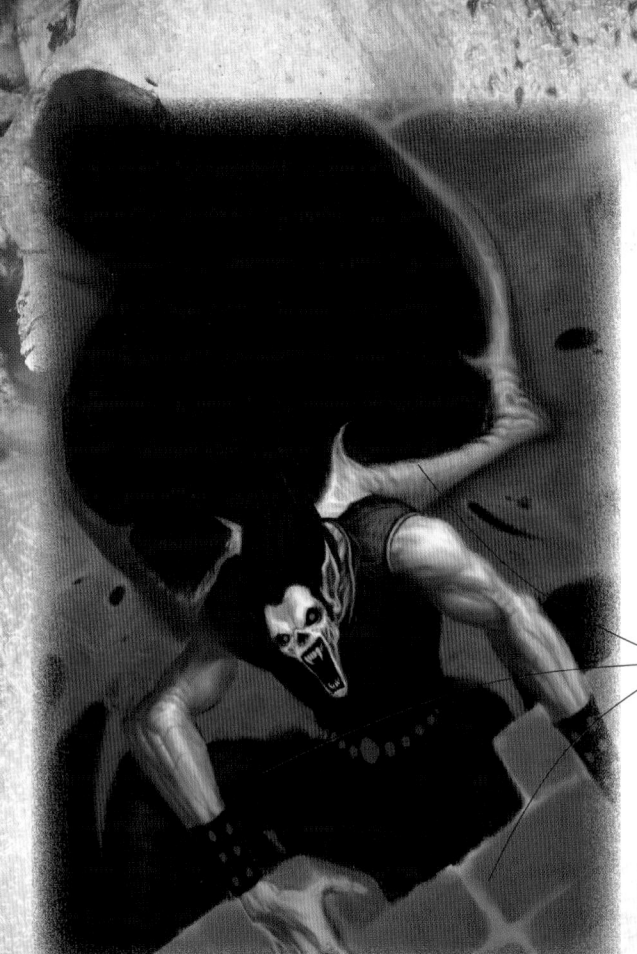

The flesh needs texture, so add this using steady, repeated brush strokes, building up the layers of colour. Remember not to have too much wet paint on your brush, and to let the paper dry out as you go. Redefine the highlights on the skin after this if necessary.

Start to pick out the individual bricks and his hand, blend in the lighting on his trousers and add more texture on his wings

 STEP 13

It's fun time! Paint in textures and details on the parts of his body that you want the eye drawn to, for example his face, shoulder and arms. Keep refining his face, highlighting those eyes and gradually work into the background to make that castle start to stand out.

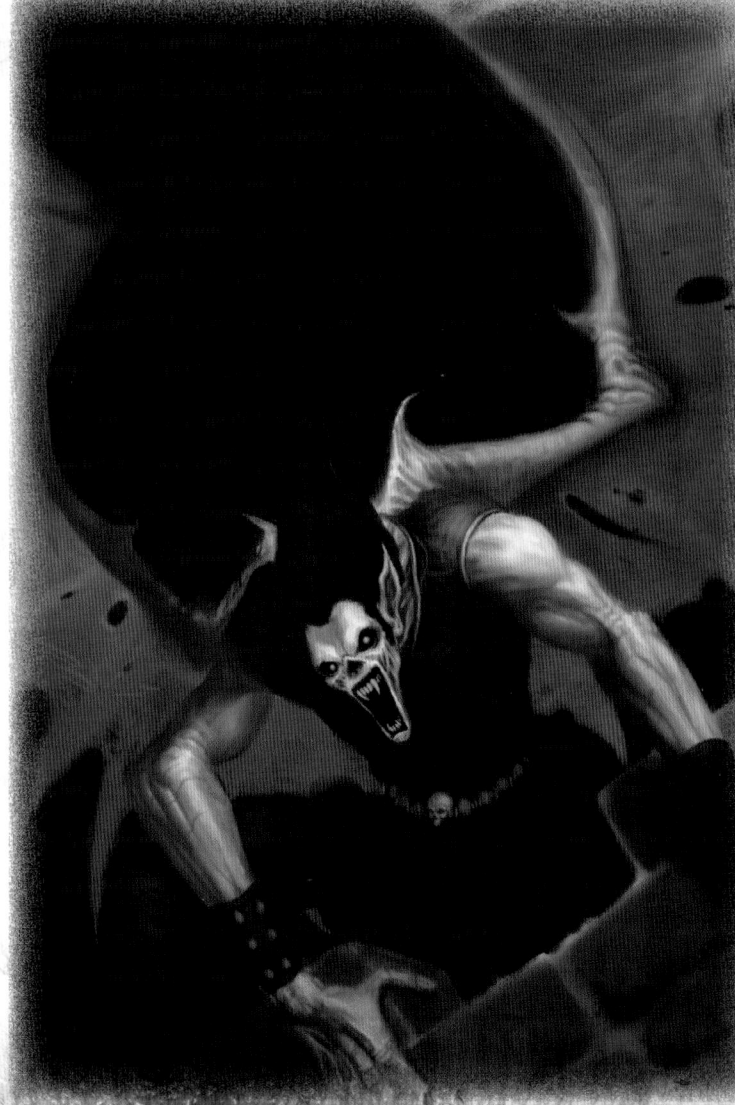

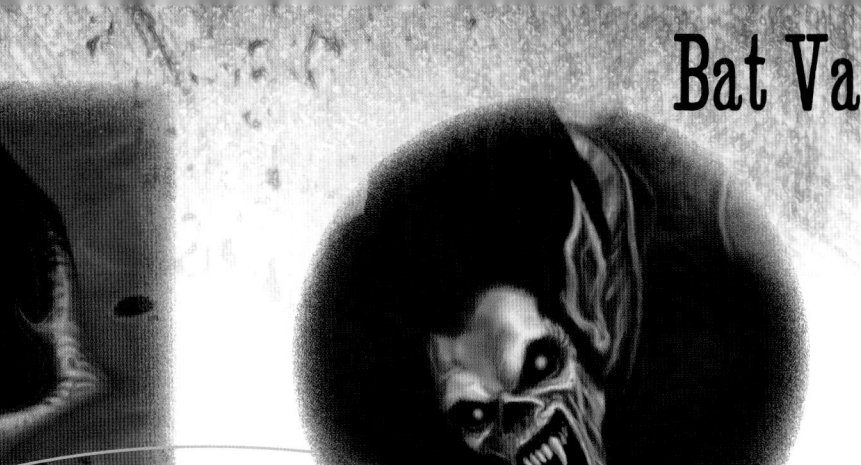

 ## STEP 14

Refine those teeth, hair and any other details such as wrinkles on his face, using a fine brush. Give him some attitude: is he smiling, snarling or both? Take the time to work your way round the image for a final time, checking that you're happy with all of the blending, shapes, textures and highlights, and ensuring that all of the pencil lines have gone now.

 ## STEP 15

These end stages are all about fine tuning, so keep working on all of those details until you're happy. The eyes in particular need to be spot on!

Pop that castle out of the background by painting in a lighter and brighter shade of red for the sky, and draw in some doors and windows with a soft yellow pencil

Add small details to his clothing and armbands

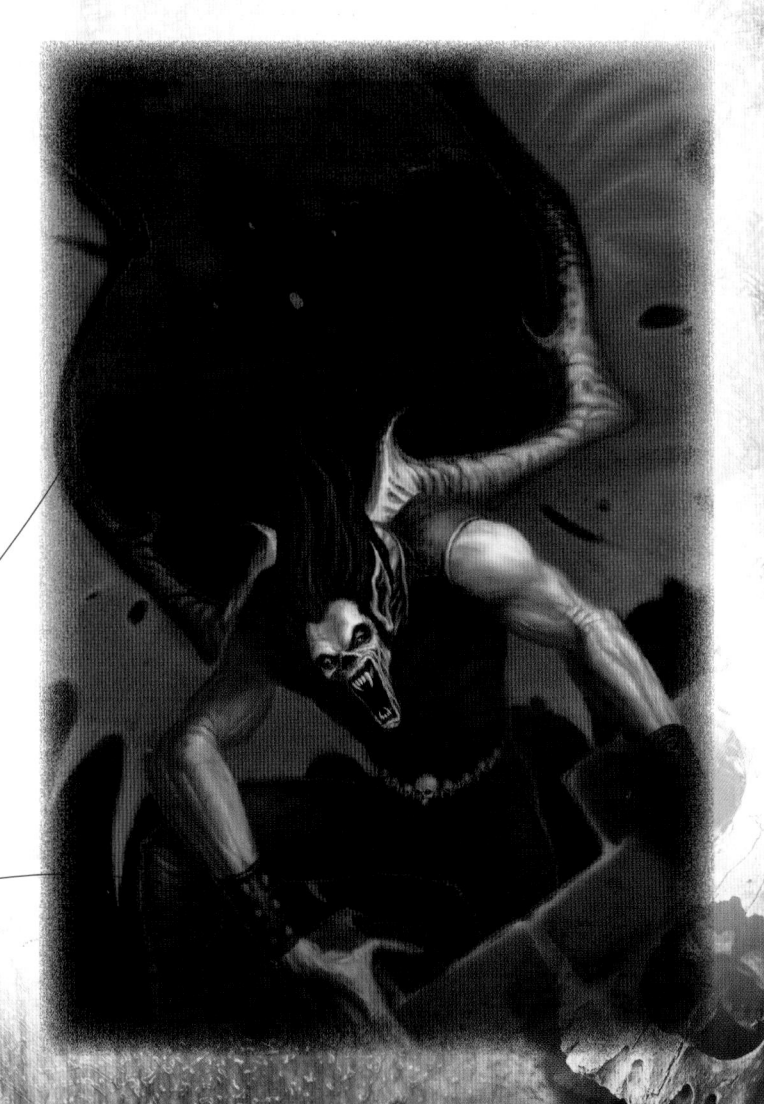

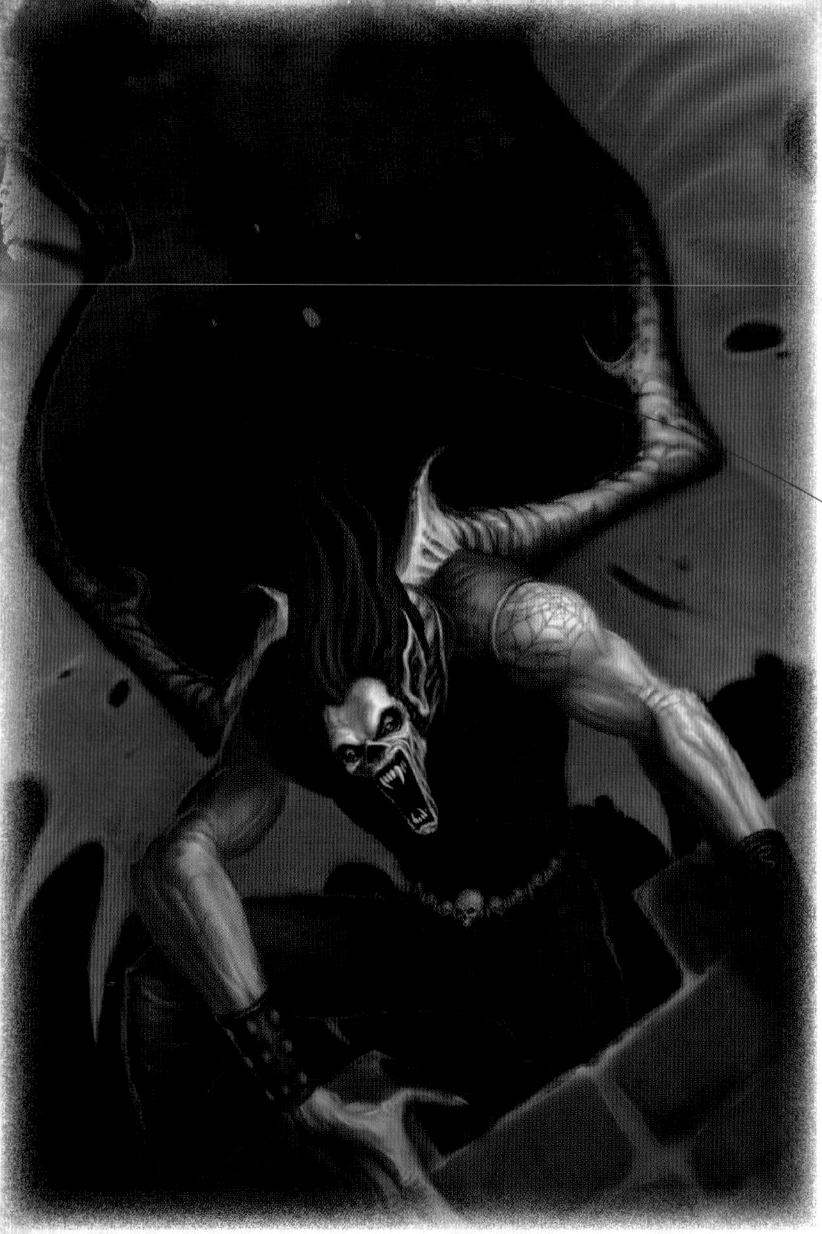

Little details, such as this reflection of the door on the ground, really add to the atmosphere and realism of the piece

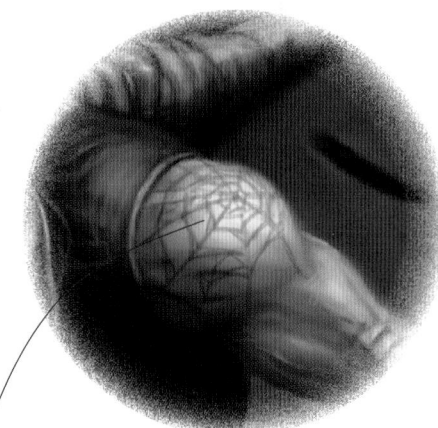

Use a pencil to add in any final details

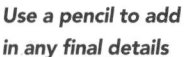 **STEP 16**

Give the sky a cloud-like texture by using a large brush and blending in the colours by dabbing.

 FINAL PIECE

Henry loves his rock music, so use a fine brush or pencil to write 'rock' on his t-shirt (or any other writing you fancy!). Add depth to the wall either by overlaying a texture in Photoshop, or by scrubbing with an old brush that's not loaded with paint. Now you just need to remember to look up when you're checking for vampires...

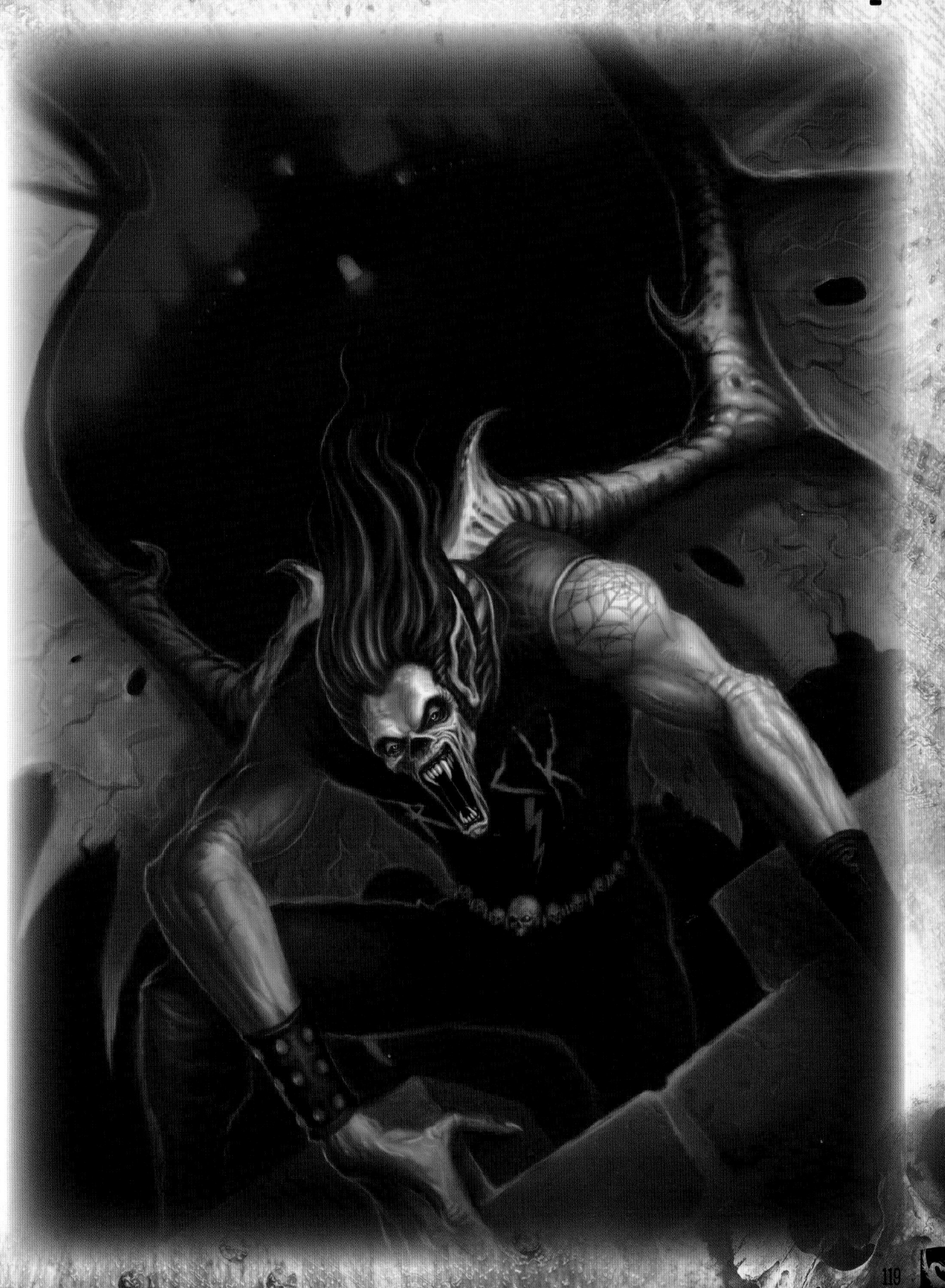

Vampire Hunter

Sam wasn't meant to be here. He wasn't meant to survive. He couldn't understand how he was still moving and breathing... no, no, he wasn't breathing! How could this be?

He remembered being attacked, his throat being bitten out by the swooping bat vampires. He didn't stand a chance. They left him for dead, laughing in their wake, mocking his humanity. Sam looked at his blood soaked hands and watched as the falling rain washed it away.

The alley was lit by one, bright, grill-covered lamp, and he stood up in its light, a pale ghost-like figure. He coughed,

and blood gushed from his mouth, spilling down his chest. He'd become one of them, he knew it. He cursed himself for being so stupid, and leaned up against the wall, head bowed. He'd kept his desperation for vengeance in check for years, but had let his guard down and now they had got him. Sam knew the cost — having dealt with these vampires for the past three years he knew what he now was. He also knew that 'The Hunger' would strike him soon — he had just a couple of hours, tops, to find the vampires. Time to make a move.

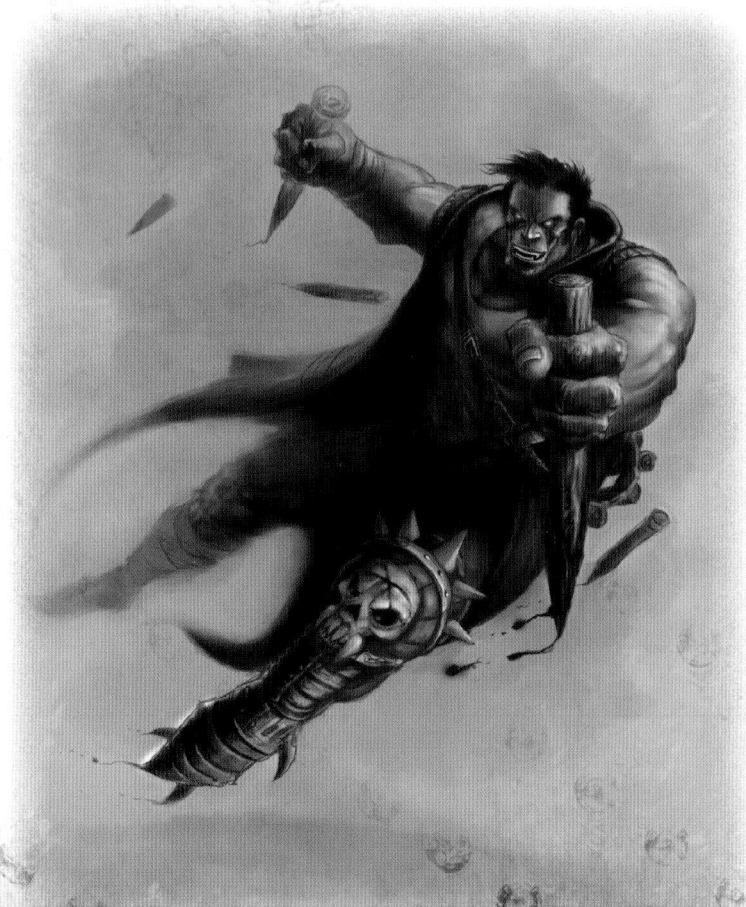

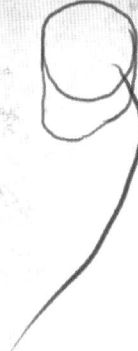

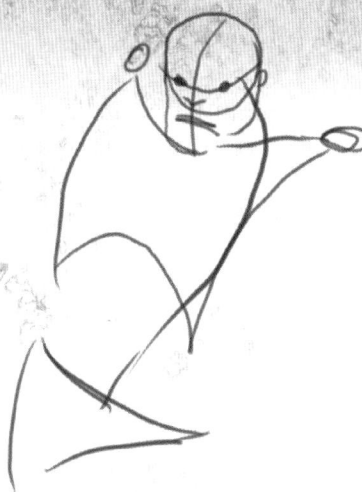

STEP 1

In this image the vampire will be diving to the side, both arms raised with stakes brandished in his hands, one leg bent towards us and his other leg trailing behind. Draw the head and spine using simple lines – the spine should be trailing off to the side to show the flow of his body jumping to one side. Sam will have a solid build, so his head should reflect this and be more rectangular in shape than usual.

STEP 2

Using basic shapes and lines, draw in the collar bones, making sure the one closest to us is a little larger to get the correct proportion and make the image look really realistic. Add in the markers for his eyes, nose, mouth and ears. A solid build means a solid, broad chest, so use your basic shapes to draw in his ribcage area. Draw in his pelvis with the bottom pointing slightly to the side following the flow of his spine.

Draw in the forearms, adding three fingers and a thumb to his right arm, which we're going to see the most of

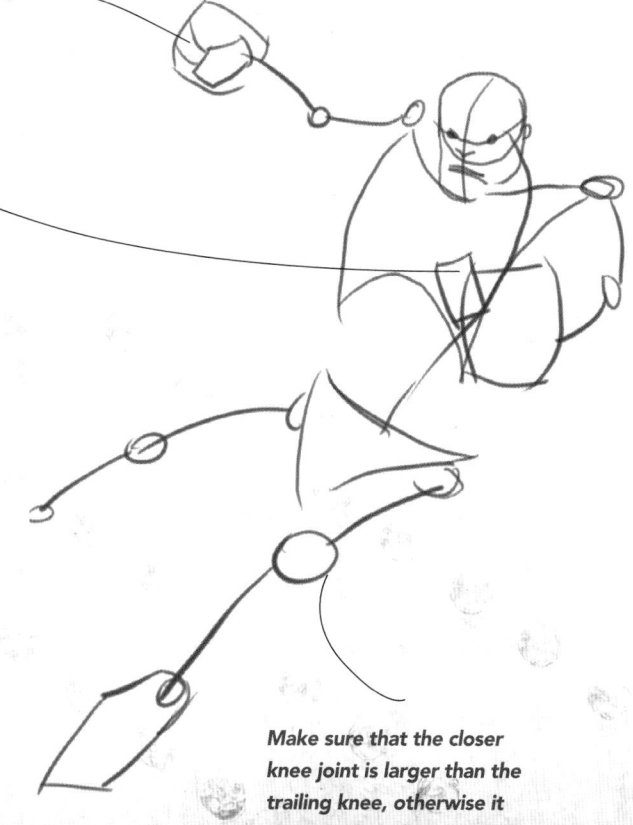

STEP 3

His far arm is going to be a little in the distance, so make sure this hand is smaller than the closer arm and hand. Remember that he's going to be holding stakes, so his hands should be in fists at this early stage. Now start work on those legs. The closer leg will be bent at the knee, while the trailing leg will be relatively straight in comparison. The front leg will be taking the weight of the hunter.

Make sure that the closer knee joint is larger than the trailing knee, otherwise it won't look realistic

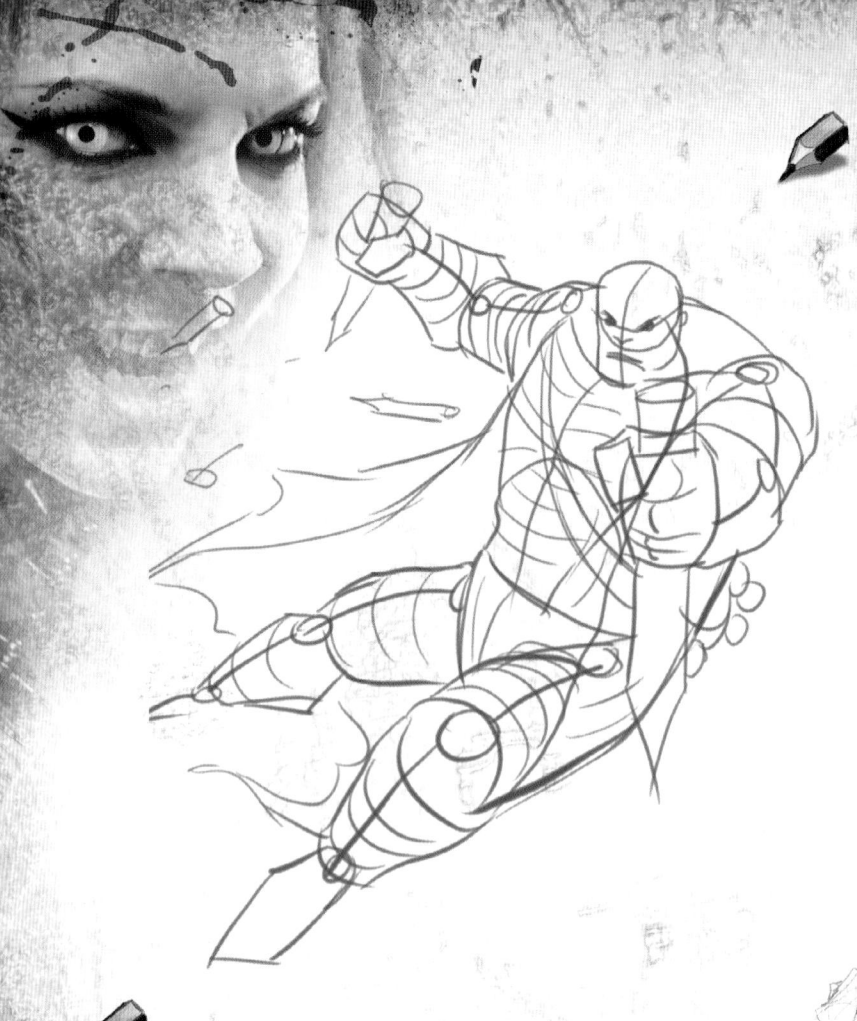

STEP 4

Now fill out the form of the vampire hunter, adding cylindrical shapes and form lines, remembering that he's a pretty muscular, chunky vampire. Check that you're happy with how he's looking, and erase any lines that you don't want. Add in the outline of the stakes here as well, and some objects flying around in the background to show that he's moving quickly.

STEP 5

Work up your basic outlines into a more finished sketch. Draw in as many details in the sketch as you like, such as a skull or two on his legs, spikes and armoured feet. He has a belt over his shoulder holding more stakes, so he's not going to run out of weapons! At this point he looks quite monstrous.

Think about how the movement of the character will affect the hair, and use this as a tool to demonstrate the action in the piece

STEP 6

Use a large, flat brush to wash your initial colour in. Keep the background colour neutral, ensuring that your colour scheme for the rest of the character will pop off it.

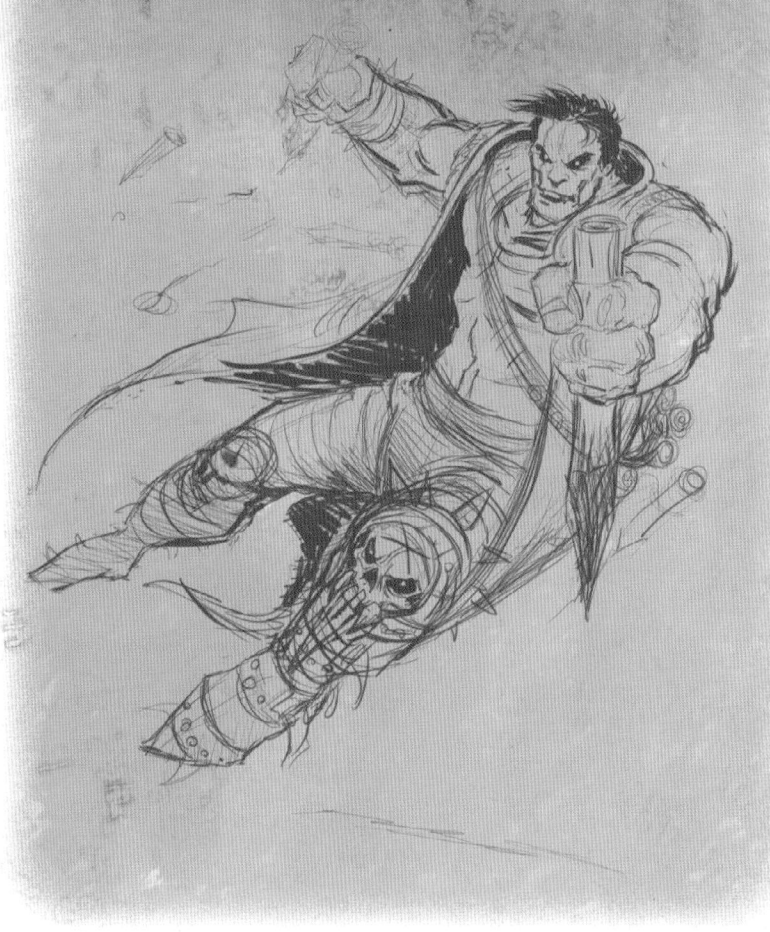

STEP 7

Decide on your light direction and start to pick out the shadows and tones. Here, the light is going to come from behind the character, which means we can get some really interesting tones on his coat and legs. Choose a darker tone of the background colour for the shadows. Just adding this tonal dimension really starts to bring the image to life.

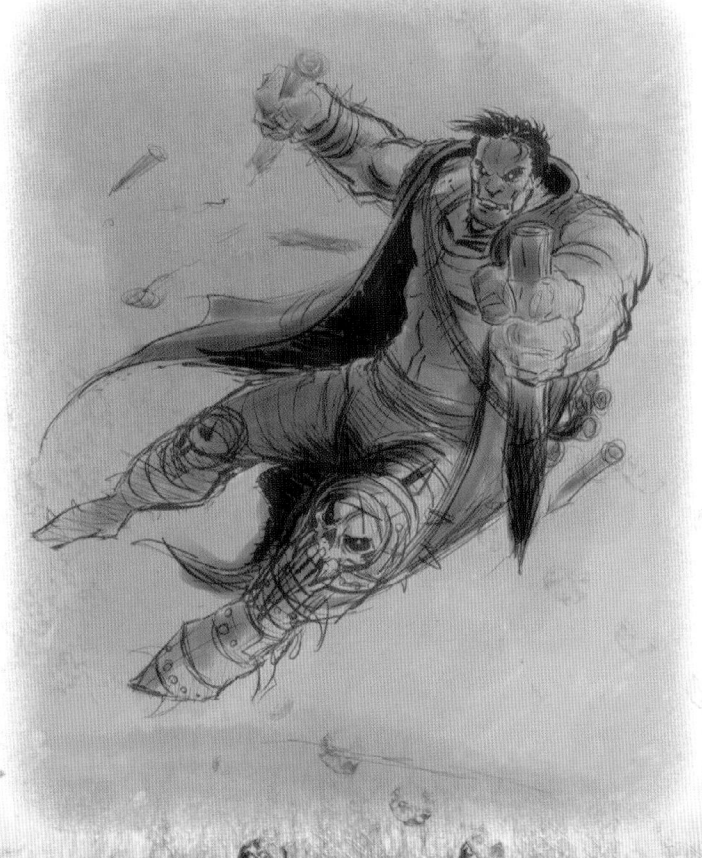

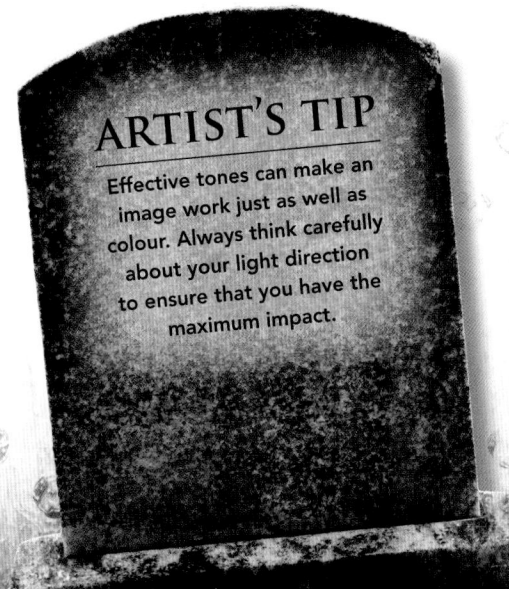

ARTIST'S TIP

Effective tones can make an image work just as well as colour. Always think carefully about your light direction to ensure that you have the maximum impact.

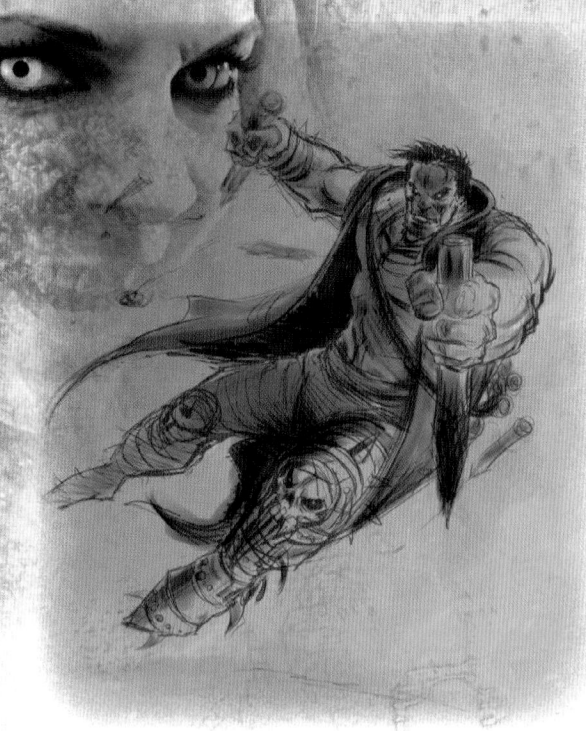

STEP 8

Work around your image intensifying and deepening those shadows. Add a wash of red or a small amount of deep brown to the background to give it some depth and texture. Adding this makes the background part of the whole composition, rather than a plain wash for the character to sit on.

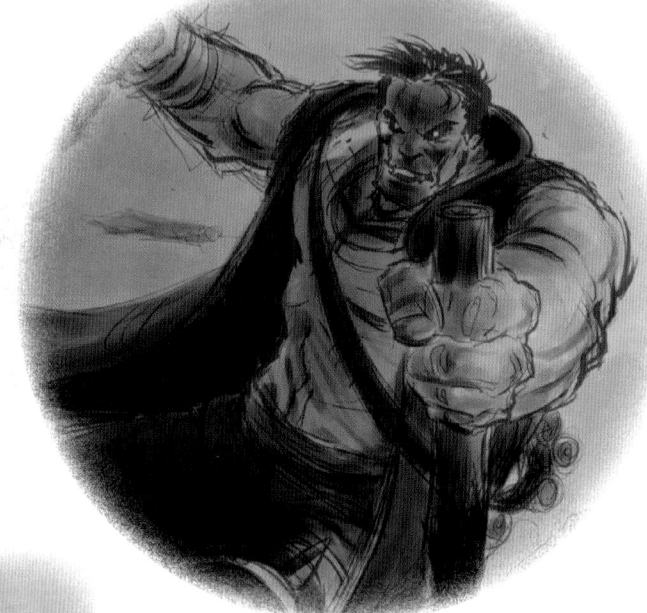

STEP 9

It's time to paint in some colour washes. He has grey/blue clothing, and a dirty grey/yellow shirt, with greyish flesh. You don't have to stick to the colours used here – although these tones will give you a solid base to start building your texture from, experiment with some colour combinations of your own!

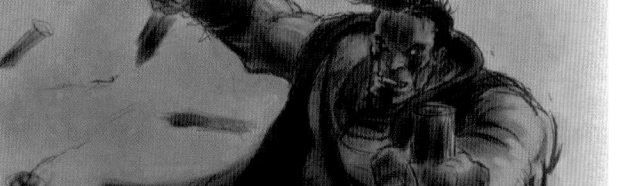

STEP 10

Start to wash some warmer colours into his flesh and the stakes, and a little more colour into the background. Decide on the colour for the armoured leg, bearing in mind where the light will fall on it and the effect it will have.

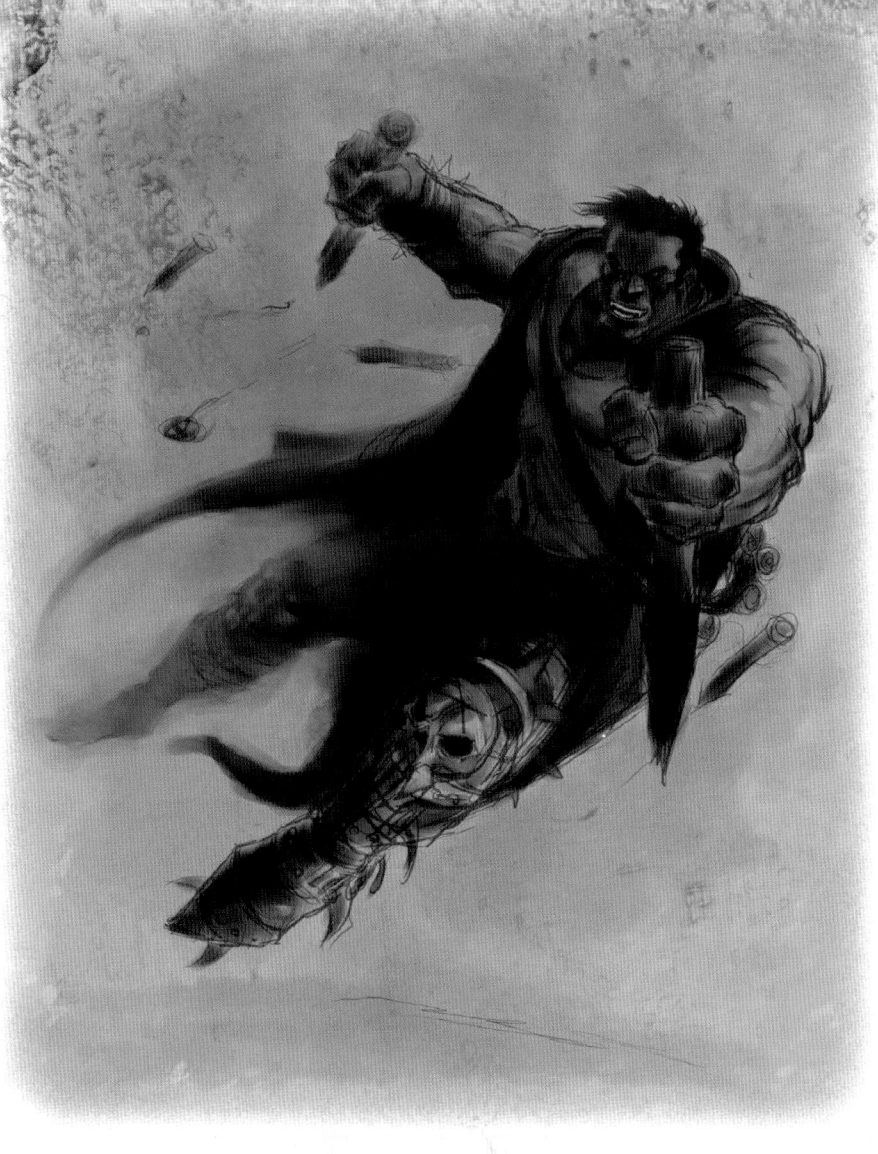

 ## STEP 11

Take the opportunity to stand back and assess what you've done. Flip the image (if working digitally) or look at it in a mirror if you're in traditional media. Check that you're happy with how everything is looking, and start to work your way around the whole image touching up the blending, especially in his jacket and trailing leg, which should appear to be fading into the distance.

 ## STEP 12

Start to blend Sam's features with a fine brush, and paint in his eyes. You need to have this vampire hunter's fangs visible, so add these in with a pencil and fine brush loaded with white paint. Check your highlights around the face, and pick out any that you feel are lacking.

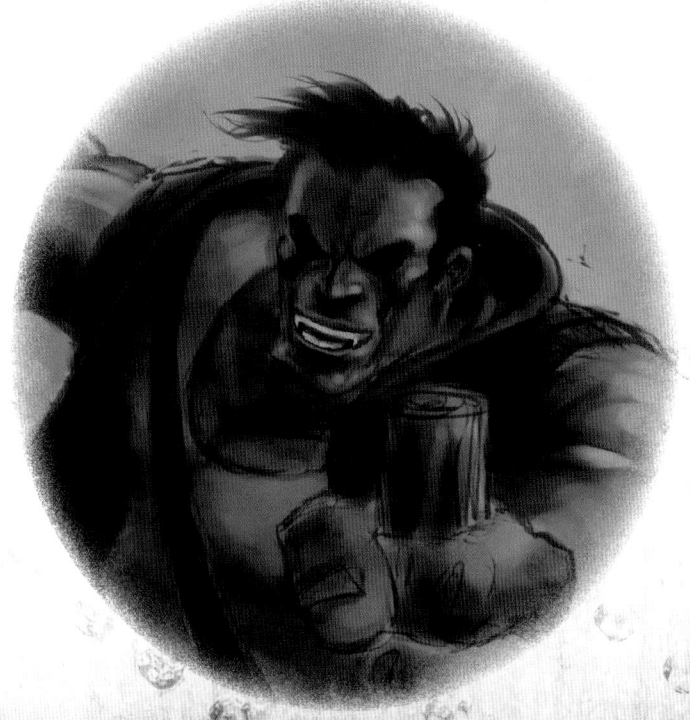

Use a grey/green wash and highlight with a lighter shade of the same colour to show up the stubble on this unshaven chin

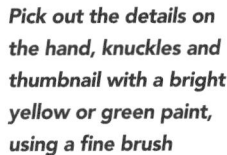

Pick out the details on the hand, knuckles and thumbnail with a bright yellow or green paint, using a fine brush

Remember that the trailing hand and leg will have much less detail and saturation than those in the foreground

STEP 13

Blend in the flesh, making sure you use some nice saturated warm colours on his face and closest arm. His trailing arm will have less saturation and detail. Using a reference if necessary, try to add some creases on his shirt, remembering that they follow the flow of the body. Begin to pick out those finer details, especially on the armoured leg.

FINAL PIECE

So nearly there! Use a sharp pencil to select details on his belt including the studs, buckles and tears, and paint another stake on his belt. Add in some trailing lines of blood to one of the stakes to really help to show his movement. Paint these with a deep red and highlight with a bright and saturated warm colour, such as red, orange, or yellow. Finally, wash some saturated orange onto his face to help to draw our eyes to this area. Have you seen any vampires lately?

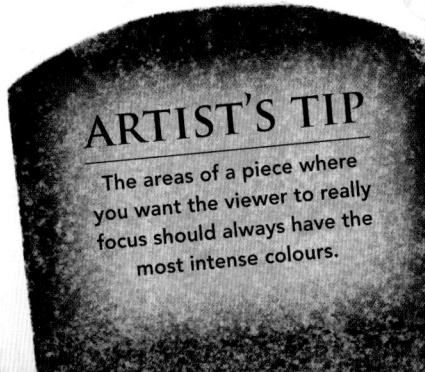

ARTIST'S TIP

The areas of a piece where you want the viewer to really focus should always have the most intense colours.

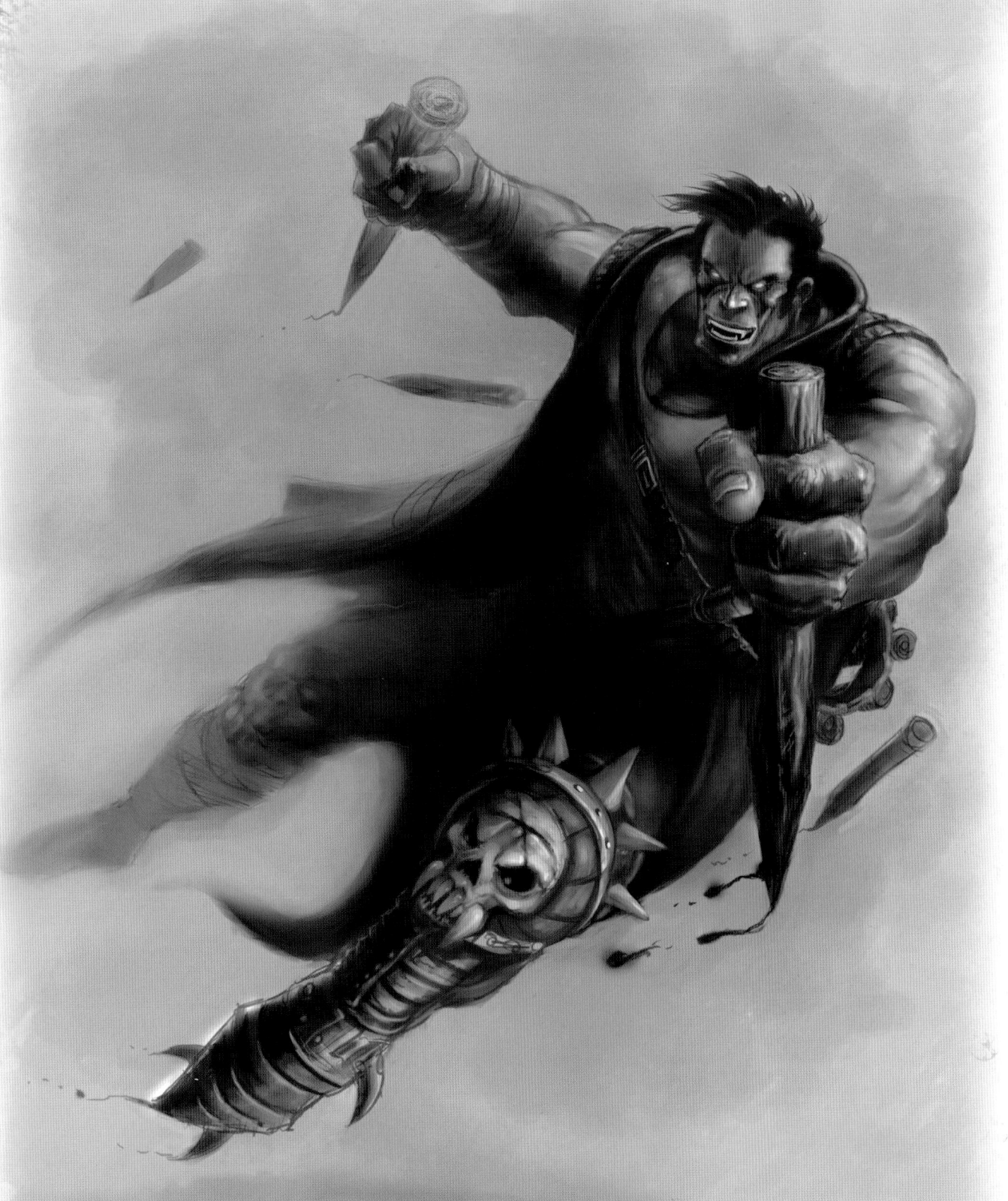